THE
Westminster Pulpit

VOLUME IV

THE
Westminster Pulpit

VOLUME IV

The Preaching of

G. CAMPBELL MORGAN

WIPF & STOCK · Eugene, Oregon

Wipf and Stock Publishers
199 W 8th Ave, Suite 3
Eugene, OR 97401

The Westminster Pulpit vol. IV
The Preaching of G. Campbell Morgan
By Morgan, G. Campbell
Copyright©1954 by The Morgan Trust
ISBN 13: 978-1-60899-313-0
Publication date 1/15/2012
Previously published by Fleming H. Revell, Co., 1954

CONTENTS

CHAPTER		PAGE
I	Thou Shalt Remember	9
II	The Untrodden Pathway	22
III	The Grace of Giving	35
IV	Restlessness and Its Remedy	48
V	Righteousness or Revenue	59
VI	Unpardonable Sin	71
VII	Shining Faces	85
VIII	Life; in Flesh, or in Spirit	97
IX	The Spirit of Christ; The Supreme Test	110
X	Horizoned by Resurrection	123
XI	How to Succeed in Life	136
XII	My Lambs—My Sheep	149
XIII	But!	162
XIV	God in Christ	176
XV	The Set Time	188
XVI	God's Fighting Forces	202
XVII	The Secret of the Lord	216
XVIII	The Mind of Christ	229
XIX	Keep Yourselves in the Love of God	243
XX	Divine Selection	256
XXI	Final Words	269
XXII	The Strength of the Name	281
XXIII	The Optimism of Faith	294
XXIV	The Verdict	307
XXV	Salvation in Zion	320
XXVI	The Rights of God	322

The Westminster Pulpit

VOLUME IV

CHAPTER I

THOU SHALT REMEMBER

And thou shalt remember all the way which Jehovah thy God hath led thee.
DEUTERONOMY 8:2.

WHEN THESE WORDS WERE UTTERED, ISRAEL WAS AT THE parting of the ways. A change was imminent, both of leaders and of circumstances. Moses well knew that very soon he would lay down the burden which he had borne so long and so bravely, and that another would be commissioned to lead the people. He knew also that they would very soon change the circumstances of the wilderness for those of the land flowing with milk and honey.

In this book of Deuteronomy we have his final charges to the people, charges resulting from experience and expectation. Standing among the people whom he loved so well; with whom he had so patiently borne; with whom he had been so righteously angry; he looked back over the years, and on into all that he knew lay before them, because God "made known His ways unto Moses"; and spoke to them out of the fulness of his heart.

In reading these closing messages of the great leader, one of the most impressive notes is that of his anxiety that the people should *remember*. He recognized the influence of memory. He knew perfectly well that, properly stored, it is a perpetual inspiration to present endeavour; and consequently one of the great forces that makes the future. He also recognized the subservience of memory to will. He knew that it can be trained in certain directions, and to the retention of certain definite facts. Consequently, he was careful to charge his people with that which they were to remember.

Evidently, there is not only the historic setting, and the philosophic basis, but the religious purpose of this text. Moses was desirous of directing the memory of the people to supreme matters, urging them to look back, but to look back from the right standpoint, and to see things in the right relationship; to see, moreover, the real things, and the abiding things; the things therefore worth remembering.

The word here translated "remember" means quite literally to mark. "Thou shalt mark all the way which the Lord thy God hath led thee." The pictorial suggestiveness of it is that of the chart, the map, or the way, on which certain facts were to be marked, and thus fixed upon the memory.

The true backward look is that which sets the past in relation to God; that which lays to heart the lessons God has intended to teach by the experiences of the past; and is that which always has the future in mind. Let us attempt thus to remember all the way along which the Lord our God has led us.

First, then, let us remember the past in its relation to God.

When Moses did this, he was careful to note three things about it. They were: to remember God's deliverance, that He brought them out of Egypt; God's leading, that He led them through the great and terrible wilderness; God's resources, which were placed at their disposal.

These people had been brought out of Egypt and its bondage to God, and to that freedom which was perfectly conditioned within government and within law. This was fundamental, and this they were charged never to forget. Take the Old Testament and read right through it, listening to its teachings; and whether you are reading its devotional literature, or that which is distinctly prophetic in the sense of the forthtelling of the Divine will, you will discover how constantly these prophets, seers, and psalmists, took the people back to Egypt, and the fact of their deliverance therefrom. That was absolutely fundamental.

The history of this people began when they were brought out of Egypt.

And so Moses, charging them to remember, put that as the first fact, "the Lord thy God . . . brought thee forth out of the land of Egypt, out of the house of bondage." They were a special people on the ground of deliverance, and they were to place all the past, the immediate past, the past forty years, in relation to that beginning of deliverance when God broke the power of the oppressor, and led them out into the place where it was possible for them to live the life of faith, the life of direct and immediate obedience to Himself.

In all our backward looking, we are to remember that the life of faith begins in that hour in which He looses us from our sins, and makes it possible for us to obey His Kingship and His government. When we look back, we must put everything in relation to that initial deliverance by which God freed us from sin and its bondage, and brought us into relationship with Himself. That is what we fail to do very often. We look at the incidents of our life, and the happenings of the days, and we fail to set them in relation to that fundamental fact of our redemption by blood, and our relationship to Christ upon the basis of sin forgiven and peace with heaven.

If the Old Testament writers constantly referred the

people to their coming out from Egypt, the New Testament writers as constantly refer us to redemption, and to our oneness with Christ by the mystery of His Cross. I can only quote the old and familiar illustrations, and surely no other are needed. "Husbands, love your wives, *even as Christ also loved the Church*." "Exhort servants to be in subjection to their own masters . . . that they may adorn the doctrine of God, our Saviour"; that they may in the obedience of their everyday life show that fundamental fact of their relationship to Jesus Christ.

So we are to remember back far enough, and by so doing, begin to realize the fact that all the details of life are related in the purpose and economy of God to that first deliverance by which He brought us to Himself by putting away our sins.

How often we forget that first thing. God never forgets it; and no day dawns but that the affairs of home, and the affairs of the office, and the affairs of business are, in His economy, being overruled to the working out into perfection that fundamental relationship to Himself that commenced in the hour when He loosed us from our sins, and brought us into relationship with Himself.

Second, he charged them to remember all the way along which God had led them. There is nothing more beautiful in the book of Deuteronomy than the different passages in which Moses insisted upon that guidance of God. "God . . . went before you in the way, to seek you out a place to pitch your tents in." I can never read that without feeling how wonderful a declaration it is. I see that moving camp in the wilderness, for forty years hither and thither, backward and forward; and the movement seems such a haphazard business. It was not so. God always went before them, and chose the place of their camping; and when the sun went westering, and the cloud halted, and they paused and erected their tents, it was always on ground which God had chosen. Moreover, He accompanied them upon the march. They came to no rough and rugged desert but that He was there too. They came to no long stretch of level country which wearied them, but that He was with them. They came to no hour of difficulty and perplexity but that He was there; and He granted them the shining of the fiery pillar at night, and the mysterious mist of the cloud by day, as signs and symbols of His abiding presence.

Through all the way, there was movement toward the purpose that He might "do thee good at thy latter end." They had come forty years before to the same margin of the land, and the book of Numbers is the story of retrogression, and backward marches. Yes, but that is not all the story. God led them back that they might go forward. He led them circuitously that they might go straight. He led them through the terrible wilderness that they might come to the ultimate triumph.

Let us look back. Think of any day you please, the darkest or the brightest, the saddest or the gladdest, and whether it be shadow or sunshine, the rough or the smooth pathway, these same things are true. First, in every day we walked in works which He had before ordained that we should walk. And we found grace to help in every time of need. All things have been working together for good to those who love Him. Delay has been in order to speed. Denial has often been His choicest gift. Or, to borrow that quaint and yet true statement with which you are all familiar, the disappointment over and over again has proved to be His appointment. Look back over the way, and see if these things be not so. If for the moment there may be some who are in the midst of darkness and difficulty, and cannot see the ultimate, then hear the testimony of those who have passed through long and weary marches, and they will tell you that they would not have missed Marah with its bitterness for all they possessed; that they would not have missed if they could the darkest day, because they have now come to see how God led them that way, and that it was a way of purpose which was beneficent, and out of the darkness has come the light.

Look once again. Moses reminded these people that they had been supplied with necessities. I like the fine discrimination of his method. What are the things he told them that God had given them? Raiment, and bread, and water. They had received a great deal more than these. But what he laid upon their memory was the fact that things absolutely necessary for life God had been providing for them. For forty years, in spite of all their murmuring and unbelief, and difficulty and suffering, there had never been a day when they had lacked necessary things.

May we not look back and say the same. What good things have we lacked? A great many things we have desired that we have not had; but did we need them? There may have been hours in which we felt sure that the supply would fail; but did it fail? There may have been days when we felt perfectly sure that the cause was lost and hopeless, and there could come no succour, not even the bare necessities of the occasion, but did things turn out so? If this congregation could but become vocal with its own experiences, what tales we should hear of wonderful deliverances, of hours out of which we have been brought, in which, as we entered them, it seemed as though we must die; of days when it seemed as though the last prop had been knocked from under us, and all chance of our accomplishing the desire of our heart had gone for very lack of strength. But we are here this morning, remembering the way along which the Lord our God has led us.

And yet there is, I think, a deeper note in the text and in the injunction. Moses attempted to teach these people the necessity for learning the lessons God had to teach them. And these lessons are threefold. Three things he distinctly tells us lay in the purpose of God, as He delivered and led His people, and supplied their need.

The first is this, "That He might humble thee"; and the second is, "That He might . . . prove thee, to know what was in thine heart"; and the third is, "That He might make thee know that man doth not live by bread only, but by every thing that proceedeth out of the mouth of the Lord doth man live."

That He should humble us. How we shrink from that word. Answer my inquiry in your own heart, quite honestly. Do you ever read the passage without feeling some little resentment at the word? "The Lord thy God hath led thee these forty years in the wilderness, *that He might humble thee.*" Do we not feel a little at war with the idea that the purpose of God is to humble us? And yet, my brethren, if we do, it is because we are interpreting the meaning of the word and suggestion by what we know of man's method for humbling other men. Let us interpret the word by the whole economy of God. I ask you to remember this fact, that pride is the most ghastly of all human failures. It demonstrates ignorance. It is not necessary that I stay to illustrate it. You know perfectly well that among your own acquaintances the proud man is an ignorant man, and pride foreshadows ruin. The old Book is still true,

> Pride goeth before destruction,
> And a haughty spirit before a fall.

Pride is hated alike by God and man. Then, let us read once again. "He humbled thee, and suffered thee to hunger, and fed thee with manna." God's purpose is to produce the character which is the opposite of pride. All God's methods tend toward humbling. His deliverance only comes to a man *in extremis*. It is when the strong and self-contained swimmer is about to sink for the third time that the mightier swimmer has the chance to save him. God only begins His great deliverance when a man says, I can do nothing of myself. "He humbled thee." God's leading of His people is always leading through the pathless wilderness. God's supplies for His people always come out of the unknown. We say that today this is not so. Think again. That story of water out of a flint, and manna raining upon people is of yesterday. Today we know where we get our supplies from. Are we quite sure? Oh this age that thinks upon the surface of things. Get back behind your loaf of bread, and back behind your flour, and you have golden harvest. Where did that come from? Oh, we ploughed and sowed. And then what happened? There is always the touch of God if you will wait long enough to feel it. God is forevermore bringing to His people supplies out of the unknown. If a man is to be delivered, he will be delivered when he feels he cannot help himself. If a man is to be led, he must be flung into the wilderness where there is neither map nor guide post. If a man is to depend on God, and lose his arrogance and his pride, he must receive his supplies from One Who brings them from the unknown resources.

Then remember the beauty of humility. Humility always veils its face and worships. Humility makes friendship. Oh, you can have acquaintances who are not characterized by humility, but that thing in your nearest and dearest friend that makes him or her your friend is humility. Humility serves forevermore. God has been leading you through the wilderness to humble you; not to break your spirit; not to make slaves of you; but to free your character from all the things that He hates, at the root of which is pride; and to make you meek and humble and lovable. That is the first lesson, and God is still doing that same thing; and if we can only see these things in their larger outlook, we shall look back and thank Him for every day when we were at the end of self and compelled to depend upon Him.

The second lesson is that God delivers, and leads, and supplies in order that he may prove. This does not at all mean that God needs to find out what is in us; but that He wants us to find out what we are in ourselves. Therein is revealed a perpetual method of God. God brings us into circumstances which will reveal the hidden facts of our nature to ourselves. Those who know most of the Divine government, will know what I am trying to say. There are incipient forces of evil in our lives. We do not know that they are there, but God knows that they are there. Rebellion lurks in the nature even while I sing the song of loyalty on a sun-shiny day. God will put me into a day with no sunshine, and bring the rebellion out, that I may know it. Blasphemy may lie in the depths of my nature, even while I offer praise. Then God will lead me by some pathway where that inner thing shall come out to the light. Cowardice may be in my heart even while l sing, "Stand up, stand up for Jesus, Ye soldiers of the Cross." Then, before many days have gone, I shall be in a place where that cowardice will be manifested. Hatred may be in my spirit while I preach on "Thou shalt love the Lord thy God." Then He will place me in some circumstance that will manifest it. Dishonesty, impurity, greed; all these may be hidden beneath the surface. Then He will lead me into places where they will be revealed.

If that were all I had to say, it would be too awful a

thing to say. But, there is something else to say, and I hasten to it.

The third lesson is that we may "know that man doth not live by bread only, but by every thing that proceedeth out of the mouth of the Lord doth man live." "That" is a great word quoted by Jesus in the wilderness, a word constantly spoiled by imperfect interpretation. Do not be alarmed if I say that it does not refer to the Bible only. It includes the Bible, but it is something greater, profounder than the Bible. Let us take the illustration. These people were in the wilderness where there was no bread. How was He going to feed them? They knew how to get bread. They had seen the process in Egypt. They had gone out and flung their corn upon the land when the Nile had left its rich deposit. So they had gotten their bread. But there was no Nile running through the wilderness. They could not fling seed corn there. Or, if these men knew something of the methods of the land to which they were going; there was no yoke and no plough in the desert. God wanted them to know that they never got bread from the Nile, and as the result of their own toil. They obtained it from Him. "By every word that proceedeth out of the mouth of God." Let a man live in the Divine ordinance, in the Divine government, in the Divine will, and the desert will blossom as the rose, and out of the nothing will come the everything, and out of the *is not* will come the *is*.

Thus, He not only put His people into circumstances to develop their own inner evil and bring it to the light, but into circumstances to bring these men into such knowledge of Himself as would drive them to Him, that He might correct the evil, and put it away, and redeem them, and perfect them.

We have often said that man's extremity is God's opportunity. But I would like to put that in another way, for the purpose of this meditation, a more striking way. Man's extremity is man's opportunity for finding himself, and finding his God, and so finding life. I charge you remember, and if you will do so solemnly, you will come, I am perfectly sure, to agreement with me when I say that the richest hours of the past were the hours of extremity, and the hours of darkness, the hours when we were at the end of ourselves; the hours when we discovered something in us that appalled us, because these were the hours when God came into visibility. No bread, but it rained from heaven. No water, but out of the flinty rock it gushed. No way in the dreary wilderness, but He chose the places where we pitched our tents.

Then God help me, I will put my head on the pillow, and go to sleep. He is always appearing in the hour of man's extremity. I remember the day of desolation, darkness, despair; I was done, I was beaten, I was at the end of everything; and then there came a light, and a glory, and a supply, and a deliverance, and God. Those are the great days in life. It is by these things that men live, not by rose gardens, and not by the hills and valleys to which they are going. There is danger in them, and that is what Moses is going to tell them.

Let us come briefly to the last of these things. The true backward look is the look that looks on. The forward look to these people was one of hope. Better times were coming, better circumstances were coming. They were coming to a garden, and Moses is a poet of no mean order, as he describes the wonderful garden, "a good land, a land of brooks of water, of fountains and depths, springing forth into valleys and hills; a land of wheat and barley, and vines and fig trees and pomegranates; a land of oil olives and honey; a land wherein thou shalt eat bread without scarceness." A good time coming? No. "*Beware* lest thou forget the Lord thy God." Oh there is great suggestiveness in this, heart of mine, listen to it. There is graver peril in prosperity than in adversity. The peril of self-satisfaction, "My power and the might of mine hand hath gotten me this wealth." The peril of self-righteousness. Lest you shall say in the land, "God has put us into the land because we are such good people." No! Neither by the might of your hand, neither by the goodness of your heart are you the people of privilege.

"Beware." It is when the sun shines that most souls are shipwrecked. In the day of storm we are driven to God and find Him. In the day of calm we trust in ourselves, and lose God. Therefore, remember, if the future has rosy tints upon it, beware. Now do not let anyone misunderstand me. If we remember God we may go into the sunshine, and succeed; and get out of the sunshine its honey and its sweetness and its strength. But, because of the grave peril of prosperity, it is well to remember, and so to remember as to put all the immediate past into relation with the fundamental deliverance; to remember in such a way as to discover the goings of God in all the past, leading, and guiding, and choosing, and directing, and making us hungry as well as making us full; and to remember the past with the eye upon the future.

So, to remember is first of all to repent. I, this day, do remember my sins. Well, do not shirk the business. Look at the devilish thing, look it in the face. Do not let the devil persuade you it did not matter very much. Oh, it was damnable, it hurt God, it harmed your brother! Look your sin in the face until your heart is broken! It is out of such remembrance that deliverance comes.

But to remember is not only to repent, it is to believe.

> His love in time past
> Forbids me to think
> He'll leave me at last
> In trouble to sink.

And I sing the song of deliverance for today and tomorrow whenever I remember.

Therefore, so to remember is to praise, to hope, and to dare.

So let the backward look be one that in its final value is an onward look. Then God will lead us into the land, and He is able to keep us there as well as in the wilderness.

CHAPTER II

THE UNTRODDEN PATHWAY

Ye have not passed this way heretofore.

JOSHUA 3:4.

Last Sunday morning we looked back. This morning we look on. The Children of Israel are still seen at the parting of the ways. There is some change of circumstances from those at which we looked before, but it is a slight one so far as the hosts are concerned. They are still on the margin of the land. We spoke then of the fact that change was imminent, the leaders were about to change, the circumstances were about to change, the wilderness was passed, and the land was immediately before them.

When we turn to this book of Joshua, we find that Moses, the servant of God, has entered into rest, and Joshua has taken his place as leader of the nation. Behind the people there is the history, and the great lessons learned through that history.

Among the last words of Moses to them had been those which formed our text last Sunday morning, "Thou shalt remember all the way which Jehovah thy God hath led thee." Standing upon the margin of the land, behind them lay the deliverance from Egypt; the guidance of God for forty years in the great and terrible wilderness, and the daily supply of daily need. They possessed, moreover, the lessons learned through the experience of the past; that first of humility, for He led them and suffered them to hunger, and fed them, that He might humble them; that secondly of the discovery of themselves—for I think you will agree when I say that the people who stood on the margin of the land for the second time after forty years had learned a great deal about themselves that they did not know before; and finally that of the discovery of God in many an hour of extremity and many a place of difficulty.

Now before them lay the great unknown. Joshua said to them, "Ye have not passed this way heretofore." There were certain things about the future which they thought they knew, but of none of them were they absolutely certain. There were things about the land which had been reported to them as a people forty years before, which, doubtless, many who were then but children would nevertheless remember; facts concerning its mountains and valleys, its rivers and rills, its cities and its people, but nothing was certain, nothing was definite. The future was all unknown.

So this morning we stand at the parting of the ways. We attempted a week ago, as the Old Year was passing from us, to consider the responsibilities of memory. We attempted to emphasize the teaching of that last word of Moses, and to show that in remembering we must put the past into relation with God; must attempt to learn the lessons He has intended to teach, and must recognize that the true look back is a look on.

I propose to continue that subject this morning, by asking you to consider the responsibilities of anticipation. Here again I shall seek the contextual light of the story, for while we live in other times, and our manners are different, and in many things we have changed radically and completely from these men of a bygone age; yet in all the essentials of our human nature, and in the master principles that govern human life, we are the same as they; and, therefore, from the picture on the old page we may gather light for the new history.

There are two things of which I want you to think with me. First, of the uncertain future; and second, of the certainties of the future.

"Ye have not passed this way heretofore." The future is all uncertain. That is a fact which needs no argument in the case of sane men and women. It is only insanity that gazes into crystals, and examines palms, and seeks to listen to wizards and witches that peep and mutter. If my words in this connection are few, I do not think they are unnecessary, especially in this quarter of London. I pray you remember that it is only insanity which imagines that anybody can discover the secrets of the future. Therefore, with this congregation I will not argue it. The future is unknown, is utterly uncertain.

If the fact of its uncertainty is thus recognized, let me speak of the fascination of that uncertainty. There is to every healthy mind a fascination about the unknown. That explains the perennial interest which is attached to the passing of one year and the beginning of another. As a matter of fact, there is no new year and there is no old year. These are things of human almanacs, human calendars and human calculations. I believe, and I say this quite frankly and of growing conviction, that the nearer we live to God the less we care about times and seasons of any kind. We come to a recognition of the fact that time is eternity. Suns rise and set, and seasons pass; and these are the only marks of time in the Divine economy. Those of our Januaries and Februaries, and Sundays and Mondays, are pagan. When presently the great Kingdom of God comes, we shall never talk of January or Sunday. Our friends, *the Friends,* are ahead of us when they speak of first day, and second day. Yet there is a fascination in passing from one year to another, and there is a value in our marking of the passing of time in this particular way. We have halted and looked back. Now we are halting to look on. Who of us here this Sunday morning has not been dreaming dreams about the New Year; wondering, with healthy wonder, what it is bringing to us, what the ever receding curtain of mystery will leave revealed in the foreground of experience? There is a great fascination about the uncertainty of the future.

This fascination is born of two things, one lower, the other higher. Let me speak of the lower first. It is born of the passion for the new that ever burns in the heart of humanity. If I speak of that as the lower, it is only by comparison with the other, for it is not essentially wrong. It is one of those master instincts of human nature that we do well to recognize, and attempt to direct along true lines. The passion for the new, for discovery, is in every healthy human heart. What do you mean by a newspaper? What is the fascination of the newspaper? The finding out of things not known, the entering into the discovery of the larger whole. Do you remember Kipling's lines about the explorer? In those lines there lies a philosophy applicable not only to the geographical explorer, but to all human life:

> There's no sense in going further—it's the edge of cultivation,
> So they said, and I believed it—
> Till a voice, as bad as conscience, rang interminable changes

> On one everlasting whisper day and night repeated—so
> Something hidden. Go and find it. Go and look behind the Ranges—
> Something lost behind the Ranges. Lost and waiting for you. Go.

That is the passion of exploration, and it creates the fascination of the unknown in the New Year.

The higher motive, or the higher reason of that fascination, is the desire for the better. The passion for the new is true and right, but it is the lower. The higher is the desire for the better. Oh, those vows and resolutions of the New Year. They are so multiplied that even the newspapers gain some amount of humor out of them. Yet they are tragic and pathetic and human. Promises made with the dawn of the dead year, broken, scattered all along the line, until one is ashamed to look back upon them. Yet they were fine, true, noble; they meant well. Today we are making them all over again. If there is any gladness in our heart about the New Year, it is that we see in the future a chance of being better. The glamour of it, the fascination of it is in all our hearts. "Ye have not passed this way heretofore." We pause and listen to the voice that comes singing out of the unknown, and it is the voice of hope.

But think not only of the fascination of the unknown, think also of the fear of it. This is as certain, as positive a quantity in our outlook as is the other. We know not what the future has hidden in the way of opposition; what forces are hiding behind the mountains, or lurking in the mists that lie along the valleys. We cannot tell how deep is the river, how tortuous the path through the mountains, how many robbers lie ambushed, suddenly to swoop down upon us. We are ignorant of the forces that are against us in the coming year. Their number, their nature, their methods are all unknown. So it was with these people upon the margin of the land. They had become accustomed to the perils of the wilderness, but those ahead were unknown. Consequently, there was fear as to their ability to cope with the difficulties that lay ahead.

And so it is with me. If I do not know the foes, how can I be sure whether my own strength is equal to them. Here I halt upon the margin of the New Year, feeling its lure, its fascination, its appeal; and yet, in an almost greater degree, fearing it, dreading it. If I do not stay for illustration, it is because your minds will act more rapidly than my speech can. In your business, in your home, perhaps in the weakness of your physical frame, or in the trembling mental unrest of which you are conscious, are unknown possibilities of opposition. Are we equal to them? So felt these men on the margin of the land, and so feel we. We have not passed this way heretofore. It is all strange, all new, and while it fascinates us it fills us with fear.

Yet once again. In thinking of the uncertain future, while we admit the fact, recognize the fascination, and know the fear; let us ever remember the force of it, the value of it, the strength of it.

What is the force of uncertainty? It is a force in the life because it is the inspiration of effort; and a call to preparation. If I knew all the facts of the coming year, I might be careless. I do not know them; and out of the mystery and fog and silence there breaks one voice, "Watch!"

Said Joshua to the men encamped near the river, with the land before them and the wilderness behind them, "Sanctify yourselves: for *tomorrow* the Lord will do wonders among you." Tomorrow for God: today for you. Today for you because you do not know tomorrow. Consequently, the force and value of uncertainty is that it compels me to seek to put my life into right relation with the forces that are equal to tomorrow. It compels me to make preparation for effort, to quit myself like a man that I may be strong; for if I am to march one step at a time, one day at a time, in the midst of forces that I do not know, over territory that I have never traversed, and if I have to deal with new unfoldings of mystery, it behoves me to be equipped, and to be ready. Herein lie the values of uncertainty.

But now turn to the second consideration, the certainties of the future. "Ye have not passed this way heretofore." If this does suggest indeed, the uncertainty of the future, and remind me that the pathway is an unknown one, I am constrained to inquire whether there are any certainties with which I may take my way into the unknown tomorrow. I want to answer that inquiry in the very simplest way by saying that there are three certainties with which I may face the uncertain future. I will name them. The first is the past. The second is the present. Though it appear a paradox, the third and the most certain is the uncertain future.

The past. Let us get back to this borderland, to this place by the Jordan. Look at these people. "Ye have not passed this way heretofore," but Moses had already said, remember all the way you have passed. Their first certainty was the past.

As you face the new, never forget the old, for the most absolute certainty that we possess as we face the uncertain is that of the things of the past. Deliverance prophesies deliverance. Guidance predicts guidance. Supply promises supply. Let me make this a little more geographical. There is a river in front of us. Then measure the river by the sea. He divided that, He can divide this. There is an unknown land before us. Measure the unknown land by the unknown wilderness. But passing into a new country, we shall need to be fed with bread and water. Measure your hunger in the new land by the manna in the old.

The one thing no man can take away from me as I face tomorrow is yesterday. You may confuse me about the problems of next year, but you cannot confuse me about the solutions of last year. You may tell me of all the perils and difficulties and dangers that are ahead, but on the pathway o'er which I have passed lie dead my foes. I have sung a song on the deliverance side of the Red Sea; Jehovah hath triumphed, His people are free, and I do not think you can frighten me with a running river when I have seen the sea divided. Therefore, I look into the future and it is all uncertain, and I come to it with the certainties of the past, with the deliverances wrought, the prayers actually answered, with the supplies that have come out of the nowhere into the here. That is the first certainty, and it is a great one. Doubt very much the man or the philosophy that asks you to doubt your own experience. There are moments when we are inclined to do it. It is quite a commonplace thing for men to say to me, and to each other, I doubt not when speaking of these things, I am sometimes tempted to doubt whether there was ever anything in it all. Do not be tempted to doubt your past triumphs. Lay hold upon the things that you have in the actuality of your experience. Make them new by remembering them perpetually. Make them forceful by allowing them to become the inspiration of all your endeavour. There are men and women in this house who come to the New Year full of dread. Look back one moment. Yes, it is good to do it in silence, when the preacher has no word to say. I cannot tell you what to look at, but you know. That day when the bitter waters were sweetened, when after the long desert tramp you sat down at Elim. Oh, we have had the experience. That is our one certainty as we look on. You cannot take that away from us. You can mystify us about our theory, but you cannot mystify us about the things we have been brought through.

Then we also have as certainties the lessons learned. These we dwelt upon last Sunday. Let us reckon on them as certainties. We have learned the lesson of humility, learned it through crushing and breaking, sorrow and difficulty, but let us be glad if we have learned it.

Then again, there was the discovery in ourselves of some things that we did not know, and would rather not have known, or so we think; the startling surprise of the evil thing in us, which some hour of trying circumstance brought to light; that hour, when we who had cursed Peter for his cowardice were cowardly; when we who had denounced Judas for his treachery were traitors. Thank God, as I face the New Year I know it. I have found it out. I am not in half so much danger from that discovered evil as I was before it was revealed. You failed, my brother, in some dire disastrous moment you fell into some gross, venal sin. If you will only live in the light of that warning, you can climb on your dead self to better things. You have learned your weakness, and you will avoid the very street in which you fell! You will be careful to have no business transactions with the man who persuaded you to do the mean thing! You have found out that you could do a mean thing. You did not think you could, but you are safer for having found out. It is a great thing when a man has found out where his weakness is. Where I am weak I become strong, through the knowledge of the fact.

And finally, in the past we have discovered God. Now we are going to abbreviate our dictionaries by cancelling the word extremity, for we have found out that it is when we are at our extremity that the door of opportunity is opened for our discovery of God, and our entering into all the possibilities of His power. These are the things of the past, which are our certainties as we face the New Year.

Then there are the certainties of the present. To these people they were the sacramental symbols, and the living leader.

When Moses passed, Joshua remained, and what Moses could not do Joshua could, and that because Moses was dead. If you question that statement, remember what we read in the second verse of the first chapter, "Moses My servant is dead; now *therefore* arise, go over this Jordan." The death of Moses was necessary to progress into the land.

These then were the things of the living present, the sacramental symbols and the living leader. Why dwell upon the sacramental symbols? Because here was a change. These people possessed the Ark before. Yes, but they had not followed the Ark, but the cloud; and they would never see it again; the cloud of fire by night, and the mist and mystery by day had ceased. They had a new pathway to tread, with a different method of guidance. They who had waited for the moving of the cloud were now to wait for the moving of the Ark and the priests. The cloud was the provision for the wilderness. God was changing His method with them. They were to live not by a particular sign, but by the word of the Lord. They would never forget that the Ark came out of the cloud. It was in the mystery of the cloud that enveloped the mountain that Moses had the pattern of the Ark given to him. But henceforth the cloud was withdrawn, and the Ark remained. It was not for them to question, or to desire to retain the past; but to be thankful for the present provision, and to obey.

What application has this to us? We have the present as well as the past as we come to the New Year. And in the economy of God there remains for His people one visible, tangible, sacramental symbol, and it is the Bible. That is not a subject which I am going to discuss or deal with fully. I make the assertion and leave it for you to think over. The only sacramental symbol God has left in this world is not bread, or wine, or water, but the Word written. We have that still.

To us remains also a living Leader. If we want to understand all that is included in this face, we shall not stay in the book of Joshua. In the letter to the Hebrews the writer says, in effect, Moses led you out, but he could not lead you in. Joshua led you in but he could not give you rest. Now there is one greater than Moses and Joshua Who leads out, and leads in, and gives rest. We must discover Him in spiritual communion.

Do you doubt at that point, my brother, my sister? Nay, do I doubt? Are we in danger of doubting? Let us think once again. The whole superstructure of our moral and spiritual life depends upon the living presence of the living Christ. This Bible is only the sacramental symbol. It is a great certainty, but do not worship it. In the name of God, do not worship it! It is the living Leader Who is the supreme certainty for the days to come. Are you not tempted to say, "If I could but put my hand upon the hand of His flesh I should know Him better." Not at all. The men who did it never knew Him until He withdrew the hand of flesh and came in spiritual power at Pentecost. These frail hearts of ours still hanker after the hand of flesh upon which our hand might rest, something more present, more tangible, of which we might be sensible; but He is as definitely in the midst of us, as positively by the side of every pilgrim of faith, aye, and more so, than was Joshua present to the hosts of old. Thus we have in the present the Word, written and incarnate.

The final certainty is the future. The past is past. I cannot go back. The present is passing, and I cannot hold it. Twenty minutes ago I was talking of the present. That is now the past. We say, "Tomorrow never comes." As a matter of fact we never possess anything certainly except tomorrow. Everything else is shifting, changing, gone. The future is mine! That is the truer word; it is the word of the man who struggles up after his fall; the word of the man who builds his castle in the air; the word of the man who feels the lure of the coming days. The future is mine. That is true.

Thus here we stand, on an ever moving present, between an irrevocable past and a challenging future. I repeat the phrase already used more than once, the lure of the future is on our spirits. How shall we meet it? The answer is in these early chapters of the Book of Joshua. There is a special word here for the leaders, a special word to Joshua. Now for the moment Joshua becomes the symbol not of the lonely and supreme Leader, Christ, but of all those who are put into places of oversight. What is the word to leaders, preachers, teachers, prophets, overseers? "Be strong and of a good courage." If you read all that first chapter you will find that that was a call to Joshua by God and by man. God said to him, "*Be strong and of a good courage*"; and presently, when he charged the Reubenites, and the Gaddites, and the half tribe of Manasseh, as to what they were to do, they said, "According as we hearkened unto Moses in all things, so will we hearken unto thee: only the Lord thy God be with thee, as He was with Moses . . . *only be strong and of a good courage*." God said it, and man said it.

It is so today. The appeal of God to those who are charged with leadership is, "Be strong and of a good courage." Let not your heart faint. Do not tremble. Do not play the coward. The appeal of humanity to the leaders of the Christian Church is the same, "Be strong and of a good courage." If you tremble, no victory will be won.

How shall we meet the future? What is the word to the hosts? This also have I recited, "Sanctify yourselves: for tomorrow the Lord will do wonders among you." How were they to sanctify themselves? With regard to the past, they were to remember! With regard to the present, they were to see the Ark, to keep at a sacred distance from it, and to follow it; to discover that it was the new symbol of their relationship; to treat it with holy reverence; to follow it. Their relation to their leader was to be that of loyalty, so long as he was loyal to God.

What of the future? With the inspiration of the past filling the soul, with the certainty of the present enabling the life, they were to go in and possess.

Thus let us go forward to face each day in the name of the Captain of Salvation. Oh, but giants are there! To be slain! Walled cities are there! To be taken! Difficulties await us! To be overcome!

So may God give us grace to follow our greater than Joshua into the unknown tomorrow, and to possess it in His name, and for His glory.

CHAPTER III

THE GRACE OF GIVING
A Million Shillings!

See that ye abound in this grace also.
2 CORINTHIANS 8:7.

THE PASSAGES READ FOR OUR LESSON HAD SO EVIDENTLY A local and immediate application that they seem to have very little value for us. I am glad that the local coloring has faded, because in proportion as that is so the lines which are vital and essential stand out in clearer relief. I need hardly remind you that if a great deal of this is of the nature of faded color, there are things that none of us would care so to describe. For instance, no one would say that the color is faded from this statement, "Ye know the grace of our Lord Jesus Christ, that, though He was rich, yet for your sakes He became poor, that ye through His poverty might become rich." Because of that one verse the chapter is worth reading; worth reading if only to see the use the apostle makes of that great truth; for it is a significant fact that the verse with which we are all so familiar, the verse that is enshrined in the very heart of the Christian Church, is one that occurs in the midst of a chapter which we have admitted is full of local coloring. In that fact there is revealed a method of apostolic writing and teaching that I am very anxious we should constantly recognize.

These New Testament teachers never dealt with local matters by local methods; they forevermore brought to bear upon the temporal, the eternal. Whenever they touched something that was the subject of a day or of an hour, they did it in the atmosphere and spirit of the eternities. Not merely when they wrote to saints, calling them to the life of full sanctification; not merely when they wrote the great document of human salvation; but when they wrote about the relation between husband and wife, between fathers and children, between masters and servants; and when they had to do with so commonplace a matter as a collection, they adopted the same method. They corrected the wrong things of the passing moment by bringing them to the measurements of the undying ages. All false conduct which they desired to set right, they approached with eternal and abiding principles.

Because I am desirous that we should understand the place of giving in Christian life, I want to speak of the New Testament ideal thereof.

The chapter from which the text is taken clearly sets forth that ideal. The source of Christian giving is suggested in the opening verse, "Brethren, we make known to you the grace of God which hath been given in the churches of Macedonia." The grace of God bestowed upon His people is the source of all giving. The spirit of giving is also revealed. The Macedonian Christians were eager in their desire for fellowship. They gave beyond the expectation of the apostle, in that they gave themselves to God, and then gave themselves to the Lord's service, and consequently, not merely out of their wealth but out of their poverty, they gave more than they were able. The method of giving is revealed in the same words. They gave themselves, and their gifts followed. Finally, the great arguments for giving are stated. The first is that of the things they possessed, "Ye abound in everything." Notice that the *everything* in the apostolic thinking does not take into account what some men may have lacked, material wealth. "Ye abound in everything, in faith, and utterance, and knowledge, and in all earnestness, and in your love to us." Upon the basis of that abounding wealth he appealed to the Corinthian Church, "See that ye abound in this grace also." His final argument is that of the verse which we read, "Ye know the grace of our Lord Jesus Christ, that, though He was rich, yet for your sakes He became poor, that ye through His poverty might become rich." The word here translated "poor" occurs nowhere else in the New Testament. It is the strongest use of the word that it is possible to make. It indicates absolute pauperism. He became so poor that He had absolutely nothing more to give away. The local coloring has faded, thank God that it has, for the living figures and abiding principles and eternal realities flame upon the page in all the greater brilliance and radiance for the fading of the local colors.

Some five or six years ago, in a Northfield Conference, Mr. John Willis Baer, who was then Secretary for Christian Endeavour for the world, was conducting a question box. He took out of the box the question, "How shall we raise money for Foreign Missions?" His answer was as quick as the crack of a pistol, and as forceful: "Don't raise it, give it." In that answer is the solution of the whole problem which confronts us at the present hour. If funds are lacking to carry on the work of God in the far distant places of the earth, it is because the Church has become so busy raising money that she has ceased to give it.

Every method for raising funds for Missions that is spectacular, worldly, and commercial, I hold to be out of harmony with the will of God, and in the long issues calculated to hinder and not to help. If we can but return to the simple and profound principles of the New Testament in the matter of giving, we shall never have to call a halt, or beckon the workers back, in order that we may close fields into which they have entered because the Church at home is not conscious of an opportunity, or is not ready to sacrifice in order to enter a field.

What is the basic principle of giving? It is declared in one word, which I have already quoted in this chapter. I take it out of its context. It does not belong only to this chapter, for it is stamped upon the pages of the New Testament. It is the word *"fellowship."* "Beseeching us with much entreaty in regard of this grace and the fellowship." If we may but come to an appreciation of the meaning of that word in all its applications, we shall have touched the profoundest basis. What is fellowship? Those of you who worship here regularly must be patient if I now repeat in this connection what I have said in other connections. The word translated "fellowship" is one of the richest words in the New Testament. So rich in suggestiveness is the Greek word "Koinonia," that not even the revisers found it possible to express it in all connections by one English word. When I take up my New Testament I find the same Greek word is translated "communion, communication, distribution, fellowship." I find, moreover, that its kindred word, "Koinonos," is translated "partaker, partner." Whereas there is something very dull in the repetition of a group of words like that, the very repetition helps us to see the richness of the word. There is one passage in the New Testament which admits us to the heart of its meaning. It occurs in connection with that fascinating picture of the early church, when it is declared that the disciples had "all things in common." The Greek word so translated is the root from which our word fellowship comes. Fellowship with God, therefore, means that God has placed all His resources at our disposal, and that we, dare I say, have placed all our resources at His disposal? I dare not; I dare say only that we ought to place all our resources at His disposal. That is exactly what the apostle meant when he wrote to the Corinthian Christians, "We make known to you the grace of God . . . ye abound in everything . . . see that ye abound in this grace also." The grace of God to you is that He has put all His resources at your disposal. Your grace is to be manifested in that you put all your resources at His disposal. That is perfect fellowship. Tell me, if the whole Christian Church understood, and lived in the power of such fellowship, would there be any need to ask the patronage and help of godless men to carry on godly work? Would there be any need whatever to recall from the field loyal hearts who are suffering and serving, but who must be brought home owing to lack of funds? This is the difficulty. God has put all His resources at our disposal, but we have not put our resources at His disposal. That is the foundation principle that ought to underlie all Christian giving.

Let me break up that foundation principle into two working principles: "Ye are not your own; for ye were bought with a price," and "Whatsoever ye do, do all to the glory of God." If in the consciousness of fellowship with God, if in the activity of placing at His disposal all our resources, we remember that we ourselves are not our own, but His; and if in all the activities of everyday life we make His glory the one supreme, master-passion, then we are applying these working principles, and we shall find that they will produce all that is needed for the doing of God's work in the world.

The principle for practical application is found in the first passage I read. I think it is well that I read the actual words again. "Upon the first day of the week let each one of you lay by him in store, as he may prosper, that no collections be made when I come." To me, to read that, and then to think of the habit of the Church in raising money, is to see how far we have wandered from the apostolic ideal. The only use the churches through this country seem to have today for the preacher is for him to visit them in order that there may be a collection. Out of twenty-five letters I receive asking me to preach, I am safe in saying that twenty of them say, "We are in need of funds, and your visit will enable us to raise them." The apostle says "that no collections be made when I come." In order that it may be so, the true method of giving is stated. The giving of the Christian man is to be personal; let every man. It is to be regular, upon the first day of the week. It is to be perpetually readjusted, according as God has prospered. I hear a great deal about the tithing of incomes. I have no sympathy with the movement at all. A tenth in the case of one man is meanness, and in the case of another man is dishonesty. I know men today who are Christian men in city churches and village chapels, who have no business to give a tenth of their income to the work of God. They cannot afford it. I know other men who are giving one-tenth, and the nine-tenths they keep is doing harm to their souls.

Turning from the principles, I want to say a few words about laws and regulations. We are to arrange our substance as Christian people on the basis of recognition of the fact that all is His. Consequently, it is not that I am to give Him a tenth or a part, and hold the rest to spend according to the dictates of my own desire. The Christian man must recognize that not a tenth, but ten-tenths, belong to God. He has no right to spend anything save in accordance with the Divine will. May I put the case quite simply for the youngest Christian here. Out of my income I am to spend so much on food, clothing, shelter, mental culture, recreation, and all to the glory of God. If the method of my eating is not for the glory of God, then I waste God's money. If the method of my dress is not according to the glory of God, then I violate the principle of Christian life and of Christian giving. I must do all to the glory of God. In order to be giving directly and immediately to the actual work of God, therefore, there must be a recognition of stewardship, and that means careful disbursement, not only of your hundreds and thousands, or millions, but of your pence and shillings. We have no right to disburse money without investigation. If your conscience is not at rest about a society, you have no right to buy off a collector with a subscription. We need a new sense of stewardship in the heart and conscience of Christian people in all of this matter.

If we lift this whole question on to this level, certain things will happen. First of all, we shall be forever at an end of spasmodic giving in this missionary matter. When once the Church comes to the sense of responsibility on the basis of fellowship, and on the principle of stewardship, we shall never again hear of the annual missionary Sunday. The whole of our churches are under the curse and ban of it, both in regard to information, inspiration, and giving. Systematic and regular giving will cancel all spasmodic giving, which creates crises, and hinders the work of God.

Again, if these principles once be recognized and acted upon, there will be an end forever of that carelessness which never readjusts conditions. There is someone who has been giving to a missionary collector a guinea subscription for the last twenty years. Twenty years ago that man's income was not a fifth of what it is today, yet he is going on in the same way, a guinea a year! To come to the consideration of these things in the light of the New Testament ideal, will mean constant readjustment, sometimes lessening your giving in honesty, or increasing it in response to the increasing prosperity of the days.

If in the Christian Church at this hour, in this country, there could but be the realization of this New Testament ideal and these New Testament principles, the result would be that of making forever unnecessary all questionable methods of raising money. What is the reason that the missionary societies lack funds? Is it that the Church lacks fulness of life? Or is it that the Church has become lamentably ignorant of New Testament teaching? Or is it both? Are not these two things very closely interrelated?

In a word or two let me illustrate the application of these principles. I maintain that every Christian Church should put first things first. I maintain that it is of the very essence of the Church's life that the first of her income should be spent, not on herself but on the work of her Lord, and not on the work of her Lord at her doors, but on the work of her Lord in the far distant places of the earth. It is not for any reason of sentiment or purpose of boastfulness, but because we believe it is the Divine order, that out of all collections taken in this church the first tenth is set aside for missionary work. As I say to my friends in the provinces when they come to Westminster and put a sovereign on the plate, two shillings of it goes to missionary work beyond our own borders.

There is a peril in that which we need to recognize and avoid. The peril is that when this is done the Christian men and women in the church may imagine that their individual responsibility is fulfilled. By no means. I pray you think carefully; if we had not tithed our income for these three years would you have given any less to the collection? I trow not. Your giving has been the giving of your worship, your expression of gratitude to God for the benefits He has conferred upon you. The giving of the tithe is the giving of the corporate church, and not the giving of the individual members. Think of it carefully, and see that your individual responsibility abides. Tithing of collections must not be allowed to weaken personal responsibility.

As in the church life first things should be put first, so also in personal stewardship, first things must be put first. Note that the Corinthians did this. Paul says, "Now concerning the collection." When? Immediately after the great passage on the resurrection, the chapter of the final issues of Christ and Christianity, the chapter that climbs the heights until the challenge to death is heard; "O death, where is thy victory? O death, where is thy sting? The sting of death is sin; and the power of sin is the law: but thanks be to God, who giveth us the victory through our Lord Jesus Christ. Wherefore, my beloved brethren, be ye steadfast, unmovable, always abounding in the work of the Lord, forasmuch as ye know that your labour is not vain in the Lord. Now concerning the collection." Put the collection in the full tide of your spiritual life. Put the collection in full relationship to the highest, noblest doctrines of the faith. Hold your offering in the supernal light of the resurrection of the Son of God. Put your giving in relation to the life that was won out of death.

The inspiration of giving must be the grace of God, the love of God. There comes back to me a story, I cannot forbear telling it even though perchance I may have told it before, because it had such an effect upon my own life. Hudson Taylor told me this story the last time I saw him in this world, the story of how, long years ago, there came into his room, on his birthday morning, his own little girl, and she brought in her hand a most mysterious-looking arrangement, so mysterious that Hudson Taylor did not at all know what it was.

She said, I have brought you a birthday present. He took it in his hand and looked at it. It was a matchbox, into one end of which she had driven a knitting needle, and into the other end a pin, and had somehow fastened some cotton to the pin and to the top of the knitting needle. Being only a man, and not a mother, he said to his girlie, "Well, darling, what is this?" "Oh, father dear," she said, "I knew it was what you would like. It is a missionary ship."

There is the whole philosophy of Christian giving. The heart of the child knew full well the love of her father's heart, knew that the thing he most longed to possess was a ship, and she made one for him. There is no one in this congregation who will dare to laugh at that missionary ship.

The years passed, and there came a day when the girl had grown to womanhood, and once again she came to her father in China on his birthday, and she said, "Father dear, I have brought you something for your birthday," and he said, "What is it?" She continued, "I want to introduce to you the first Chinese woman that God has used me to lead to Christ." The potentiality of that Chinese convert lay in that matchbox, knitting needle and pin.

There is the plane of Christian giving. What does God want? What is His heart set upon? Before every present you buy which is worth anything, you say: I wonder what he wants. I wonder what would please her. That is the true genius of giving. That is what the child did before she made the ship. Such giving comes out of real love.

If we could but get the Church here! If instead of desiring to keep up an appearance of respectability there were a great, passionate, surging love for God and the things that God loves, all our financial problems would be at an end, and then as young men and maidens come up and ask to be sent out—and they are coming all the time—we would not have to tell them there is no place for them, no method of training them, but out of the fulness of funds we could get them ready, and send them forth to the work of evangelizing the world.

My last word to you is of our own Society in this respect. Doubtless many of you know that the London Missionary Society is asking that before the last day of March there should be given to it from the churches of our order a million shillings. I know perfectly well how easily people say, Another appeal! and down it goes into the waste-paper basket.

I wish you would think about that appeal. What does it mean? It is an appeal for money to wipe out a deficiency which at the present moment is £37,000, and before the end of the year in all probability will be £50,000. How has this deficiency come about? I reply at once, the deficiency is due to the success of the work. The deficiency is due to the fact that God has answered prayer and blessed the workers. We have sent forth workers into the distant fields. They have succeeded. If they had failed there would be no deficiency. I want you to think carefully of this when you are facing the subject of missionary giving, that planting a missionary, or a mission station, means not merely the amount needed to support him or it for a year, but more the next year, and more the following year if he succeeds. I have in my hand an article which appears in the January number of the London Missionary Society's *Chronicle*, in connection with this appeal, which I propose quoting to you. It puts the whole case in a nutshell. The writer says:—

> The deficits have occurred because the Board has been sanguine enough to "Budget for a Rise" in its income, which "rise" has not been realized, at least to the extent anticipated. But surely, after such experience, twice or thrice repeated, this habit of "Budgeting for a Rise" ought to have been discredited? Well, the Directors have, after all, but afforded

another example of the triumph of Hope over Experience. Though having had experience that the income had not risen as expected, they still hoped that it would do so. Who can blame them for persisting, at least for a while, in the belief that the churches would *not* allow the rose tree to be cut down on the very day when it was blooming?

That is the whole story of the deficiency. Do not blame the Mission House. You business men, if you are at all anxious about the Mission House, investigate its methods and discover that the cost of administration in the London Missionary Society is under two shillings in the pound, which amount includes all secretaries' salaries, the whole administration, and the cost of all the literature issued. It is a smaller amount than is spent by any of the other large Missionary Societies. Do not blame the Mission House. Do not blame the missionaries for succeeding. Blame the Church, that she is out of fellowship with her Lord, that she is not true to the doctrine of fellowship, that while God has placed all His resources at her disposal, she has not placed all her resources at His disposal.

Supposing these million shillings are not forthcoming, what then? The result must be curtailment. There must be the closing of some part of the field that we are at present occupying. It means cutting down the rose tree somewhere in the day of its blossoming! Is that to be our reply to the opening doors of opportunity?

I came, as you know, back to my work this winter from one month spent in going to different places on this great missionary enterprise. When I went out for that month's campaign, I stipulated, as did my brethren, that I was not to talk about money. I did that because I believed, as I still do believe, that the true way of dealing with the financial problem is by deepening the spiritual life of the Christian Church; but when the hour has come that the Board has to consider whether it must cease work begun, and call men and women home, in the name of God, it is time we spoke of finance; and I have tried to put this subject where I think it ought to be put, on the highest level and on the profoundest foundations.

And what does it all come to in the end? What is to be the reply of this congregation to that appeal? In the light of that appeal, as it covers the churches of England and Wales, before the end of March, in addition to the subscriptions of our members, in addition to the tithe, we at Westminster ought to send to the Mission House £200. It could be done, it will be done without any difficulty, if we all will put this matter on the basis of the New Testament ideals. Let no youth or maiden, no man or woman, who can only give out of poverty, withhold the shilling because it is only a shilling, and let those whom God has blessed with more, exercise that same function of stewardship, and give as in the presence of your Lord.

To me it would be almost heartbreaking if we had to close any field, or call back any workers when as never before the Master is opening up the world and bidding us enter in. It would be to the great joy of my heart if this congregation made its response without any organized collecting. I very much shrink from that. I hope it will not be necessary. If we will all send in our penny or sixpence, or shilling, or pounds, or scores or hundreds of pounds, during the next three months it will be easily accomplished.

I do desire that at Westminster, where God has so graciously blessed us, we shall make our response to our Society and help them at this time.

I thank you for the patience with which you have heard me. Believe me, I have spoken out of my heart. I now leave the matter with you.

CHAPTER IV

RESTLESSNESS AND ITS REMEDY

Who will shew us any good?

PSALM 4:6.

THAT IS NOT THE INQUIRY OF THE PSALMIST. IT IS A QUESTION which he quotes, in order that he may reply to it. Let us, therefore, read not only the inquiry but also the answer:—

> There be many that say, Who will shew us *any* good?
> Lord, lift Thou up the light of Thy countenance upon us.
> Thou hast put gladness in my heart,
> More than in the time when their corn and their wine are increased.
> In peace will I both lay me down and sleep;
> For Thou, Lord, only makest me dwell in safety.

"Who will shew us any good?" So far as we are able to judge from the pages of history, humanity is one in all ages. There are changes upon the great stream of human life, but they are surface changes; changes in manners and in methods, and even in the maxims of men; but underneath is the same human nature, asking the old questions, making the old complaints, and wondering with the old amazement. Humanity today is confronting the problems of long ago. In the process of the ages they come to the surface, and men attempting to answer them, find themselves again and again unable so to do, and decide presently that they will abandon the effort, and the problem sinks back in the tide and is forgotten. It reappears, and when it reappears we call it new, but "there is nothing new under the sun."

In the days of the Psalmist he said there were people who asked, "Who will shew us any good?" It is the language of a man who, looking back, is dissatisfied, looking around him is full of cynicism, and looking on is pessimistic. It is the language of restlessness and dissatisfaction. The question is being asked today by men in utterly different circumstances. Satiated men, overfull, full to repletion, come at last to the moment when they say, "Who will shew us any good?" Hungry men, conscious of the pinch of poverty and the pang of want, gaunt, desperate men say, "Who will shew us any good?"

Successful men, using the word as the world uses it, men who seem never to have failed in any enterprise their hands have touched. We watch them as they climb from point to point, until at last we think of them as having achieved the most remarkable success, and then they come and sit by us and say, "Who will shew us any good?" "Vanity of vanity, all is vanity."

Men who have failed, for some reason we are never able to discover, there are men who always seem to fail; trial after trial, attempt after attempt, effort after effort, but always beaten, always a little lower, until at last with heartbreak they say, "Who will shew us any good?"

Is it not worth our attention that men in such opposite circumstances make the same inquiry? Does not that fact suggest that the inquiry is a revelation of some underlying malady which is independent of circumstances; the full man, the hungry man, the man successful, and the man of failure are alike disappointed. Let us hear their challenge. It is sounding in our ears on every side. This age is peculiarly restless. There is a hot feverishness manifest on every hand expressing itself in a thousand ways and with ever varying emphasis. I venture to say that you can express the whole of it in this old, simple, blunt language of my text, "Who will shew us any good?" Is life worth living?

Have we any answer to that inquiry? In reply to that inquiry concerning the inquiry, I would say at once, yes, we have an answer. The answer is as old as the inquiry. The answer lies here upon the page of this ancient psalm. While men may quarrel about the authorship and about the date, I am infinitely more interested to discover its consciousness of human unrest and its answer. Here is the answer:

> Lord, lift Thou up the light of Thy countenance upon us.
> Thou hast put gladness in my heart,
> More than in the time when their corn and their wine
>   are increased.
> In peace will I both lay me down and sleep;
> For Thou, Lord, only makest me dwell in safety.

Am I not right in saying that is an all-sufficient answer? Has not the consciousness of this congregation agreed as to the accuracy of that answer? "Who will shew us any good?" said the restless, feverish men of the psalmist's day, and he replied, the source of good I will declare, "Lord, lift Thou up the light of Thy countenance upon us"; the experience of good I will recount in your hearing,

> Thou hast put gladness in my heart,
> More than in the time when their corn and their wine
>   are increased;

and finally, I will give you the result of this goodness, "In peace will I both lay me down and sleep." "Who will shew us any good?"

Is that the inquiry that was hot in your heart as you found your way to the sanctuary tonight, my brother? Is that the question you are asking, sister mine, after all the attempts to satisfy the craving of your fine nature with the things of dust and the excitements of the world? Tired, broken, disappointed, angry, cynical, do you say, Is life worth living?

I pray you listen in the sanctuary to this great answer, "Lord, lift Thou up the light of Thy countenance upon us," which being interpreted, may thus be explained. This man, and those of us who take our stand by his side in testimony, declare that we find good where God found it and finds it. If that declaration seems for the moment to wander a little away from the meaning of the Psalmist when he said, "Lift Thou up the light of Thy countenance," I beseech you keep that word in mind while I depart to a distance only that I may come back to it to discover its richest meaning and profoundest intention. We find good where God found it. Where did He find it? We read those old and familiar words in the first chapter of Genesis. I want you to be quite simple and like little children, and see what the first chapter of Genesis says. Light, the earth and the sea with all its myriad forms, the sun in the heavens in the daytime, and the silver queen of night, all the flowers, the birds of the air, and the fish in the sea, and the great creatures on the earth, and man; and God said these things are good. "Who will shew us any good?" Wherever you are you are near to some of these things. God says these things are good. Turn a deaf ear to the man who tells you they are evil. They are not evil. Do not believe the man who affirms that this is a wicked world. It is an absolutely untrue statement if by the world you mean the earth God created. These things are good. Light is good. The earth with its store of wonders is good. The deep and fathomless ocean of which the finest thing in literature is in the Bible, "Thy way was in the sea, And Thy paths in the great waters." The ocean is good. All the flowers and fruits of the earth, the fauna and flora of nature are good. The brightness of the sun, and the sunlight in either winter or summer; the radiance of the moon and the pictures she flings upon the sky as she plays with the clouds; these things are good. The fish in the sea, the fowls of the air, in every sense are good. You are living in the midst of these things and are saying, "Who will shew us any good?"

There is something wrong somewhere. Step a little higher and look once again at the Genesis picture. This time not at isolated items which in every case God pronounced good, which in every case rested the heart of God, and at last so rested Him that He hallowed the day of rest as a memorial of His own satisfaction with the things in the midst of which you live your life and I live mine. Climb a little higher and what are the conditions which are presented to your vision in this early chapter. The first is that of the supremacy and sovereignty of God. The second is that of the viceregal dignity of man. He is made a little lower than God, and is given dominion over all the creation beneath his feet. The third is that the creation potentially is waiting for the touch of men in fellowship with God to answer him in laughter and flowers, the abundance of harvest, yielding up to him the deep and profound secrets that lie within her bosom. If you will take one step higher and look no longer at isolated items, no longer at the condition, but look at the spiritual suggestiveness of this first chapter of Genesis with its picture of original conditions, what do you find? A picture of fellowship. A picture of co-operation. A picture of happiness. A picture of fellowship between man and God, and between man and everything beneath him; and therefore, between everything beneath man and God, through the instrumentality and mediation of man.

Man in rebellious selfishness shuts God out of his life. There is the tragedy of it all. As God is my witness, the last thing I desire to do is to speak in metaphor, or to look at dim and distant pictures. If you came here tonight saying, "Who will shew us any good?," the root trouble with you is that you do not know God. I will make that affirmation on the positive side. No truly Christian man or woman ever asks that question. The man or the woman who by grace has come into fellowship with God says, "Thou hast put gladness in my heart. More than they have when their corn and their wine are increased."

> "In peace will I both lay me down and sleep:
> For Thou, Lord, only makest me dwell in safety."

If you are hot and restless, unable to sleep, unable to find anchorage, crying out in the agony of your soul, "Who will shew us any good?" Is life worth living? The reason is that you have lost touch with Eden. You have lost consciousness of God.

Now some of my young friends are saying, We understand the reason for that very peculiar reading in Genesis, but why did you turn to Matthew? I read that old story of the baptism of Jesus, and of the word that came out of heaven, because there, in the Man of Nazareth coming to fulness of human life and just entering upon the ministry to which He was ordained, I find God's new resting place. If that sentence sounds a strange one let me tell you just what I mean. In Genesis, God saw that His creation was very good, and He rested; and then came the tragedy of rebellion, the tragedy of sin, and man lost his rest. When man lost his rest through sin, God lost His rest, and never found it again until He rested in His Beloved. "In Whom I am well pleased." Pleased with earth and air and sun and flowers and fish and fowl, the whole creation; pleased with man, but wounded in man's apostasy, God never found rest again, until He found satisfaction in the perfection of the humanity of Jesus. If you should be inclined to charge me with imaginative interpretation, I pray you hear me while I quote the words of Jesus upon a memorable occasion. Passing through the Bethesday porches, He saw a man who had been for thirty-eight years in the grip of infirmity. He healed him, and when men criticized Him for working a miracle on the Sabbath day, He answered, "My Father worketh even until now, and I work." You must interpret His word by His miracle. He claimed in that moment to be identified with God in activity, and what was the activity? It was activity in the presence of human limitation resulting from sin, the activity which wrought against the thing that spoiled until it was spoiled, and man remade.

But the earth when it was created did not yield up its secrets, did not sing its songs, did not come to the full manifestation of its potentialities. Man was there to discover its secrets under the guidance of God, to make it sing its songs, to bring its potentialities out into flower and glory. There are most curious notions abroad in the world about the garden of Eden. I have seen pictures of it. They are almost invariably pictures of impossible Italian gardens, through the wonderful pathways and amidst the curious flowers of which man is seen walking. I do not so read my Bible. I read, "The Lord God planted a garden eastward, in Eden," that is, fixed its habitation, marked its limitations, arranged its boundaries, and put man "into the garden of Eden to dress it and to keep it"; made him responsible for it, put him there that he might delve, in order that presently to his unutterable amazement and growing wonder, flowers might grow, and fruits might ripen; put him there that through the process of the cultivation of that planted garden, under the government of God, he should bring to light its hidden secrets. Every rose that blooms lies potentially in mother earth, but it never blossoms to perfection until man's hand has worked in co-operation with Divine power. That is the picture that I find in Genesis. It is a picture of fellowship and co-operation, and therefore of happiness. No one in Eden's garden said "Who will shew us any good?" God said it was very good; and man, yielding obedience to the throne of the Eternal, and exercising authority over everything beneath him, said, it is very good. There was no restlessness, no feverishness, no disappointment, until—ah me, that is the root of the malady—I leave the *until* incomplete.

You say, "Who will shew us any good?" God help you to see the tragedy of all this. It is not true of all of you. Some of you find perfect rest in one little plot of your garden because you find God in every blade of grass. "Who will shew us any good?" say they, and they cross the great Atlantic back and forth and play bridge and never see the beauties of the sea or listen to the anthem of the hurricane! They play cards ceaselessly, and then say, This voyage is very tiresome! "Who will shew us any good?"

Man out of harmony with God has lost the key to nature, and has lost the capacity for rest, and is hot and feverish and restless. The Man of Nazareth realized the first intention of God. In Genesis I read that man was given dominion over the fish of the sea and the fowl of the air and the secrets of the earth. In this Book of Psalms I find the question asked, "What is man that Thou art mindful of him?" Singing up out of the Psalmist's essential humanity came the answer,

> Thou hast made him but little lower than God,
> And crownest him with glory and honour.
> Thou madest him to have dominion over the works of
>   Thy hands,
> Thou hast put all things under his feet.

But I cannot find that man, until I come to the gospel stories, and then the writer of the letter to the Hebrews quotes the ancient psalm and says, "We see not yet all things subjected to him. But we behold Him Who hath been made a little lower than the angels, even Jesus." If you watch Jesus at His work you will see the perfect Man mastering the secrets of nature. His miracles are attestations of His perfect humanity rather than demonstrations of His Deity.

Why do I linger here so long? Because to eyes that have ever looked upon the Son of God, the picture is full of glory and beauty. Yet I have another purpose. If in the things I have now endeavoured to say, you have caught a new consciousness of the perfection of the Man in Whom God found His rest, follow Him to the end, I pray you. What is the end of His life? The cross. What is the cross, "Who will shew us any good?" There He is, spoiled, mauled, murdered by men who ask that question. God came incarnate into the lives of the multitudes who had lost their vision of God, and "There is no beauty that we should desire Him." Therefore He was bruised and broken. "We did esteem Him stricken, smitten of God, and afflicted." We were wrong. "He was wounded for our transgressions, He was bruised for our iniquities: the chastisement of our peace was upon Him; and with His stripes we are healed." Incarnate God is upon the cross.

Is that the end? Is that the last word? By no means. Another man is hanging on a cross by His side, a thief, a robber, a malefactor. Out of the strange mystery of crucified iniquity there comes this weird and awful cry addressed to the central figure, "Jesus, remember me when Thou comest in Thy Kingdom." From the lips paling in death comes the regal answer, "Today shalt Thou be with Me in Paradise."

I see the first gleam, it is not the full light, but the first gleam, the accursed tree is the healing tree. The cross erected by man's sin is enwrapped in the Divine determination to save. By that sign of the cross, I know that all the tragedy is being dealt with, and that man can be remade. Behold Eden, and out of its ground came thorns, a curse upon man's sin. Behold the cross, and see the thorns are plaited into a crown bathed in blood on His brow. Coincidence do you say? There are no coincidences as accidents in the economy of God. Just as Mrs. Browning sang truly when she sang that the chaffinch implies the seraphim, so that crown of thorns reveals the way by which God deals with the malady, in order to bring man back into the consciousness of rest and of goodness. By that cross men may be repossessed of Eden.

Yes, you say, you mean that if a man shall trust in that cross he will find his way to heaven. I certainly do mean that, blessed be God, but I mean something else. I mean that by the way of the cross, by man's restoration through that cross into the place of fellowship with God upon the ground of sin forgiven, man can find his way into Eden here and now in this world. Do not let us be afraid of the simple illustrations with which we began, the light, the earth, the sea, the sun, the moon, the stars, the flowers, the birds; all the things of the earth; man can go back and find delight and rest in all these. You have often heard the saints singing it, and they mean it if they know the cross,

> Heaven above is softer blue,
>   Earth beneath is softer green;
> Something lives in every hue,
>   Christless eves have never seen.
> Birds with gladder songs o'erflow,
>   Flowers with deeper beauties shine,
> Since I know as now I know
>   I am His and He is mine.

"Who will shew us any good?" The Psalmist's answer is the only one—

"Lord lift Thou up the light of Thy countenance upon us." You have lost this world, because you have lost God. You find no rest in your own garden because you are out of fellowship with the God of the garden. You are tired of everything in this life because God made you for Himself, and you cannot satisfy the clamant cry of your deep, profound life apart from Him. It is quite impossible.

Shall we not get back to Him? You say, The journey is so long. No, there is but a step betwixt thee and God. At this moment, while the preacher is uttering his last words, and while the men and women who are sitting next you know nothing and can know nothing of the transaction, you can return to Him, and the light of His countenance will be lifted upon you, and the gladness that is greater than the gladness of plenty of corn and wine will fill your heart, and the peace of God which passeth all understanding will garrison your heart, because you are right with God. May He bring us to the trysting place in His grace, and constrain us to that return which means perfect rest.

CHAPTER V

RIGHTEOUSNESS OR REVENUE

Ye cannot serve God and mammon.
MATTHEW 6:24.

THESE WORDS OCCUR IN THAT PART OF THE MANIFESTO OF Jesus in which, after enunciating His laws for the government of human life, both in its human and Divine relationships, He declared the necessity for a super-earthly consciousness in dealing with all the things of the earth.

You will at once recognize that the paragraph which I read to you this evening, beginning with His charge, "Lay not up for yourselves treasures upon the earth, where moth and rust doth consume, and where thieves break through and steal; but lay up for yourselves treasures in heaven," is a paragraph bringing those who listen to the King face to face with the truth upon which He perpetually insisted, that it is impossible to live the earthly life as it ought to be lived unless there is an abiding consciousness of things above and beyond the earth.

In the course of this particular instruction, He warned His disciples and all the subjects of His Kingdom against two perils, those of covetousness and of care; the two opposites, the desire to possess, and the anxiety lest not enough may be possessed to meet the bare necessities of life. His charge against covetousness closed with these words, "Ye cannot serve God and mammon." They are emphatic, clear, and final, and constitute one of those brief declarations of which it is almost impossible to miss the meaning, unless we come to the text with prejudice, and desire to read into it things that are not in it, "Ye cannot serve God and mammon."

This evening I propose, first, an examination of these words of Jesus; and secondly, an immediate application of them.

First, then, let us take the statement itself, "Ye cannot serve God and mammon." Three words arrest our attention; the emphatic words around which all the rest are grouped, and to which the rest do but serve as connecting links to create the declaration. The three words are God, mammon, serve.

Because it is always necessary to get back to the simplest and most elemental things in our study of the words which fell from the lips of Jesus, I am going to ask you to take these words one by one, and examine them, before we consider the declaration. Let us for the moment put the whole declaration out of mind; we will come back to it, for the text is the message of the evening. In order that we may return to the declaration and consider it, let us then look at the words God, mammon, serve. If I am to understand this declaration of Jesus, I must seek to find out what He meant by God, what He meant by mammon, and what He meant when He used the word serve.

This is a very large inquiry, and one to which for a perfect answer it would be necessary to take the whole scheme of His teaching as you find it in the gospel narratives. I suggest to you that we take another method in order to answer the inquiry, which I think will be perfectly fair. In the whole of this Manifesto what conception of God is manifest?

Mark carefully this thing. He neither argued for the

existence of God, nor attempted to define the mystery of the Divine nature. So far as the teaching of Jesus is concerned, we are left without anything in the nature of definition. He came and exercised His ministry, taking God for granted, never occupying one single half-hour in defending the doctrine of His existence, or in defining the nature of His Being. Therefore, if I would know what He meant by God I must listen for the incidental things, and must pay attention to the underlying conceptions which manifest themselves through those incidental references. In order to find these, I read again this Manifesto of the King, going through it merely to take out of it the direct, immediate references to God which occurred in the course of its deliverance. With what result? The first reference is in the fifth chapter and the eighth verse, "Blessed are the pure in heart: for they shall see God." The next is in the ninth verse, "Blessed are the peacemakers: for they shall be called the sons of God." The next are in the thirty-fourth and thirty-fifth verses of the same chapter, "Swear not at all; neither by the heaven, for it is the throne of God; nor by the earth, for it is the footstool of His feet." In the forty-fifth verse, "That ye may be sons of your Father which is in heaven: for He maketh His sun to rise on the evil and the good, and sendeth rain on the just and the unjust." In the forty-eighth verse, "Ye therefore shall be perfect, as your heavenly Father is perfect." Then I read through chapter six and I find these references, "Your Father Who is in heaven," "Thy Father which seeth in secret shall recompense thee." "When thou prayest, enter into thine inner chamber, and having shut thy door, pray to thy Father which is in secret, and thy Father which seeth in secret shall recompense thee." "Thy Father Who seeth in secret shall recompense thee." "Behold the birds of the heaven . . . your heavenly Father feedeth them. Are not ye of much more value than they?" "If God doth so clothe the grass of the field, which today is, and tomorrow is cast into the oven, shall He not much more clothe you, O ye of little faith." "Your heavenly Father knoweth that ye have need of all these things." "If ye then, being evil, know how to give good gifts unto your children, how much more shall your Father which is in heaven give good things to them that ask Him." These are the references He made to God, never arguing for His existence, never defining His being, but, incidentally, referring to Him.

From these I discover a God of essential purity, the pure in heart shall see Him; a God Who is a God of peace, the peacemakers are His children; a God Who is a God of authority, supremacy, power; heaven is His throne, the earth His footstool; a God Who governs in all things in the material world, and is in that sense a God of providence, making His sun to shine, sending His rain; a God of perfection, "as your heavenly Father is perfect"; a God rewarding men, recompensing men in the sense in which the great word appears in Hebrews, "He that cometh to God must believe that He is, and that He is a rewarder of them that seek after Him"; a God of infinite resources, caring for the birds, clothing the flowers, giving food and raiment to all who put their trust in Him. This is not exhaustive, it is only suggestive. If we let the sublime and glorious thought of God, which evidently filled the soul of Jesus, break upon our consciousness as the result of these incidental allusions, we shall see what He meant when He said "God."

Turn to the next word, *mammon*. The word represents wealth, material possessions not necessarily in particular quantity, but the fact of them, material things. The only place in which the word occurs in the New Testament is here in the Manifesto, and once when Christ, speaking of material wealth, said, "Make to yourselves friends by means of the mammon of unrighteousness; that, when it"—the mammon—"shall fail, they"—the friends—"may receive you into the eternal habitations." What then is mammon? What is mammon according to the conception of Jesus? Something about which men should never be anxious. Something which God knows men must have. Something which God promises He will add in the proper measure and proportion to men according to their need, "Seek ye first His Kingdom, and His righteousness; and all these things shall be added unto you." Something which a man may so use as to transmute it into infinite possession in the land of life which lies beyond. The word suggests material possessions, nothing inherently evil, and nothing necessarily improper.

I turn to the third word, *served*, which need not occupy us above one minute to understand. To serve as does a slave, for the word is one that suggests bond slavery. Its root suggestion is, to be bound by. The inter-related word in the text is master. "No man can serve two masters." "Ye cannot serve God and mammon." It is a word which suggests the supremacy of another; the idea is that of being mastered, and of yielding supreme obedience.

My own conviction is that my task is now really accomplished, that every man and woman can come to this simple statement and see its true impact and discover its true meaning, "Ye cannot serve God and mammon."

This is not a comparison of equal forces in opposition to each other. Jesus is not putting God on that side and mammon on the other as necessarily antagonistic. Had this text said, Ye cannot serve God and the devil, it would have been quite another thing. I am not saying that that is not true, but that is not the text. The underlying thought, the suggestiveness, the philosophy of the text is not the same as it would be under such circumstances. Jesus is not putting God and mammon necessarily into opposition. Everything that mammon connotes is in the Kingdom of God. It has its place in the fulfilment of His purpose. He knows man's need of material things. He will add to man the things he needs. Mammon can be the means to the highest ends. It is possible for man by means of mammon to make friends who will receive him into age-abiding habitations. There is nothing inherently evil in it. The tragedy suggested is not that of man standing between two forces that are forever in opposition, choosing which he will serve. Mammon is simply non-moral. Lay your hand upon a coin, I care not what the coin, a sovereign or a copper, and think with me. That coin is non-moral. There is no inherent evil in it. There is no inherent good in it. The questions of right and wrong lie wholly in the spiritual nature of man, and mammon is affected thereby. You can take that coin and put it to such base uses that it will damn you. You can take that coin and put it to such good uses that it will make you richer forever and ever.

Christ does suggest two possibilities which are in opposition. The one, that man can serve mammon. The other, that he can serve God. What is it to serve God? To be His bond-slave, yielding all to His absolute supremacy. The abandonment of everything to which the name of God connotes, purity, peace, and all those other facts of which we spoke. That is a possibility for every man and nation. There is the other possibility, to serve mammon. To be the bond-slave of material possessions, and every poor man can be that; to yield wholly to the sway of the things which are only material; the abandonment of the life to husks. Jesus declared the possibilities to be mutually exclusive. To serve God and be His bond-slave. To serve mammon and be its bond-slave. To serve God is to command mammon, not to serve it. To be wholly yielded to God is to be the master of all material things, not to be bound in slavery thereto. To state the case from the other side. To serve mammon—to live saying only, What shall I eat, what shall I drink, wherewithal shall I be clothed, and how shall I possess these things, is to dethrone God. "Ye cannot serve God and mammon."

Take two illustrations. First, an individual one. Here is a man standing at the parting of the ways, facing a moral crisis. He knows perfectly well that two ways are stretching out from the point where he stands. He knows perfectly well that he is at a moral crisis in his life. What are these two ways? There is the way of temporal advantage, and there is the way of eternal advantage. These things are not always, necessarily, forever antagonistic to each other, but the hour comes in which they are in opposition. Which will the man do? That is the hour of crisis. We leave him at that point.

Take another illustration, a national one. The hour has come in the history of a nation when two ways lie out before her; one is the way of righteousness. Let us abbreviate the word and make its impact greater, *rightness*. Let us further abbreviate the word, the way of *right*. What is the other way? The way of revenue. These two things are not altogether, always antagonistic. They are not necessarily in conflict. There is a way of revenue which is the way of righteousness. There is a way of righteousness which is the way of revenue. But the hour comes in the history of a nation when these two are in opposition. There is the crisis. That is an hour of destiny for the nation because it is the hour of crisis.

Take your two illustrations again and let me say a second thing. We have seen the crisis, mark the choices. I see a man standing at a moral crisis, at a place where two ways meet, the way of temporal advantage and the other way of eternal advantage. I say to that man, "Ye cannot serve God and mammon." Which will you serve? I say to the nation, as the nation stands at the parting of the ways, when the hour has come that she must decide between righteousness and revenue, "Ye cannot serve God and mammon." Which will you serve?

I go back to the individual in the place of crisis, in the place of choice, and I now look for the consummation. He says, "I will seek first the Kingdom of God." Then all the things which are necessary to him will be added unto him. In that hour, when he has made God supreme, he has come to mastery over mammon.

I go back to the nation and watch her as she makes her choice. I inquire what the consummation will be. I see the nation decide that "righteousness exalteth a nation, but sin is a reproach to any people," and make her choice to do right at all costs, and I see that nation never lacking the revenue necessary for the maintenance of her moral integrity and abiding strength. "All these things shall be added unto you."

You will notice there are no neutral tints in this sermon. I stand here tonight first, always first, so help me God, as a minister of Jesus Christ, but I stand here as an Englishman. It is time that we have done with neutral tints, and that we come back again to the clear dividing lines of Jesus Christ. "Ye cannot serve God and mammon." You say, Is there not such a thing as policy? The Church has nothing to do with it. The Church of God must stand in every hour of crisis by the side of the individual man, in the presence of the nation, insisting upon the hard, clear, sharp, beneficent dividing lines which the Christ of God creates; to the right or to the left, life or death, light or darkness, heaven or hell, for the man or for the nation. "Ye cannot serve God and mammon."

What is the application? You will find in the pews a pamphlet scattered broadcast. My only regret is that I was unable to secure enough to be sure that every man and woman would go home with that pamphlet in their hands at the close of this service. I want those of you who are interested and can lay hands upon one to take it home and read it. That is the second part of my sermon. I cannot pause to read it, neither is it necessary that I should. It is from the pen of a man for whom we all thank God, Mr. Arnold Foster, one of our missionaries in China.

Tomorrow a conference will meet in Shanghai. How many of us know of it? Does the Christian Church in England know of it? I have seen some incidental references to it, some few things said concerning it in the religious press. I have seen more in what men call the secular press than in the religious. The Church of God is asleep about this matter. What was the genesis of that Conference? The answer is in the pamphlet on pages five and six. There Mr. Arnold Foster tells us that this Conference is the outcome of an approach made by the United States Government. What is the constitution of the Conference? Twelve nations are to be represented, China, Japan, Siam, Persia, Russia, Germany, France, Great Britian, Italy, Holland, Portugal and the United States of America. For what are they gathering in Shanghai? The answer is given in the pamphlet. To consider, "The character of the opium habit as a habit. The results of opium on the Chinese as a nation. The volume of the trade, its sources of supply, and the rights of the traders." That is very technical. I do not profess to understand diplomacy or policy. All these things are very necessary I suppose. It is necessary that our Government should send these commissioners. I am profoundly thankful she has consented to do so and that they have gone.

Nevertheless, there is a sense in which the whole thing is a farce. We know perfectly well what the opium habit has done for China. We know perfectly well that the blame and shame is on us. If there were such a thing as a national conscience that was worth anything, we should blush to remember that America had to ask us if we would not consider this problem.

Well, the Conference is to meet. Its object is thus stated, "Suggestions of measures which the respective governments may adopt for the gradual suppression of opium cultivation, traffic, and use within the Eastern possessions, thus assisting China in her purpose of eradicating the evil from the Empire." I quote from the communication sent out to diplomatic agents by the United States State Department.

England has twice declared, through her elected representatives in Parliament assembled, that the opium traffic is "morally indefensible." Since doing so, within the last two years, the Government has steadily resisted China's own efforts to rid herself of it. It is said that we must proceed slowly, that there is the need of policy. I know nothing about policy. I face the facts. I stand in the presence of China's undoing, and I can hardly speak of this thing as I feel it. I know perfectly well that some people will say, the preacher was in danger of getting excited. I am terribly in danger of it. I can hardly possess my soul. Where attempts have been made in certain quarters, during the last two years by China's government, to put an end to this traffic, our Government, by its agents and representatives, has declared that it cannot be done because of existing treaty rights, and that there must be a gradual ending of the thing. That is where we are.

This is not a question of politics, party politics. By unanimous vote, not merely of men sitting on one side of the House, but of the whole Assembly, England has said through her elected representatives, this thing is morally indefensible: but we are halting. Why? There is only one word. Revenue! India is perpetually quoted if we urge haste. Make your calculations of what it would mean to end the traffic forthwith, and then remember that the amount of money necessary for the doing of it, costly though it would be, falling upon this nation by way of taxation, would not begin to compare with the two hundred and fifty millions spent on the Boer war, and the forty millions we have added to our annual expenditure as the result of it. I am not dealing with the Boer war. It may have been absolutely necessary. It may have been a piece of devilry. I do not know or care anything about that now. The fact is that for purposes of wrong or right we spent that money. Here is a great nation crippled, blighted by a traffic we have forced upon her, and we are now standing at the bar of an awakening world conscience. The world is watching this conflict. The representatives of these other nations, however we may question it or wonder about it, will be principally interested to see what Great Britian suggests or is prepared to do. What a chance we have, not wholly to redeem the past—that we can never do—but to set ourselves right with China. We profess an interest in China. Here is our opportunity. What a chance to show the awakening world conscience that we prefer righteousness to revenue.

Has Christ anything to say to us, to England? Who am I? I am but a voice crying in the wilderness. How can I speak to England, or to governments? I may not be able to do so, but I must speak as I can. I say here tonight solemnly in the name of God the Father, the Son, and the Holy Spirit, the word of Christ to this Government and to this nation at this moment is no other than this, "Ye cannot serve God and mammon." If we serve God we shall prefer righteousness to revenue. If we serve mammon, we shall put revenue before righteousness. If we do that, then it would be for the benefit of the world and all the coming ages that we should cease to talk about God. It is this attempt to persuade ourselves that we can still be Christian and worship God, while we persist in the wrong and shameful thing for the sake of revenue, that is harming the Kingdom of God, and flinging a blight o'er all the earth.

The issue is clear cut and definite. To serve God is to co-operate with Him, and to have done at all costs with the thing that is blighting another people. To serve mammon is eventually to be destroyed by God.

We need to be saved from our national pride, from this actual devilish conviction that neither God nor man can harm us. Already the judgment of the moth and rottenness—to use the language of one of the old Hebrew prophets—is upon us. Already, everywhere there are evidences of weakness. I say again, I have said it in other connections, our safety is not in the two-power standard. I am tired of the monotony of the phrase. Our safety is not in the new territorial army. If we do wrong persistently, we are doomed as the nations of the past have been.

Now is the hour of the Church. She should be gathering everywhere in assembly for prayer and humiliation, and insistence upon this great truth. Half the resolutions passed in our denominational assemblies and Free Church Council Federations are of little importance in the light of this. What we need is to come to the knowledge of the fact that we stand nationally at the parting of the ways.

When I have said all, I have not said half that should be said. When I have said all, the last thing and the best thing is that I should get down, and that you should get down before God, taking the sin of our nation into our own hearts. We make our boast that we are of Great Britian. Her shame is ours also. Let us get down before Him in humiliation. Let us cry to Him that He will at this moment guide, direct, and deliver us from this shame, to the glory of His name.

CHAPTER VI

UNPARDONABLE SIN

Verily I say unto you, All their sins shall be forgiven unto the sons of men, and their blasphemies wheresoever they shall blaspheme: but whosoever shall blaspheme against the Holy Spirit hath never forgiveness, but is guilty of an eternal sin.

MARK 3:28, 29.

IT IS IMPOSSIBLE TO OVERESTIMATE THE SOLEMNITY OF THESE words of our tender and compassionate Redeemer, yet they have always been considered difficult of interpretation, and strange, I had almost said wild, theories have been based upon them. I personally believe that much of the difficulty of interpretation is due to lack of the childlike heart, and a simple method in approaching them.

I think I speak for all Christian workers—and by Christian workers I mean all preachers of the gospel, or teachers, or individual workers who know what it is to come into personal dealing with men and women about spiritual things—when I say that at some time or another someone has come to you and told you that they fear they have committed the unpardonable sin.

After some years of such work, and after having met with very many such cases, I have come to this deliberate conclusion, that when a person is obsessed by the idea that he or she has committed this sin, such obsession is the result of Satan's attempt to harass a saint, rather than his effort to destroy a sinner. If that may seem a somewhat strange thing to say, I want quite simply to attempt to make clear what I mean by it. I speak now entirely from experience, and experience may not be trusted as infallible foundation for dogmatic statement. Speaking entirely from experience, I declare that I have never yet found a man or woman, hard and rebellious and determined in sin, possessed by that particular fear. It is always the fear of the sensitive soul, always the fear of some trembling child of God. I do not say that it is always the case, but I do say that I have never met an exception. Therefore, I have come to the conclusion that Satan never destroys men by making them believe that, but he does harass the saints by attempting to make them believe that.

A method I have invariably followed for many years in dealing with those who come to me and say that they have, or that they fear they have committed the sin against the Spirit which has no forgiveness, is that of asking them this question: If you have committed this sin, will you be good enough to tell me what it is? I have never yet found a person possessed of the fear that they have committed it who could tell me what it is.

Notwithstanding all this, the words are full of solemnity. Jesus uttered no idle words. No words that fell from His lips are more full of startling arrest than these. No words are more calculated, or ought to be more calculated, to make men pause and listen and think, and search their own hearts: "Whosoever shall blaspheme against the Holy Spirit hath never forgiveness, but is guilty of an eternal sin." Immediatately, let me mention one matter, so that I need not pause to refer to it again. The change in the versions is all-important. In the Authorized Version it reads, "Is in danger of eternal damnation" or condemnation. Here is one of the cases where there is absolutely no doubt that the text was incorrect. The translation resulted from the fact that the King James translators followed the translation of Tyndall, which translation was based upon the text of Erasmus, and there is no question that at this point it was at fault. Now that other texts are at our disposal, it has been found that Jesus said a far more solemn thing, a far more searching thing than that man blaspheming the Spirit is in danger of eternal judgment, punishment, or condemnation. He declared that such a person is, not in danger of, not even guilty of, in our sense of the word guilty, but to be more literal and in this case far more accurate, he that committeth this sin is in the grip of an eternal sin. Such is the strong and startling word of our Lord.

I detain you yet another moment by way of introduction as I ask you to remember that this most solemn thing was said in immediate relation to perhaps one of the most gracious things that ever fell from His lips, and that is why I read the twenty-eighth verse as well as the twenty-ninth. Hear again the twenty-eighth verse, "Verily I say unto you, All their sins shall be forgiven unto the sons of men, and their blasphemies wherewith soever they shall blaspheme." Not all their sins *may be* forgiven, but *shall* be forgiven. It is one of the greatest words He ever uttered about forgiveness, a word in which He virtually declares that the value of His Cross covered the whole race, and that the redemption He provided was for all men; that sins, not *may be*, but *shall be* forgiven; except that sin which He here described as blasphemy against the Holy Spirit.

We shall better understand the meaning of our Lord if we interpret His words in the light of the whole Bible. Therefore I want in very brief words to cover a large area in the next few minutes, as I remind you of what the Bible teaches concerning the Holy Spirit of God and His mission in human history. Having considered that it will be pertinent for us to inquire reverently, "what is the sin against the Holy Spirit." From these two lines of consideration we may draw lessons of practical application which shall be by the help of God for our own profit in this evening hour.

What does the Bible teach about the Holy Spirit? No one can be at all acquainted with this Library without knowing that the Spirit of God is referred to from the beginning to the end; yet that there is a distinct difference between the teaching of the New and the teaching of the Old Testament. They are not contradictory. They are complementary; yet if I had no New Testament, the doctrine of the Spirit's activity would be other than it is. Go back in memory to your Old Testament, and passing over it in rapid survey, think of what you find in it concerning the Spirit. His work is referred to in the first chapter of your Bible, the Spirit brooding over chaos, the agent through whom the will of God was wrought out so that cosmos came out of chaos, light from darkness, order out of disorder. I pass along over the pages and I find ever and anon, some individual at a crisis who, for a special purpose is spoken of as acting in co-operation with the Spirit. The Spirit was with Joseph and he was able to explain dreams. The Spirit fell upon Bezaleel, and he was able to be a cunning worker in gold for the beautifying of the house of God. The Spirit laid solemn imprisonment upon Balaam, and he was compelled to utter blessing when he desired to mutter cursing. The Spirit clothed Himself with Gideon, and Gideon became the deliverer of his people from Midianitish oppression. The Spirit fell upon Saul, and even he for a time was among the prophet. The Spirit spoke through the prophets, gave them visions and voices, and made them the messengers of Jehovah. You will notice, moreover, through all the Old

Testament, that the Spirit was forever associated, according to the thinking of these men, with Jehovah Himself, working with Him in wonderful fellowship. I may quite reverently borrow the language of the letter to the Hebrews concerning the method of revelation in the past, to describe the method of the Spirit in the Old Testament as "at sundry times and in divers manners." The Spirit fell upon men, equipped them, passed away from them. As I look back over the history which the Old Testament reveals, I see the Spirit of God interpreting the will of God to men when they specially needed it, equipping men for their work in crisis. No system of teaching is given concerning His work, but He is often referred to; so I find through my Old Testament the presence of the Spirit in the history of men.

I come to the New Testament and immediately find that I am in a new age. One Man is presented to my view, born of the Spirit, anointed by the Spirit, filled with the Spirit, led by the Spirit; one Man Who passes before my view from Bethlehem to Calvary, all the while in living co-operation, fellowship, partnership, and harmony with the Spirit of God. During the last days of the life of that Man, I listen as He teaches the group of His disciples truth concerning the Spirit of God, to which men had never listened before. He told them distinctly what the mission of the Spirit should be, when presently, as the result of His own work, that Spirit should be given to men. He made a distinction which I want you to note, the Spirit would no longer visit them fitfully, but He would abide with them forever. He would no longer come to them for special revelation of the will of God, but He would remain to tell them the secrets of God in the commonplaces of life as well as at crises. He would no longer anoint them merely for some hour of crisis, some day of battle, some delicate piece of workmanship, but He would be with them all the days and all the hours, and in all places, in all the activities of life.

Jesus declared that the Spirit should be sent from the Father through Himself, as the result of His own work. He declared that the work of the Spirit should be that of making Him, Christ, living and real in the experience of men. His work was to be Christocentric in the profoundest sense of that word. To the disciples of Jesus, He was to reveal Jesus when He was absent in bodily presence, bringing to their minds all the things He had said, leading them into all the truth concerning the Christ. He was to be the advocate of the absent Christ in the lives of His disciples, and so their Comforter, strengthening them, disannulling the orphanage which they would experience when they lost the vision of His face and the sense of His human nearness.

He also declared that the Spirit would have a special mission in the world beyond His mission to the Church: "He, when He is come, will convict the world in respect of sin, and of righteousness, and of judgment; of sin, because they believe not on Me; of righteousness, because I go to the Father, and ye behold Me no more; of judgment, because the prince of this world hath been judged."

We, therefore, have not to consider the ministry of the Spirit prior to the coming of Christ. We have to consider the ministry of the Spirit subsequent to that coming, in its new aspects, new relationships, new meanings, and new purposes, all of which result from the mission of the Christ.

Therefore, let it be understood that the work of the Spirit in the world is not to make Himself the consciousness of the Church, but to make Christ the consciousness of the Church. The work of the Spirit in the world is not to present Himself, or offer Himself to the world. The work of the

Spirit in the world is to present Christ, to offer Christ to the world.

The Church of God all over the world is confronting a very subtle peril, that of putting the Spirit of God in a place of prominence that is entirely unwarranted by New Testament teaching. The movement associated with the phrase, the gift of tongues, at the present time has upon it the hallmark of hell. Let there be no mistake about this. The terror of it to my heart is that some of the sweetest saints of God, the very elect, are being deceived, because they lack this fundamental intelligence of what the mission of the Spirit really is. If the emphasis of any movement is on the Spirit and on gifts that prove the presence of the Spirit, know this, that according to the teaching of the Christ, that movement is out of harmony with the work of the Spirit. The work of the Spirit is to reveal Christ. The Spirit is the hidden Worker making the Christ Himself the supreme and overwhelming consciousness of believing hearts, the one and only Saviour of men who need salvation.

What then is the sin against the Holy Spirit? The answer to that inquiry can only be given as we thus understand the ministry of the Spirit. That is why I have taken so long in attempting briefly, yet nevertheless carefully, to declare what the work of the Spirit is. The sin against the Spirit is that of persistent, willful rejection of His testimony concerning Christ. There are other passages in the New Testament which have created as much anxiety, as much doubt in the hearts of some Christian people, as has this great and wonderful word of Jesus. They are all passages that refer to the sin which has no forgiveness. You will find two of them in the letter to the Hebrews, one in the sixth chapter, verses four to six, "For as touching those who were once enlightened and tasted of the heavenly gift, and were made partakers of the Holy Ghost, and tasted the good word of God, and the powers of the age to come, and then apostatized," "fell away" I have upon the page, but I use the anglicized form of the Greek word because it helps us to understand the meaning of falling away, "it is impossible to renew them again unto repentance: seeing that they crucify to themselves the Son of God afresh, and put Him to an open shame." It is quite evident that the sin for which there can be no repentance and for which there can be no forgiveness is that of rejection of the Son of God, as revealed and interpreted by the Spirit in that dispensation which had not dawned when Jesus uttered the warning, and which did not dawn until the day of Pentecost.

If you turn on in this same letter to the tenth chapter you find another warning full of solemnity, "For if we sin willfully after that we have received the knowledge of the truth, there remaineth no more a sacrifice for sins, but a certain fearful expectation of judgement and a fierceness of fire which shall devour the adversaries. A man that hath set at nought Moses' law dieth without compassion on the word of two or three witnesses; of how much sorer punishment, think ye, shall he be judged worthy," mark the sin, "who hath trodden under foot the Son of God, and hath counted the blood of the covenant, wherewith he was sanctified, an unholy thing, and hath done despite unto the Spirit of grace." I know there are other difficulties of interpretation and of exposition surrounding these two passages in Hebrews, with which I am not now proposing to deal. I have only read them that I may bring you face to face with the central thought they contain about the sin for which there can be no repentance and no forgiveness. What is the sin? The crucifixion of the Son of God afresh. The trampling under foot of the blood of the covenant, the counting of it as an unholy thing.

How then do men commit that sin? By doing "despite unto the Spirit of grace." To state the case as from the other side. What is the sin against the Holy Ghost? The sin of deliberately refusing to accept His testimony. The sin of deliberately rejecting Christ in that hour in which Christ is presented to the conscience and will by the ministry of the Spirit, so that the conscience is sure of Christ, and the will is constrained toward Christ. Conscious and willful rejection of the Spirit's revelation of Christ is the only sin for which there never can be forgiveness.

Let me put this in another form. Had these men to whom Jesus spoke committed the sin? Certainly not. They were in the neighbourhood of sin. They had been undoubtedly convinced, in the presence of His work, of superhuman power, and they had charged it upon an unclean spirit. They were not guilty of the unpardonable sin. They had not committed blasphemy against the Holy Ghost, but He warned them. If you will suffer your sense of history to help you for a moment, you will see how presently the hour came in which He departed from the world, having left behind Him the circumstances of straitening and limitation. When the Spirit came to the disciples they knew Christ better than they had ever known Him when He had been amongst them in bodily form. On the day of Pentecost when the Spirit fell, sinners in Jerusalem came to a consciousness of the meaning of the mission of Christ which they had never gained while Christ Himself stood in bodily presence amongst them and preached. He warned these men, saying in effect, you may blaspheme My name, speak against the Son of God, and all your sin of that kind shall be forgiven, but there is a new ministry to commence, a new unveiling of My presence and power to be given to you, the Spirit is coming to convict, mark the word, "of sin, of righteousness, and of judgment:

of sin, because they believe not on Me; of righteousness, because I go to the Father, and ye behold Me no more; of judgment, because the prince of this world hath been judged." If you disobey that testimony, if you refuse to yield when the Spirit interprets the meaning of My mission, then there can be no forgiveness, because in that hour you reject the Saviour and forgiveness for all sin. The sin against the Holy Spirit then is that of final and willful rejection of the Lord Christ as He is presented to the heart of man by the ministry of the Holy Spirit. That sin is committed only when the Spirit is finally withdrawn from human life, and the Spirit of God is never withdrawn from human life until the choice has been made distinctly and irrevocably in full possession of all light. Never until that solemn and awful hour is the Spirit withdrawn, and never until that hour can man have committed the unpardonable sin.

Follow me patiently, one step further. That sin cannot be committed during probation. It is not a sin of an hour. It is not a sin of a moment. It is not a sin of an act. It is a sin of attitude, definitely, persistently taken, until the choice has become destiny. When does that hour come? It cannot come while men are still in the midst of light, in the midst of the operation of the Spirit. It never comes until man crosses the boundary between this life and the life which lies beyond. This is not the day of vengeance. It is the day of grace. I may have refused, disobeyed over and over again, time after time, but the Spirit does not leave me, it does not abandon me. I am here to make this affirmation to you with all confidence, basing it upon the whole revelation of the Bible, the Spirit never abandons a man while this life lasts. God has set a limit to probation. At that hour when man passes out of the present into the larger life that lies beyond, he crosses the boundary line.

Have you ever heard the Scripture of the Old Testament quoted, "My Spirit shall not always strive," in order to declare that it is possible for a man with whom the Spirit has been striving for ten, twenty, thirty years, to be abandoned, so that he may live another ten years, lost. I declare that there is no warrant in Scripture for any such affirmation. Take that word, "My Spirit shall not always strive." It was a word of the old economy, as the Bible teaches us. It was a word used in the days when Noah preached righteousness before the flood came. When did the Spirit cease to strive with the men of Noah's day? Never until God shut Noah in, and shut them out, and the day of judgment immediately supervened. While he remained a preacher of righteousness, the Spirit was still striving with men. Lifting the ancient figure into our own age, remember this: God's Spirit never ceases to woo men until the hour comes when crossing over the line they enter upon the destiny they have created for themselves by their own choosing. If there has been no obedience to light, no response to the Spirit, then there is no forgiveness. It is the one and only sin for which there can be no forgiveness. All other sins shall be forgiven except that of refusing forgiveness by refusing the Saviour; the sin of blaspheming the Spirit, refusing His ministry, shutting the heart against His appeal, declining to answer the wooing tenderness of His ministry, or the warning severity thereof. If a man shall so choose and so rebel then the sin becomes age-abiding, it becomes eternal sin and there can be no forgiveness.

Yet hear me once again. Every time in which you refuse the Spirit's ministry you are sinning toward that sin. The final hour will never come while this life lasts. Where is that dividing line? Who shall mark it out for himself? Who shall know but that the Spirit so often refused will not be compelled to end His ministry ere the light of morning breaks because the day of opportunity shall have passed, as you shall have stepped from this room of time into the spacious halls of eternity and the spiritual world. The solemnity of the word needs to be upon our hearts. It may be that in very deed I am close to the border line, and so He who said, and said in virtue of His passion, in virtue of His cross and shame and dying, that all sins shall be forgiven, also said that if a man will not receive forgiveness by the ministry of the Spirit then there is no forgiveness, neither can there be, for the sin becomes age-abiding.

I read to you the sixty-first chapter of Isaiah. You remember when Christ passed into the synagogue and read the great words that indicated His own Mission, He read partly from that sixty-first chapter of Isaiah. Have you noticed where He ceased reading? "The Spirit of the Lord God is upon me; because the Lord hath appointed me to preach good tidings unto the meek; He hath sent me to bind up the broken hearted, to proclaim liberty to the captives, and the opening of the prison to them that are bound; to proclaim the acceptable year of the Lord," and He closed the book and handed it back to the reader in the synagogue. If you will turn to the book of Isaiah you will find that our punctuation puts a comma where He stopped, and the next sentence is this, "and the day of vengeance of our God." But He did not read that, because He had not come then for the day of vengeance. He had come to preach the acceptable year of the Lord. Over nineteen hundred years have run their course, and the comma is still there, but it is only a comma. He will come again with flaming feet for "the day of vengeance of our God." Did you notice the next phrase in Isaiah? "To comfort all that mourn." That is not a mistake. Do not imagine that the prophet has lost his way in rhetoric. It is scientific. It is systematic revelation on the highest line. "The acceptable year of the Lord"! We are in it yet, men, women and children! Beyond it the day of vengeance, of judgment, the day of the Lord, of fire and sword, thank God, upon all oppressors, and upon all wickedness. Beyond that again is the comforting of the mourning, and the establishment of the Kingdom.

Why do I refer to all this in this particular connection? Because the principle is one that I want you to discover at this point. Jesus in this evening hour, in this sanctuary, to every man, woman and child, is fulfilling His ministry by the Spirit in proclaiming liberty to the captives and opening the prison doors to such as are bound, and proclaiming the acceptable year of the Lord. There is only a comma there, and beyond it the day of vengeance of our God. Where does the comma end in your experience? When you pass out of the acceptable year. When you pass out of the gracious time, which the writer of the letter to the Hebrews describes by an ordinary word and which he dignifies with a capital letter, "*Today.*" Ere morning breaks, some of us may have crossed the line. If to the end we have refused the ministry of the Spirit, have declined to let Him break chains and open prison doors and set us free, then mark the word of Jesus, we are in the grip of eternal sin. There is no forgiveness. We pass out into the darkling void where we have lost the vision of God and the possibility of fellowship, and have become the companions of our own sins, dwellers with lust, that is, hungry, having no bread. The day of vengeance of our God has broken for no man or woman in this house.

Troubled heart, has the enemy been saying to you that you have committed the unpardonable sin? Nail that lie down in the presence of the Saviour. The fact that you are here; that your feet found their way here, even though you are filled with anxiety; the fact of the tender pain of conscience lest you may not be right with God; these are supreme evidences of the ministry of the Spirit wooing you toward the Saviour, attempting to persuade you to allow Him to loosen the bonds, unbar the doors, break the chains, and set you free. It is the acceptable year of the Lord.

Yet I could not be true to this text if I did not let my final word be its warning note. Forgiveness for all sin and blasphemy, but if I will not have forgiveness, then I commit the unpardonable sin, the sin of refusing the Christ Whom the Spirit presents. No one has committed it. Many may commit it ere a day or a week has passed. No one need commit it. Harden not your hearts while it is called Today, but answer the ministry of the Spirit Who is not making Himself the supreme consciousness of your thinking, but presents to you the Christ. Yield yourself to the Christ presented by the Spirit, and the Spirit will enter your life bringing with Him the value of Christ's death, the virtues of Christ's life, the victory of Christ's indwelling, and you will find your way into fellowship with God for life and for service.

May we feel the constraint of the Christ through the Spirit, and feeling it, yield to it, and be delivered from the sin that lays its eternal grip upon us so that there can be no forgiveness.

CHAPTER VII

SHINING FACES

It came to pass, when Moses came down from Mount Sinai with the two tables of the testimony in Moses' hand, when he came down from the Mount, that Moses wist not that the skin of his face shone by reason of His speaking with him.
EXODUS 34:29.

THIS VERSE HAS OFTEN ATTRACTED THE PREACHER, AND NATurally so. Almost invariably the attraction has been that of its declaration, that Moses wist not that the skin of his face shone. This also is natural and proper, for that is the main statement. The verse, from the purely literary standpoint, seems to blunder cumberously on its way to that main declaration. But these very apparently awkward repetitions are of great importance, and, in proportion as we grasp their significance, the main statement will become the more arresting and suggestive.

First and obviously, there is declared in this verse the fact of which Moses was unconscious—that his face shone as he came down from the Mount. Then there are the words in which the writer, undoubtedly Moses himself, accounted both for his ignorance and for the shining of his face, and the very repetitions constitute an emphasis which commands attention.

As to the actual shining of his face, he carefully explains the secret of it—"by reason of His speaking with him." He had been dealing with God, and the glory which consequently suffused his spirit shone from his face.

My purpose is to consider the story that is contained in the verse, in order that we may deduce from it some principles of permanent value, and apply them in the simplest and most commonplace realm.

In the story there are two phases. Of these the first is found last in order of statement. It is contained in these words: "The skin of his face shone by reason of His speaking with him." The second phase is contained in the earlier part of the text: "When he came down from the Mount with the two tables of the testimony in his hand, when he came down from the Mount, Moses wist not that the skin of his face shone."

We are all familiar with the traditional picture of Moses that represents him with two horns or beams of light, for beams of light constitute the significance of the horns. In all probability, that traditional picture of Moses was due to a confusion between two Hebrew words. There is a Hebrew word which signifies irradiation, a general illumination; another Hebrew word signifies to shed forth beams of light. The second of these words is used to describe a sunrise, from the view-point of the rays of light which shoot up the eastern sky. The other word describes rather a general irradiation and illumination. There is no question at all that this latter word is the true word in our text, and not the one that suggests beams of light. The fact thus declared, then, is that Moses' whole face was irradiated in a strange and a wonderful way, in an unusual manner, in a way in which those familiar with him had never seen it irradiated before. His face was transfigured; it was metamorphosed. Just as on the Holy Mount the disciples saw the Face of Jesus transfigured, metamorphosed, made radiant as the shining of the sun in his strength; so in the case of Moses what men looked upon, and looked upon with wonder, was a strange new outshining of glory, through the very form and features of the face with which they had become familiar. The deep secret of that outshining was that the spirit of the man, strange and newly illuminated and suffused with light, mastered in a new way his physical countenance. The material passed under the mastery of the spiritual, and there shone and flashed from his face a new and strange and wonderful glow.

Such an experience is by no means uncommon on lower levels. We have all seen it, more or less often, in the course of our lives, and in hours of communion with our friends. The face of a mother is often transfigured as she looks upon her child. The face of that mother is very plain and commonplace usually; but I have never seen a picture of the Madonna so beautiful as the actual face of some mother brooding and crooning over her bairn. We have seen the same transfiguring of the human countenance in the case of true love, in the shining eyes and face of a man, in the lovelit eyes and face of a woman. It has been seen again and again in the history of the world on the face of the martyr. They looked upon the face of Stephen, and it was as the face of an angel, for the light of the spiritual joy transfigured the physical countenance. Over and over again high heroism in the place of difficulty transfigures the face of a man until it flames and flashes with the courage of a god. That is what men saw, in a superlative degree, as they looked at Moses on that particular day. He came down from the Mount and they looked, and saw his face shining with a mystic light.

Moses himself in this verse declares the reason of that shining; "The skin of his face shone by reason of His speaking with him." It is very important that at this point we should have these pronouns rightly allocated. The effect produced, this transfiguration of his face, this illumination, this irradiation, was not the result of Moses talking to God; it resulted from God talking to him.

Let us try to see the occasion. In those wonderful days Moses ascended the Mount of God six times, and this was the last descent.

He had first been called to the Mount, and God had uttered to him words of the great covenant which He proposed to establish between Himself and His people, that they should be to Him for a people of His possession. Descending from the Mount, Moses had declared the words of the covenant, and the people had consented, saying, "All that the Lord hath spoken unto us we will do."

On the occasion of the second ascent, God had spoken to him in other language: "Lo! I come unto thee in a thick cloud"; and had commanded him again to descend and to set a fence about the mountain, and to warn the people to sanctify themselves, to stand apart in awe, aloof from that mountain. Going down, Moses had carried out these injunctions, and separated the people.

Again he had ascended the mountain, for the third time, to receive a further command as to the necessity for the sanctification of the people and the separation of the Mount. The third descent was to obey, and thus to make more sure the awful fact of separation between God and the people.

Then came the fourth ascent. Taking up with him Aaron, Nadab, and Abihu, and seventy of the elders, they saw God, and were not consumed. Aaron, Nadab, and Abihu and the seventy elders retired, and Moses was left alone with God for forty days, in the course of which he received the Law, and the pattern of the ceremonial worship and ritual.

Then came the fourth descent. He came down from the Mountain bearing two tables, upon which the Law was written. The golden calf had been created; and Moses, hot with righteous wrath, dropped and broke the tables of the Law.

Then came the fifth ascent. Moses went back, bearing the sin of the people upon his heart, and prayed one of the greatest prayers recorded in the Bible. He prayed that God would spare the people, and, if in no other way, that He would blot his name out of His book that the people might be delivered. In that strange and mystic hour of communion, Moses dared to ask that God would reveal Himself to him in some new way. Then it was that God told him that no man could look upon Him and live, but that He would hide him in some cleft of the rock, making His glory pass by him. The fifth descent was a return to prepare two new tables in obedience to the Divine command.

Then he ascended for the sixth time. During the period of his last presence upon the Mount, God wrote again the Law upon the two new tables, and made Himself known to him in a way in which He had never made Himself known before.

We may cover all the ground that is necessary for our present understanding of that revelation by saying that Moses had revealed to him by these words of God, that mystery of the merging of mercy and judgment in the Divine character, and in the Divine being. In words that throb with tenderness, even as we read them, the character of God is revealed as to the compassion of His heart. In words that are still vibrant with the thunder of His holiness, His character is revealed as to His holiness; He could make no terms with sin. With the strange new sense of God upon his soul, Moses bowed his head and worshipped. In response to that worship, God repeated in that hour of communion the terms of the covenant between Himself and His people, and re-uttered the words of the Law which had already been given.

In proportion as we apprehend the mystic wonder of that wonderful hour upon the Mount, we begin to understand the experience of Moses. That new spiritual illumination was so mighty, so powerful, that it irradiated his countenance.

So we come to the second phase of the story, which, as I said, is first in order of statement:

> When Moses came down from Mount Sinai with the two tables of the testimony in Moses' hand, when he came down from the Mount . . . Moses wist not that the skin of his face shone.

He had no consciousness of the light which shone upon his face. His spirit had entered into a new fellowship with God. He had fathomed yet more deeply the unutterable abyss of the Being of Deity, and his whole spirit was mastered and held and captured and illuminated by the experience.

Now note the twice-repeated declaration: "When Moses came down from Mount Sinai"; "When he came down from the Mount." That which created his unconsciousness was the Mount, and the fact that he held in his hand those two tables of stone. The Mount was the place of Divine revealing, and that is always the place of self-concealing. The measure in which a soul passes into the presence of God is the measure in which the soul becomes unconscious of itself, and rises to the full dignity of the meaning of its own experience. The deep secret of the human soul is capacity for God which is always forgetfulness of self. He had been on the Mount with God, and all his consciousness was effaced by the fulness of experience. There were no atrophied powers, there was no loss of personality; but personality rose into full spiritual health; and personality in full spiritual health becomes unconscious of itself in its grasp upon God, for the knowledge of Whom and communion with Whom personality is created.

The introduction of the words, "With the two tables of the testimony in his hand," is a remarkable one. The first two tables of the testimony upon which were inscribed the ten words of the Law had been broken; and when Moses realized that he had two new tables in his hands, a supreme consciousness of God filled his soul. Those tables were the symbols of the whole truth that had been revealed. God had declared Himself a God of compassion and of holiness, and the possession of the newly written tables ratified the declaration. That is the Biblical revelation of God from beginning to end, and here it emerges in an almost unexpected place. He is the God of the second opportunity. The Law is broken! Grace will write the words again, and send them back to men that they may try again. Moses coming down from the Mount was not thinking of himself; he was thinking of God; and the light and the glory that He had given to him changed the fashion of his countenance.

There is nothing that we need to-day in this land of ours more than faces that shine. We cannot walk our streets to-day, we cannot travel by railway train without seeing shadowed faces everywhere. The faces that we need are faces that shine, strong in confidence, in hope, in sympathy.

I hold in my hand a clipping from a recent issue of *The Bystander*.

> I fear that we English are not religious at all. (A sombre black tie as evidence of belief does not convince me. A dull-dog-look in the face is no proof of Christian conduct.) If we were really religious, we should light-heartedly wear flannels on Sundays (when weather permitted), and be merry and bright instead of hanging about like ticket-of-leave men afraid of being pulled up to report at any minute. There is

enough cant and personal cowardice in our Sunday solemnity to convict us all of hypocrisy in every hour of the day. We are afraid of our neighbours, and they are afraid of us. We believe that if we are only sufficiently miserable we shall pass muster as being respectable. I am hoping that when our boys come back this insipid "respectability" will go to blazes.

My only apology for reading so frivolous a paragraph is that there is one sentence in it of which I want to make use. Let me say that this is a clipping from two columns, the whole of which consists of the senseless patter of some writer who knows nothing of the agonies of the human soul or of the holy ecstasies of which the soul is capable. "Flannels on Sunday!" There we have the whole shallow and impertinent philosophy revealed! The one sentence I refer to is this: "A dull-dog-look in the face is no proof of Christian conduct." That is perfectly true. A dull and sombre face is a denial of Christianity. What we need to-day, I repeat, is that there should be multiplied everywhere faces that are strong, not brutal—there is a difference; faces that shine with confidence, and never are careless—there is a very clear distinction; faces that are radiant with hope, not frivolous or indifferent; faces that are sympathetic, not pitiful. The Christian face will always be a face that has in it evidences of sorrow, but shining through will be a joy that transfigures the sack-cloth. It will be the face of Jesus reproduced in measure; the face concerning which a prophet long ere He came into time had foretold, which foretelling was fulfilled; His visage was more marred than that of any man; a Man of sorrows and acquainted with grief; and yet the face of One Who could say to His disciples when the darkest clouds were gathering about Him, and the supremest sorrows were surging upon His soul, "These things have I spoken to you, that My joy may be in you."

It is now five-and-twenty years ago and more since a

very simple thing came to my own personal knowledge which profoundly affected me at the time, and from the influence of which I have never escaped. A Yorkshire factory lass had given herself to Jesus Christ; the light and the joy of it was in her soul, and her face became transfigured. She was walking up and down the platform of York Station, waiting for a train. Sitting in a first-class railway carriage was a lady of title and culture. She saw the lassie pass her carriage two or three times, and at last called to her and said: "Excuse me, but what makes you look so happy?" The girl replied: "Was I looking happy? I did not know, but I can tell you why." And she told the woman the secret of her joy. She did not know that her face was shining, but the shining face of the factory lassie arrested the woman who was in agony. The end of the story is that this woman was led to the same Christ, and her face also became transfigured.

Such shining is always unconscious. The effort to look in any particular way is always a failure. All parents know this. There are times when for some reason or another in playfulness they try to look severely at their children, when they are not feeling so. It is never successful. We cannot cheat our children so. It is equally true that when, bowing to the empty conventionalities of a degenerate society, we try and look pleasant at our guests; when we are not feeling so, we always fail, and know perfectly well that we are failing. Perhaps one of the best illustrations may be found in the realm of photography. Is there any agony greater, or any effort more unsuccessful, than that of trying to look as one wishes to look when a picture is being taken? Yet listen to me. A few months ago I was looking at a picture of a beautiful woman, and on that face all the story of her love for her man was patent. She told me that it was taken for him, and that the negative had been destroyed. How had she succeeded? Do you imagine that when she sat for that picture she was thinking about her face? Never for a moment. She was thinking of him, and forgetting herself; and so the light of her love shone upon her face.

A shining face is always the expression of a shining soul; if there be no illumination of the soul, there can be no irradiation of the face. The ghastly smirk that imitates happiness is deplorable; it is tragic. The light within which makes us forgetful of ourselves is the light that transfigures the face. As the spirit is strong in God, the face expresses that strength. As the soul is confident in Him, confidence shines from the eyes. As the spirit is full of hope on the darkest day, hope is seen upon the countenance. As the soul is sensitive to human sorrow and joy, feels the pain and the bliss of others, all the sweet sympathy is manifested upon the face.

What, then, are the secrets of such shining? Let us go back to the story. I admit that times have altered, things are not as they were; but the deep philosophy of the story abides, and its principles are of immediate application.

First, there must be time on the Mount. Time on the Mount is time in which we separate ourselves from all the things of men; time which we give to the cultivation of our fellowship with God and the things of God.

And let us not forget that time on the Mount must be spent in the interest of the very men and the very things from which for the time we have withdrawn ourselves. Moses on the Mount was carrying the burden of the people in the valley. His unconscious shining of face was the outcome of the unconsciousness of himself that made him willing to say, "Blot me out of Thy Book, if only these people can be spared."

Again, there must be silence for God; praise and prayer, but also silence! Is not keeping silence before God almost a lost art among Christian people? "His face shone by reason of

His speaking with him." Not by reason of Moses' speaking with God, but by reason of Moses' silence while God spoke to him. To silence, deliberately sought, reverently guarded, God will for ever more speak; revealing to the waiting soul new phases of Himself; unveiling the mystery of His own character; telling of mercy and judgment; repeating the terms of the old covenant that we have broken that we may renew it again, the law of life that we have violated that we may obey it.

These are the secrets of unconsciousness also. We shall return presently to the valley of our appointed task, mastered by the memory of the Mount, carrying with us the things we have heard in secret, strengthened by the revelation in loneliness. All unconscious of ourselves, we shall go, faces shining with the light.

> To the Mountains O my soul,
>   For fellowship with God;
> To the valleys O my soul,
>   In company with God.
> To the Mount of Light ascend,
>   For purity of soul;
> To the valley dark descend,
>   To make the leper whole.
> To the Mount of Life ascend,
>   For energy for toil;
> To the Vale of Death descend,
>   The demon's power to foil.
> To the Mount of Love ascend,
>   To suffer there for sin;
> To the Vale of Hate descend,
>   To succour, and to win.
> To the Mountains O my soul,
>   In company with God;
> To the valleys O my soul,
>   In fellowship with God.

In the sequel of the story we find our application. Moses had to veil his face. And why? Not because the light was too bright for those people to look upon, but because he knew it was fading, it was passing away. Paul takes up the story, and says that there is no need for the veil now, because the light that shone in the face of Jesus Christ never fades and never passes away. He also says, "We all, with unveiled face, reflecting as in a mirror, the glory of the Lord, are transfigured into the same image from glory to glory." In proportion as we know what it is to find our way to the Mount, and to see God in Christ, to hold fellowship with God in Christ, in that proportion the light that comes upon our faces shines with undimmed and growing splendour, and we have no need to wear the veil.

Does the light on our faces fade? Is the glory passing? Has all the brightness that shone from our eyes almost vanished away? Then we ought to veil our faces, or else cease to call ourselves Christians. There will be no need for the veil, if the mountain light of life and love is ever upon us, and, beholding, we reflect. So may we be men and women of shining faces.

CHAPTER VIII

LIFE; IN FLESH, OR IN SPIRIT

Ye are not in the flesh, but in the spirit, if so be that the Spirit of God dwelleth in you. But if any man hath not the Spirit of Christ, he is none of His.
ROMANS 8:9.

I PROPOSE THIS EVENING TO CONSIDER THE FIRST HALF OF THIS verse, postponing the consideration of the second half to our next Sunday evening.

Jesus Christ came into the world to save sinners. In that declaration is involved the truth, that He came to rescue man from the dominion of Satan, and to restore Him to the Kingdom of God. This involves another truth, that He does, moreover, restore man to the true balance and proportion of his own life.

The mission of Jesus Christ is not that of taking hold of human beings and changing their essential nature save as that nature has become polluted, spoiled, ruined by sin. Then He does completely change it, pardoning the sin, cleansing from pollution, remaking the ruin.

All these processes, of absolution, of cleansing, and of remaking, are in order to the restoration of man to the first Divine ideal. In this wonderful text, occurring in a supreme passage in the letter to the Romans, this truth of the restoration of man to the Divine original intention is brought before the mind, "Ye are not in the flesh, but in the spirit, if so be that the Spirit of God dwelleth in you."

The almost startling "if" in the midst of the text brings us face to face with the fact that it is possible to live a human life, in which the Spirit of God has no place; and yet the text, recognizing the Divine ideal for man, indicates the fact that in whosoever that Spirit dwells, there is restoration to the first Divine and original intention.

Let me draw your attention first of all to a very simple matter, which is nevertheless a most important one to our study. The Revised Version, when compared with the Authorized, has a certain difference which I hold to be all-important to the understanding of the real thought in the mind of the apostle when he wrote these words. The difference to which I refer is not a difference in phrasing. There are alterations and omissions, but none to which I desire to make any reference now. The difference is in spelling, and that in a very simple matter. In the Authorized Version the word spirit is spelled with a capital letter in the majority of instances. In the Revised Version it is spelled with a small letter in the majority of instances.

Let me confirm my examination of that fact to this text. Spirit of God dwelleth in you. But if any man hath not the Spirit of Christ, he is none of His." In the Authorized Version, in the three occasions where the word spirit is used in that verse, it is spelled with a capital letter. In the Revised Version the first occurrence is spelled with a small letter, and the second two with the capital letter. In the Authorized Version the thought of the verse is this. "Ye are not in the flesh, but in the spirit," that is, the Spirit of God, "if so be that the Spirit of God dwelleth in you. But if any man hath not the Spirit of Christ, he is none of His." According to that spelling, in every case in that verse the apostle was referring to the Holy Spirit. The revisers have changed the spelling of the first word so that now the intention of the apostle as suggested is different, "Ye are not in the flesh, but in the spirit," the reference being, not to the Holy Spirit, but to the spirit of man, "if so be that the Spirit of God dwelleth in you."

Accepting, without any doubt, after long and careful consideration of this whole passage, the spelling of the Revised Version, believing that the new spelling gives the most accurate interpretation; I shall ask you first to consider the facts concerning man by nature recognized by this passage, and secondly, to consider the fact concerning man by grace declared by this text.

First, then, the facts concerning man by nature which are recognized by this text. The essential nature of man is revealed by the terms, flesh and spirit. Human nature is a combination of flesh and spirit. Paul, referring to the whole of human personality in the great prayer for the sanctification of the Thessalonian Christians said: "May your spirit and soul and body be preserved entire, without blame at the coming of our Lord Jesus Christ." Spirit, soul, body: that is a recognition of the threefold fact of human personality, physical, psychic, pneumatic. Consider that threefold division well, and see what it really means. Man is spirit and flesh; man has a mind, or consciousness. If the mind becomes blank, distorted; if a man shall lose his reason; he remains flesh and spirit; but by some failure of adjustment between the spiritual and the material the consciousness ceases, or is distorted. We call that madness. The essential fact in any human life is the spiritual fact, yet closely applied to that, and apart from it there is no humanity, there is the material fact. I lay that emphasis upon the fact that mind is a possession in order that we may recognize the fact that what a man's mind is, depends entirely upon whether he lives on the spiritual side, or on the fleshly side of his nature. Here are two men, put them side by side. They are both spiritual in nature; both have bodies; they live in the same street, in the same city, in the midst of the same surroundings, but their conceptions of everything are diametrically opposed. Their minds are entirely in opposition. One man looks at another man but he does not see what his friend sees. One man looks out upon the fields and the hills, but he cannot see what his friend sees. These two men are in this Church. They are sitting side by side, you and your friend, my brother. You are both spirit. You both have bodies. You both have minds.

That is the conception of humanity that lies at the back of this great statement of the apostle. The spirit is the essential. The body is the medium through which the spirit communicates with and receives communications from everything in the cosmos external to itself. The mind is the resulting consciousness.

Pass a step further. The apostle recognizes the fact that man can live in one of two spheres; either in the flesh, or in the spirit; on that side of his nature which is of the flesh, or on that side of his nature which is of the spirit. Mark the contrast between them. A man who lives in the flesh is a man who lives as though life were limited thereby. The man living in the flesh is near-sighted; according to Peter "seeing only the things that are near." He is deaf, he never hears the voices of eternity. He counts the man fanatical or deceived who declares that he does hear them. He is suffering from paralysis in the midst of life. Whatever path he treads he arrives presently at the place of darkness and disappointment. Notwithstanding every attempt to satisfy the clamant cry of his own life, he arrives presently at the place of thirst and hunger; he comes at last to the hour when the consuming consciousness of life is lust—I use the word most carefully, not in its application to one particular form of sin, but in its accurate description of the burning desire that has no satisfaction. The man who lives on that side of his nature, in flesh, limiting his outlook by flesh, comes presently to hardness of heart; to being without faith, without hope, without love either of God or of man. That is the flesh life. These are some things Paul tells us concerning it. To live in flesh is to mind the things of the flesh. May I attempt to illuminate that wonderful word by quotation from the words of Christ. At Caesarea Philippi He said to Peter in stern language, "Get thee behind Me, Satan: thou art a stumbling-block unto Me: for thou *mindest* not the things of God, but the things of men." Peter's protest was a protest of the flesh. It was the shrinking of the flesh in the presence of the pathway of sorrow. It was the protest of flesh against those spiritual conceptions that did not fear men who killed the body, but feared only such as could harm the soul. The man who lives in flesh, minds the things of the flesh.

I particularly desire that this should not be merely the discussion of a theory. Find out where you live. Take the week that has gone. I prefer to look back rather than on. By the grace of God next week may be better than last week, if we will have it so in His strength. For purposes of personal helpfulness let your eye range over the doings of the past days, and apply to them this very simple test, which though not entirely satisfactory, will be helpful for our present purpose. With what were you principally occupied during the days of last week. The test of the hours will help you. What shall we eat, and what shall we drink, and wherewithal shall we be clothed? How shall we be able to possess more of this world's goods? How shall we minister to the comfort of these bodies of ours? How shall we enter into the pleasures of life which are wholly of the flesh? Were these the master questions of the days? Perhaps not expressed so badly as I have expressed them, but still there, absolutely dominating the life. That is life in the flesh. The man who lives there minds the things of the flesh. What else says the apostle concerning this? "The mind of the flesh is death." "The mind of the flesh is enmity against God." The mind of the flesh is not subject to the law of God. The mind of the flesh cannot please God. That is to live in the flesh, as though there were no God, as though there were no eternity, and as though life had nothing to do with any world but this, as though the last and ultimate limit were reached in the hour of death. The atheist declares that these things are so, and vast multitudes of men and women who never declare that they are so, yet live as though they were so. There are gradations of life in the flesh. There are manifestations of life in the flesh that to the common thinking of men are more vulgar than others, but in the sight of high heaven they are all on the same level. If a man lives a life of the flesh and gives himself up without reserve to all the vilest passions of his own debased nature, that is life in the flesh. Or if a man, for purely selfish purposes and selfish reasons, abstains from the vulgarities, but is without worship, has no upward look, no commerce with heaven, no recognition of a hereafter, no conception of any reality except the reality of today and the dust; he is living in the flesh as surely, and in the sight of high heaven with as pronounced vulgarity, as the man who gives rein to his lusts.

Here again I pray you do not misunderstand me. If there be no God, if there be no eternity, if there be nothing beyond the shadowy portal of the grave, well then we will make a great difference between these two men; and that is the human differentiation between respectability and vulgarity in sin. I am not here to make such differentiations. I am here viewing life in the light of this Book. I am here attempting to see humanity as it is seen from the heights and amplitudes of eternity. Life in the flesh. When you speak of your higher and your lower in that realm, you must find out how much higher or lower one is than the other, not by comparing the higher and lower in the flesh, but by comparing the whole flesh life with life in the spirit.

Turn then to the other side of the suggested picture, life in the spirit. That is life in which man recognizes that the essential part of him is spiritual, that he is not ultimately, finally, fundamentally of the dust, but of Deity; that this life is but school time, and probation, and preparation; and that all he feels within himself of essential life will come to its fulfilment and intensity beyond; the life which answers not the call of the flesh, but the call of the spirit.

All this study is illuminated by the Genesis story. There is a side of me that has come up out of the mystic, marvellous, creation of the material. I can touch the material and know it has to do with the dust. But there was a moment in the process of creation when God enwrapped that material, which in itself was infinitely higher than anything beneath it in the scale of creation, in His own breath, breathed into it forces eternal and spiritual. Thus man became a living soul. The gap between that God-breathed man and the highest form of life beneath him is the gap between eternity and time, between Deity and dust, between spiritual and material. Therein was the essential and final creation of man. A man can live on that side of his nature and what does it mean? Vision. I cannot use that word in that connection without there coming back to me a passage full of beauty and meaning in that great chapter in Hebrews describing the heroes and heroines of faith. This wonderful thing is said about one man, it is an illuminative truth, and thank God it describes exactly thousands of men today; "He endured, as seeing Him Who is invisible." If you are living in the flesh you cannot understand that, and you may just as well say so at once. You smile at it, and you pity the man who as you say thinks he sees the invisible. I want to tell you in all tenderness and gentleness, he pities you far more than you can pity him. This is not a dream. How do I know he sees the invisible? By the way he endures. The demonstration of the far vision is courageous endurance. I am not talking of a bygone age. I made my quotation from the days of old only because it has a living application. Such men are right here in this building. There are men and women here as I speak tonight who see far beyond the preacher; it would be a sorry business if they did not; they see Him Who is invisible. When my voice is no longer heard, the voices from the eternal still sound in their ears.

Life in the spirit means acuteness of hearing; a sense of power; a thrilling emotion; ecstasy and rapture, through all things and forevermore; courage of heart enabling men to endure. Life in the spirit is life indeed.

In the context, Paul describes the mind of the spirit more briefly than the mind of the flesh, and yet more inclusively. The man who lives in the spirit minds the things of the spirit, and what of them? The mind of the spirit is life and peace. If we divide this congregation by the standards of men we have all sorts of divisions, learned and unlearned, rich and poor, high and low, noble and ignoble. I protest unto you, my masters, in the name of Father, Son and Holy Spirit, that in the division of heaven we are in two classes, men and women who live in the flesh, and men and women who live in the spirit.

These are the facts recognized by my text. That a man can live in flesh with eyes shut to the eternities, with ears stopped to the voices of the infinite, and heart insensate to the nearness of God. A man can live on the spiritual side of his nature, seeing the invisible, hearing the unuttered, knowing the undiscoverable.

Now finally, I pray you notice what the text reveals concerning man by grace. That is the text. The other things have been inferences. This is declaration, revelation, affirmation. "Ye are not in the flesh but in the spirit, if——" I pause at that "if" before I pronounce the final words. I would ask you to notice how these first words make their appeal. "Ye are not in the flesh but in the spirit, if——" I speak to the men who are in the flesh, but who would fain escape the imprisonment of the flesh ere this service is over. I believe there are such here. You are in the flesh. You are saying, How can I escape this life, this prison, this bondage, this slavery to the flesh. Already my inner life is pining for something, and how I have tried to satisfy that burning thirst, that devouring hunger. Can I again cross over the line from flesh into spirit? "If so be that the Spirit of God dwelleth in you."

The mission of the Spirit of God is to restore man, first to a true relation to God, and so to the true balance and proportion of his own life. Are you living in flesh? Then hear me while I declare you are living an inverted life. The Spirit of God coming into the life of a man takes hold of that man and turns the whole life around, putting it back into harmony with the Divine ideal, putting it back into the essential meaning of its own being. Have you lived in the flesh? Then your life has been a disappointment. If some of you do not believe that yet, there are scores in this house who will bear witness to the truth of it, even though they have not yet yielded themselves to Christ.

The coming of the Spirit of God into the life of a man means that the spirit of man is taken out of the prison and put on the throne; that from that moment the man will live not in the consciousness of the near, but in the consciousness of the far, not in slavery to the cry of the flesh, but in obedience to the call of the spirit. It is by entering into the life of the Spirit of God that the change is wrought.

Let us look at this generally as I close. The test of Christian profession is in this text. If I live in the flesh I am not a Christian. I may sing all the songs in the hymn-book, and recite all the prayers that were ever written by other men, or composed by myself, study the whole Bible until I know its literature from cover to cover; but if I live in the flesh I come under condemnation. All that is the burden of the second half of my text, I utter it and postpone it. Remember that this text is the test of life. If I am living in the flesh then I am not living according to the possibilities of my own nature. I am something less than man, something lower than man, something infinitely beneath the potentialities of my own personality. This is the truth I would fain bring to the attention especially of young men in this day. Over and over again young men tell me they imagine Christianity means the ending of life. Man, it means the beginning. I mean that quite literally. It means the beginning of this life. You cannot live human life at its fullest in London if you are living in the flesh. All the gaud and glitter of things temporal are the devil's methods for drowning thought. The one thing you dare not do if you are living in the flesh is stay to think. You must away to the glaring lights and the clashing music and the paint. God help you, man. That is not life. Life in the flesh is life in prison, and in corruption. Life deteriorating, degenerating, dying, doomed, and presently damned. I pray you deliver yourself in this hour from soft conceptions of what you are doing, and come to see the horror of the whole business. You were made to lift your face to God. God has put eternity in your heart, so said the ancient preacher, and it is true. You can never satisfy the surging eternity of your own being with the nonsense of fleeting time. You can never satisfy the clamant cry of your deepest life in the painted glitter of the place of sin. Life in the flesh is disaster because it is failure.

The declaration of deliverance is here. I am flesh bound, flesh imprisoned, yes, but the I of me is not flesh. It is that which is bound, that which is imprisoned. It is myself, my spiritual nature, that which cannot die, that which presently, if I live in the flesh will pass out without a tenement into the eternities, naked, not clothed upon, having lost its way and its home. That is the essential of me and that can in these very moments, while the preacher utters his last words, in the case of every man and woman, come back into its true place through the Spirit of God. The Spirit of God is waiting to enter into fellowship with the spirit of every man, and make that spirit dominant in the life of the man, so that from that moment the flesh serves instead of masters.

The way of full life is here. The spirit of man in fellowship with the Spirit of God; then what? Then the flesh of man is ennobled because the flesh of man is used only under the direction and inspiration of the Spirit of God, and becomes the true medium through which the spirit of man enters into communication with all God's earth, and God's humanity, and God's heaven, and God's eternity.

Is that life possible? Here is the last word. Is it possible, says some man in this house, for me to be done with the flesh life and enter into the life of the spirit? Quite possible. How? By the reception of the Holy Spirit. How may I receive the Holy Spirit? In the Gospel of John is a wonderful story of how Jesus once stood in the midst of the thronging crowds at the feast of Tabernacles, on the last day, the eighth day, and He said, "If any man thirst let him come unto Me and drink. He that believeth on Me, as the Scripture hath said, out of his inner life shall flow rivers of living water." Oh, you say, what did He mean by that? The next verse tells you, "this spake He of the Spirit, which they that believed on Him were to receive: for the Spirit was not yet given; because Jesus was not yet glorified." That declaration has a historic application and an immediate application; a personal application. Historically, it meant that until He was glorified by the way of the Cross and resurrection the Spirit could not come. The personal application, what is it? A man receives the Spirit in the hour in which he yields himself to Christ. Glorify Christ, trust Him, glorify Him with thy trust, glorify Him with thy submission, by yielding thy life to Him; then what? The answer to your faith in Christ is God's gift of the Holy Spirit. One Lord, the Lord Jesus Christ. One faith, faith in Christ, the faith of the man who, conscious of sin and weary of the flesh, yields to Him. One baptism, the baptism of the Spirit whereby that man receives the Holy Spirit. Mark the process. It is an old story.

You are once again confronted by the Christ of God, the Saviour of men. Will you trust Him? Will you believe in Him? Will you yield your life to Him? Do it now, right at this very moment. Take that life of yours, in the flesh though it be, and yield it to Him.

> Nothing in my hand I bring;
> Simply to Thy Cross I cling;
> Naked, come to Thee for dress;
> Helpless, look to Thee for grace;
> Foul, I to the fountain fly;
> Wash me, Saviour, or I die.

Will you so come? In the moment in which you do, He answers your coming by the gift of the Spirit. Though there be no tongue of fire, though there be no sound of a mighty rushing wind, God's Holy Spirit enters in, and His first work is to bring your spirit out of the dust and degradation of your fleshly life, and give it the consciousness of acceptance with God.

From that moment life is new, changed, different. You live then "as seeing Him Who is invisible," in the spirit instead of in the flesh, and under the discipline of His patient grace you will come at last to glorious fulfilment, in conformity to the life of the Son of God.

CHAPTER IX

THE SPIRIT OF CHRIST; THE SUPREME TEST

Ye are not in the flesh, but in the spirit, if so be that the Spirit of God dwelleth in you. But if any man hath not the Spirit of Christ, he is none of His.
ROMANS 8:9.

TWO WEEKS AGO, WE CONFINED OUR ATTENTION EXCLUsively to the first part of this text, "Ye are not in the flesh, but in the spirit, if so be that the Spirit of God dwelleth in you." This evening we consider the sequel to that subject by taking the second part of the verse, "If any man hath not the Spirit of Christ, he is none of His."

Glancing at the verse in its entirety, we at once discover a significant and suggestive change in its expressions; "the Spirit of God," "the Spirit of Christ." Each of these phrases refers to the One of Whom we speak as the Paraclete, the Holy Spirit. This fact makes the change in the method of expression the more arresting. The second phrase has sometimes been treated as though it referred to the tone, the temper, the disposition of Christ only; so that one might read, "If any man hath not the *disposition* of Christ, he is none of His." While I hold that such interpretation is not final, nevertheless, I believe that to be the significance of the change of expression. Whereas the reference is undoubtedly to the Holy Spirit in the second part of the verse, as it is in the first part, the writer brings us in the second half, face to face with the fact that the indwelling of the Spirit of God does produce the mind of Christ. Speaking of the Spirit as the dynamic force of life, he uses the phrase "the Spirit of God." When desiring to deal with the result manifest in character, he uses the phrase "the Spirit of Christ." The first reminds us of the unseen and hidden secret, the indwelling Spirit of God. The second reminds us of the seen and manifest result, the Spirit of Christ.

The great secret of the beauty and glory of the life of Jesus of Nazareth was that He lived in fellowship with the Spirit of God. Born of the Spirit, sustained by the Spirit, led by the Spirit into the wilderness, He returned in the power of the Spirit to do His work, until He, "through the eternal Spirit offered Himself without blemish unto God." He acted in constant co-operation with the indwelling Spirit of God, never resisting, never grieving, never quenching.

What then was the result of such living? The Spirit of God became manifest in the Spirit of Jesus. While the phrase does refer to the actual Person of the Holy Spirit, it refers, nevertheless, to that Person in the manifestation of character wrought out in the mind of Christ; in the tone, temper, and disposition of Christ. Therefore, these two phrases bring us to the consideration of the seen and unseen in the Christian life and character.

May we then, reverently and carefully, attempt to consider this second half of the verse as the test of our Christianity; bringing ourselves to its suggested measurements, yielding our lives to its proposed balances, in order that we may so discover whether or not we have the Spirit of God. The absence of the Spirit of Christ demonstrates the absence of the Spirit of God. The presence of the Spirit of Christ proves the presence of the Spirit of God. Therefore, this part of the text which seems so simple in statement, flames with light and is one of the most searching tests to be found in all the apostolic writings.

I want to say one or two preliminary words on the subject of the importance and nature of character. The character of a man is expressed through his spirit, through his tone, temper, disposition. You cannot express character by the utterance of words. You do not express character finally in any particular deed. The character of a man cannot be decided by the thing he says, neither can it be discovered by the occasional thing he does. The meanest man in London may give the largest gifts to philanthropic purposes. The most generous man may have nothing to give. The saint may be discovered over and over again in some unworthy fashion of speech. The most vulgar man may drop into the language of sainthood. A man's character is always revealed in his disposition. Character is what a man is. Doing, saying, and having, possess no beatitudes. Being is crowned with the seven-fold garland of the Sermon on the Mount. Therefore, let it be perfectly understood that the final truth about a man's character is known only to God. No man can know finally the truth about the character of his brother man. The searching I suggest for my own soul and for yours in the presence of this text is not an inquisition, or an investigation of my soul by another, or of your soul by the preacher. We come together into the presence of this declaration in order that in loneliness, as between ourselves and God, we may find out whether we belong to Christ or not.

Let us then, reverently inquire what was the Spirit of Jesus.

We want to discover the mind of Christ, the tone, temper, disposition of Christ; the quality of the Spirit of God as revealed through Christ; and in order to do this we must consider the spirit of the Man of Nazareth. Forgetting for the moment the supreme fact that the spirit He manifested was the Spirit of God, for in Him Deity was unveiled, we come to the human level and inquire, what was the mind of Jesus, what were its notes, its qualities?

You realize at once that the preacher has asked a question that is very difficult to answer, for how is it possible to express with anything like brevity or accuracy the truth about the Spirit of Christ? Ask me concerning His words, and I could give you some account of them, materially at least, realizing more and more their intense spiritual values and my inability to fathom their profoundest deeps. Ask me about His deeds, and I can follow Him from place to place, and tell you of the deeds done, and the wonders wrought, but to see the Spirit of Christ is more difficult.

I am impressed first by the fact that the Spirit of Christ was characterized by simplicity rather than by complexity. I am impressed secondly by the fact that the Spirit of Christ was characterized by serenity rather than by feverishness. I am impressed finally by the fact that the Spirit of Christ was characterized by sensitiveness rather than by callousness.

Simplicity. Allow me to attempt to illustrate what I mean by simplicity. Nothing impresses me more as I read the story of Jesus than the fact that He never seemed to need to prepare for any occasion. He was always the same, transparent, natural, simple. Complexity may be defined by another term, hypocrisy. The Spirit of Jesus was absolutely devoid of this in any form. His was the simple life, the life in which there was no twist, no iniquity. With an artlessness that arrests, He spoke the things of His inner life in the presence of men. He said things which from the lips of other men would have sounded of the very essence of egotism. Yet, in His own age, the things He said did not surprise. Standing one day in the midst of a critical, hostile crowd, Jesus said, "I do always the things that are pleasing to Him." Imagine any other man saying that, and let the man of your imagination be the man you think most of as a spiritual leader; what would be the result produced in your mind? From that moment you would begin to question his sincerity. Yet, in the Gospel of John the statement which follows that declaration is this, "As He spake these things, many believed on Him." That was the result of the transparent simplicity and honesty of Jesus. We may put the whole matter in quite another way, expressing it in fuller language in His own words, "I am the Truth." Not that I preach it, teach it, expound it, not even that I hold it, but that "I am the Truth." There was perfect harmony between every side of His nature. He had no hidden chamber, nothing secret. As I watch Him through all the story of His life, I am growingly impressed with the simplicity of His Spirit. I need not pause to say that simplicity does not mean superficiality, but transparency. If you think of a great pool upon the rocks, it is simple when you can see through the limpid waters all the things that lie upon the rock foundation. The Spirit of Jesus, the disposition of Jesus, was that of absolute, transparent simplicity.

Serenity. I am impressed increasingly by the serenity of Jesus, by the fact that in hours when all others seemed to be swept by storms, or moved by excitement, He alone was quiet, calm, and full of dignity. If ever the great word of Scripture was fulfilled in human life, "He that believeth shall not make haste," it was in Jesus' life. One pauses as the illustrative pictures pass through the mind. Let me take one of the last. If ever there was an hour in His life when one would have expected to see Him moved as by tempest, it was that hour in which He approached the Cross. Yet the one calm, dignified, unruffled man was Jesus. The Roman Procurator, used to scenes of the kind, able with an iron hand to quell rebellion, was strangely perturbed. The priests were roused to white heat in their anger. The populace, fickle as it always is, was clamouring for blood. The one silent, calm, serene Spirit was that of the Christ.

Sensitiveness. Jesus came into the presence of no natural emotion which He did not share. In the presence of joy, He was joyful. In the presence of sorrow, He was filled with sorrow. If He came into the presence of the brokenhearted, widowed mother, as she followed her only son to burial, all the sorrow of her heart entered into His. If He came to the house of the marriage feast, all the gladness and joy was in His own heart. He was keenly sensitive.

These are ultimately truths about the Spirit of God, truths about God Himself. "In Him there is no darkness at all." The whole nature and method of God is that of profoundest and almost overwhelming simplicity. God is not forever changing as man is. He abides unchanged through all the processes of human change. He is forevermore a fire, either destroying or purifying, according to the nature of that which comes within its sweep. He is forevermore the sun of life, either producing fruit or burning to destruction, according to whether it touches a tree planted by rivers of water or stubble.

I need not remain to argue the serenity of God. The fact is that in the day of clash and catastrophe He is still unmoved, unafraid. "He shall not fail nor be discouraged till He have set judgment in the earth," till He have established His law in the affairs of men. We are discouraged, we are full of feverish excitement, we must demonstrate in order to make people believe. The serenity of Jesus was the serenity of the Spirit of God, which is the serenity of God.

Moreover, the sensitiveness of Jesus was the sensitiveness

of the Spirit of God, and the very sensitiveness of God Himself. Faber sang truly when he sang that earth's sorrows are most keenly felt in heaven. I venture to add the declaration on that earth's joys delight the heart of God.

This was the Spirit of Christ. Simplicity, serenity, and sensitiveness, have we these? If we lack them we lack the Spirit of Christ. If we have not the Spirit of Christ it is because we have not the Spirit of God, for He ever produces these very manifestations. "If any man hath not the Spirit of Christ, he is none of His."

Where shall we apply the test? Let us understand that the examinations of God are never special, are never fore-announced. All the method of human examination is utterly different to the method of Divine examination. The tests of the spirit come not at the announced hour for which we may specially prepare, but in the ordinary pathway of human life, or perchance in some unexpected crisis. If the crisis be expected it ceases to be a day of testing. It is along the line of the commonplace that I am to discover what spirit mine is. I am to find out, not tonight in this sanctuary, whether I have the Spirit of Christ; it is impossible to do it here; it must be done tomorrow, in my home, in my office. The spirit of a man is tested in adversity of prosperity, in the place of obscurity, or the place of popularity, in time of defeat or the time of victory, and most often, amid the thousand and one trifles of the busy hours.

Let us observe in general terms how spirits are tested in such circumstances. It is the hour of adversity, storms are sweeping, so that we are inclined to say with Jacob of old, All these things are against me. That is the hour in which the spirit is tested. One man in such an hour gives way to despair, gives up the struggle. Another is characterized by his patience, by his quiet endurance. The one is fretful, quarrelsome.

complaining. The other is quiet and peaceful. What is the difference? It is the difference of spirit. It is the difference of tone, temper, disposition. One man is living in the flesh. The other man is living in the spirit.

Or it is the hour of prosperity when everything is succeeding. Everything touched turns to gold, success attends every effort. That is the place to try the spirit. In that hour, one man becomes noted for his arrogance, his overbearing disposition, his contempt for the man who fails. But another man in that hour is characterized by beneficence and a desire to hold out a helping hand to the man who is struggling. One man makes his prosperity the throne from which he grinds his fellow beneath him. The other makes prosperity the hearth to which he invites his neighbour to share his hospitality. What is the difference? It is the difference of disposition. I am prepared to say that in a sense neither man can help what he does. He is doing what he is. The profoundest fact concerning him and his character is being manifested.

Or again. Here are two men, both in the place of obscurity; suddenly removed, it may be—let me speak in the realm of my own calling, my own work, and leave you to make the application to yours—suddenly removed from the place of conspicuous service to some place of obscurity, like Philip taken from the rush and glory of a great revival in Samaria to the desert loneliness, to talk to one man riding in his chariot. One manifests bitterness, complains that the fates are against him, that men do not appreciate him, and spends all his days murmuring against the hardness of his lot. The other faces the desert and there sheds the fragrance of a sweet and beautiful content. I do not say he wastes his sweetness on the desert air, never was there such a mistake made. Sweetness is never wasted, even on the desert air. If some bird in its flight shall drop a seed on some fertile soil and it comes to flower, if no human eye sees it, God gathers the fragrance, and it is sweet and beautiful to Him. What is the difference between these two men? It is the difference of spirit.

Or, on the other hand, a man is brought from obscurity to popularity, to use the word of the world, and immediately becomes proud and distant, forevermore rejoicing in the fact that he has become conspicuous. Another put into the same position comes and brings with him all simplicity, all humility. Humility never announces itself. The man who tells you that he is serving God in his humble way is the proudest man for five miles round. Humility, like love, "vaunteth not itself, is not puffed up, doth not behave itself unseemly." In the light of conspicuous success, or popularity, the man of the Christ Spirit is simple, sweet and full of everything that woos men, soothes their weariness, heals their wounds, and helps them upon the way.

Yet again, it is the hour of defeat. One man becomes a coward and the other man becomes a hero. A hero in defeat, you say. Yea, verily. It takes more heroism to suffer defeat than to win a victory. There is a fine air of dignity about some men in the hour of defeat. When men go to pity them, or condole with them, they can do neither, because of the heroism with which they suffer defeat.

Or it is the hour of victory. One man becomes a tyrant and the other manifests great gentleness.

Or most often, amid the thousand and one trifles of life, the spirit we are of will manifest itself in the midst of the commonplace trifles of our own home life far more than anywhere else. I think I had better leave you to make the applications. The late breakfast may prove whether or not you are a Christian, more than the song in the sanctuary. I do not say that to make anyone smile. If you are laughing at your own folly, repent of it. Come to an understanding of the fact that a man is revealed, not on the public platform, you cannot know him there, but is revealed in the little incidental things of his home life. There are men to whom the papers would give whole columns of notice, but if we could have the story of their wives, and we never can, for woman is far too heroic, we would know them as non-Christian, notwithstanding all the papers say. It is the spirit, the tone, the temper, the disposition that is supreme. If any man have not the creed, not the orthodox view; No, "If any man hath not the Spirit of Christ, he is none of His."

As I have already said, I am not bringing you to a judgment throne as though I were the judge. God forbid, I am a sinning man. I am not asking you to accept the opinion of friend or neighbour. I will not accept your opinion, I care nothing for it. I am absolutely independent of it. I have lost all fear of what you say or think concerning me. Nevertheless, in the inner secret shrine of my deepest life, I stand in the presence of His judgment bar, and I know that my relationship to Christ is tested by my spirit.

I do not think I would dare come to that text if it were not for the first part of it which we have already considered, "Ye are not in the flesh, but in the spirit, if so be that the Spirit of God dwelleth in you." I go back to it because there are those who are saying, Such a judgment seat as that condemns us! If our Christianity is to be tested not by our creed but by our spirit, then we are guilty. There are those who, saying that, are now inquiring, How can we have that Spirit of Christ? How can we become like Him? How can we be rid of the thousand and one hypocrisies that have blasted our lives, and find our way into the simplicity of absolute truth? How can we be freed from the dastardly conventionalities which make us lie in polite society, and find our way into the straight and enduring grandeur of simple truth?

How can we find our way from the panic that so often seizes us, the feverishness that makes us impulsive, and makes us fail; into the quiet, dignified serenity of the Spirit of Christ? How can we escape the callousness that for long time has made us incapable of tears in the presence of sorrow, or of laughter in the presence of joy? How can we escape from the spirit which is the spirit of the self-centered, flesh-mastered life, and find the spirit which is the spirit of the God-centered life?

Now the inquiry is answered, "Ye are not in the flesh but in the spirit, if so be the Spirit of God dwelleth in you." Remember this; I say this especially to young men and women who are struggling toward the ideal, seeing it in its beauty; remember that you cannot create spirit by the government of externals. By saying I will never again speak an unkind word, you will not create the kind spirit. Sooner or later, the actual fact will flame out again. If your spirit is unkind, for a long time out of self-respect you may curb your tongue, and prevent the poisoned word, but the hour of provocation will come and it will break loose. Not by the government of externals is the spirit ever remade.

I go a step further than that. Not by admiration or imitation does reproduction ever result in matters of the spirit. There is the vision glorious, of the simple, serene, and sensitive Christ. I will admire it. I will imitate it. I will make Him my Exemplar. These things will never reproduce His likeness. There will be but bitter disappointment for the man who attempts imitation of Christ, apart from the necessary preliminary.

Then how can I have the Spirit of Christ? The Spirit of God is alone equal to producing the Spirit of Christ. "The fruit of the Spirit is love." Unless the Spirit of God is there, the Spirit of Christ will never be there. Unless the unseen Spirit is there, the manifest Spirit must necessarily be absent. So, therefore, that which we need in order that we may have the Spirit of Christ, is the Spirit of God Who clears the vision that we may see indeed the ideal, and Who does infinitely more, who supplies the virtue in order that we may imitate the ideal in strength. The indwelling Spirit of God transforms the spirit of man until it becomes in very deed the Spirit of Christ. Brethren, do you not know it is true? Have you not seen it so? Have you not seen the man fierce and unkind become gentle and patient by the indwelling of the Spirit of God?

Finally, let us remember that the matter of supreme importance is that of our spirit. What is your disposition? How many a man is blaming his father for his disposition. How many a man is saying, Everything is against me, I inherited this from my father. "The fathers have eaten sour grapes, and the children's teeth are set on edge." Absolutely untrue. That proverb became current in the days when Israel sat by the waters of Babylon and mourned over their fathers' sins; until Ezekiel and Jeremiah alike nailed the bad coin to the counter forever by saying, This is not true, "Ye shall not have occasion anymore to use this proverb in Israel." If your teeth are on edge, you have been at the sour grapes! I grant you your evil disposition, but remember this, it can be changed, or I have no gospel. In its place there can be the very Spirit of Christ. That is the supreme matter. Oh, it is important what a man believes, or disbelieves; but these things are important only as they manifest themselves in works. The creed that does not blossom into conduct and become gracious character is of no value whatever. It is the spirit that matters. If that be true, how many un-Christly things are done in the name of Christ. I have heard the orthodox faith so preached as to drive men and women away from Christ. It is the spirit that matters.

This also let us remember. We too often attempt to correct the center from the circumference. Let us rather correct the circumference from the center, by handing over all our lives to the Christ Himself and so receiving the Spirit of God. When that Spirit of God is enthroned, we live no longer in the flesh but in the spirit, and then, not all at once, for the full fruitage of Christian character does not come in a moment to perfection; first the blade, then the ear, then the full corn in the ear; but when the Spirit of God is in the life there will be the first promise of the Spirit of Christ, and we shall "grow up in all things into Him Who is the head."

I urge that we all come to this judgment seat alone, when the service is over, when the preacher's voice is silent, when the associations of the sanctuary are gone; with our own New Testament let us go somewhere by ourselves, and let us inquire if we have the Spirit of Christ. If not, know that it is because we lack the Spirit of God; and knowing that, let us crown the Christ by trusting Him, and so receive His Spirit that we may become like Him.

CHAPTER X

HORIZONED BY RESURRECTION

Declared to be the Son of God with power, according to the spirit of holiness, by the resurrection from the dead.
ROMANS 1:4.

THESE WORDS CONSTITUTE THE SECOND PART OF A DOUBLE statement concerning one Person. That Person is indicated by a reference preceding the statement and by an explanation following it. The reference you will discover in the beginning of verse three:—"concerning His Son." The explanation is contained in the closing part of verse four:—"even Jesus Christ our Lord." Between this reference and this explanation we find the twofold statement concerning the Person thus referred to.

> Born of the seed of David according to the flesh.
> Declared to be the Son of God with power, according to the spirit of holiness, by the resurrection from the dead.

If for purposes of illumination, I may take from each of the two parts of the words necessary to discover the simple contrast, we have this result. Paul says concerning this Person Whom he first designates "Son of God" and finally refers to as "Jesus Christ our Lord," two things. First, according to the flesh He was "born of the seed of David." Secondly, according to the spirit He was "declared to be the Son of God with power . . . by the resurrection from the dead."

The first part of the apostolic declaration is simple and needs neither argument nor explanation, "of the seed of David, according to the flesh." The second part of the declaration was sublime and it was impossible—if I may thus interpret the method of the apostle—for him to write the second part without some qualification. "Of the seed of David according to the flesh," is a perfectly simple and natural declaration; but when he turns to the other side, "according to the spirit," he has to qualify, "according to the spirit of *holiness*"; or even more accurately as I think, "according to a *holy spirit*." "According to the flesh" He was of the seed of David, and Paul knew that no argument of that fact was needed. But, "according to the spirit," the essential matter in that human life, there was a difference. The spirit of this Person was holy. All the values of this differentiation are discovered when we reach the eighth chapter of the epistle. Therein the apostle is careful to distinguish between flesh and spirit in every life. In flesh, and in spirit, are the two sides of every human life. They were both present in the life of Jesus. His flesh was "born of the seed of David." His spirit must be described. It stands alone. There never was such another. It was a holy spirit, the spirit of holiness. In flesh He was absolutely of our humanity. In spirit also, and yet different. Numbered with transgressors, separated from sinners. In flesh, of our humanity. In spirit essentially the same, but in character different—holy.

The evidence of His being of the seed of David was abundant and convincing. The evidences of His being the Son of God were abundant but not convincing. The evidence did not convince because those who observed were incapable of judging, for they were spiritually blind. The men who looked at Jesus in the days of His flesh were quite capable of judging material things, fleshly things; they could trace genealogies, and discover racial traits; "according to the flesh, born of the seed of David."

According to the spirit—they said He was a gluttonous man and a wine-bibber, the friend of publicans and sinners. They did not know Him. They could not be sure of Him. The evidence of Divine Sonship were those of holiness. His thoughts, His words, His deeds, all of them were the vehicles through which the essential and awful purity of God sounded and shone upon the ways of men. "When we shall see Him there is no beauty that we should desire Him." Not that He was devoid of beauty, but that men were so blind they could not see it. The evidences of fleshly relationship were abundant and convincing. The evidences of Divine relationship were abundant, but not convincing, because men had lost their spiritual vision and were incapable of judgment. If you object to that interpretation, how do you find it in the world today? Is the man of the world of today capable of judging of the beauty of holiness? Is not the sanctified life still the sport of the worldly man? If you dare to season your daily speech with the salt that tells that you have traffic with eternity, the worldly man sees nothing beautiful in it. He shrugs his shoulders. That is the new method of persecution, seeing that the rack has gone out of fashion. He smiles, and perhaps holds you in contempt. Some of you hold the saints in contempt because you are blind and cannot discover the beauty of holiness.

How shall this Man be proven the Son of God as well as Son of man, seeing that the holiness of His spirit does not appeal to men? "Declared to be the Son of God with power, according to the spirit of holiness, by the resurrection from the dead." It is that declaration of the text which we are now to consider. In order to do so, confining ourselves entirely to this half of the great statement concerning the Person, we must carefully understand what this thing is that the apostle wrote. May I change the phrasing, not that I can improve upon it, but that sometimes by a change of words we are introduced to the meaning which we miss by very familiarity with the older formula. So I read the text thus, "Who was distinguished," and that word must not be taken in the general sense in which we speak of a man as being distinguished.

"Who was *marked out* as the Son of God with power through the means of the resurrection of dead ones?"

May I further change the text, this time not by translation in other words, but by paraphrase.

"The resurrection of dead ones set Him with powerful effect upon the horizon as the Son of God."

I do not suggest that that is translation, so those of you who are reading from the Greek New Testament need not be anxious. I do not intend it as interpretation. Those of you who are familiar with the passage in the Greek will discover that I have dared to take a Greek word and Anglicize it. What is this word "declared," "distinguished," "marked out?" It is the word from which we have derived our word horizon. What is the horizon? The boundary. What is a boundary? The end? By no means. It is the beginning. If only I could transport you to the sea, you would understand my text. Standing on the land's last limit there stretches the sea with its movement and its rhythm, its music and its laughter. What beyond? The horizon, the boundary. Is that the end? That is the beginning. Everything between me and the horizon I can comprehend. The mystery begins where the horizon bounds my vision. It is limitation. The limitation is only the limitation of my vision, not of the essential fact. According to flesh, everyone can read the story, "born of the seed of

David." According to the spirit, "*horizoned* as the Son of God by the resurrection of dead ones." Resurrection demonstrated the essential truth concerning Him. Apart from the resurrection, He is "born of the seed of David"; a great and gracious fact, and no one imagines I am undervaluing it. My heart exults with the Apostle John who handled Him. I am glad that men of my kith and kin nineteen hundred years ago did actually lay hands upon the warm flesh of the Man of Nazareth. That, however, is not all. That is not the final fact. If you make that the final fact, your Christianity will be a diminishing quantity, losing all its essential virtue and all its power of victory; until presently you will put Him by the side of Confucius, Buddha, and the rest; a sorry spectacle over which angels might weep. There is something else. He is the Son of God according to the spirit of holiness; and He is demonstrated as such, horizoned as such, flaming out as the sun upon the horizon, and rising to meridian glory, by way of the resurrection. That is the supreme value of the resurrection. The resurrection is the unanswerable demonstration of the profoundest fact concerning the Christ, that, namely, of His Divine Sonship.

In order to gain appreciation of this, let me take you very quickly along three lines of consideration. First, the truth that Jesus was the Son of God, as apprehended before the resurrection. Second, the truth that Jesus was the Son of God, as apprehended after the resurrection. Third, the resurrection as the means of demonstration.

First, the truth as apprehended before the resurrection. That is to say, I suggest that we shall, for a few minutes only, put ourselves back among the disciples before that event happened which we celebrate today.

I take up my New Testament and go through the gospel stories and find three titles of Jesus constantly recurring, "Son of Man"; "Son of God"; and "The Son," without qualification. I have nothing to do with the title "Son of Man." That put Him into immediate relationship with humanity. I take the title "Son of God." Please forgive the statistical way of stating this, I only desire to leave an impression upon your mind. It occurs in Matthew nine times, in Mark four times, in Luke six times, in John eleven times. Of course some of those occasions overlap, it does not at all matter for my present purpose. I find in Matthew that He is called the Son of God six times by men, three times by devils. Mark records two occasions when men so designated Him, and two occasions when devils called Him "the Son of God." Luke gives one occasion when a man called Him that, and four when devils so named Him, and one when an angel declared Him to be the Son of God. I come to John and I find six occasions when man referred to Him as the Son of God, and five when He so named Himself.

Take the other title "The Son," more splendid perhaps than the other because of its independence of qualification. Adjectives are often the means of weakening the glory of substantives. The proportion in which we can use substantives alone, apart from adjectives, is the proportion of dignity of statement and suggestion. Matthew has the description "The Son" four times, Mark once, Luke three times, John fifteen times. That phrase, according to the records, never fell from the lips of devil, or man, or angel. It is the peculiar phrase of Jesus.

With these figures in your mind, let me take another survey of these gospels. Christ did claim for Himself, by direct use of the title and by constant assumptions of commonplace speech, that He was the veritable Son of God. That fact was attested in a supernatural way on two occasions, when heaven's silence was broken and the Divine voice was heard. "This is My beloved Son, in Whom I am well pleased" so at baptism; "This is my beloved Son, in Whom I am well pleased; hear ye Him"; so on the holy mount. The fact was witnessed by devils, as when one said to Him, "I know Thee Who Thou art, the Holy One of God," and another "Thou art the Son of God," and yet another "What have I to do with Thee, Jesus, Thou Son of the Most High God? I adjure Thee by God, torment me not." That fact was once confessed by a man amid the rocky fastnesses of Caesarea Philippi, when answering the challenge of Christ Himself he said, "Thou art the Christ, the Son of the living God."

If you will go over these occasions, I can but suggest the line, you will find that every confession of Sonship was closely associated with the thought of holiness. "My Son, in Whom I am well pleased," that is the declaration of His holiness. "I and the Father are one." "I do nothing of Myself, but as the Father taught Me, I speak these things. . . . I do always the things that are pleasing to Him," all that is the claim of holiness. "Thou art the Holy One of God," "Thou art the Son of God"; so evil recognized His holiness. And surely you will agree that Peter meant that when He said "Thou art," not the prophet foretelling, but the Messiah fulfilling.

That is a rapid survey of those days prior to the resurrection. What shall we say of it? The fact of His Divine Sonship was breaking on the consciousness of men. It was only the flush of dawn upon the dark sky. Men did not know Him as the Son of God. Peter confessed Him as the Son of God, but immediately afterwards rebuked Him, and by his rebuke demonstrated the fact that he had no full conception of the thing he had said. There He lived amongst men, holy, undefiled, spotless, pure, the Son of God; and they were puzzled, they wondered, but they did not fully comprehend.

Turn over the New Testament to the remaining part of it. How far was the truth of the Divine Sonship apprehended after the resurrection? To an audience such as I am addressing this morning, the inquiry carries its own answer. We know full well that all the thought of the other writings of the New Testament are saturated with the conception of the Divine Sonship of Jesus. It was the central conviction concerning Him. It was the constant reason of loyalty to Him. It was the persistent burden of testimony concerning Him. I will not weary you with saying things about that conviction. Let me rather end this section of our study with two quotations:

"Who is the image of the invisible God, the firstborn of all creation; for in Him were all things created, in the heavens and upon the earth, things visible and things invisible, whether thrones, or dominions, or principalities, or powers; all things have been created through Him, and unto Him; and He is before all things, and in Him all things consist."

That is the vision of Jesus Christ which flamed upon the consciousness of believing men after the resurrection.

Or, take another quotation which you may consider anonymous or which you may attribute to the same pen, I care not:

"God, having of old time spoken unto the fathers in the prophets by divers portions and in divers manners, hath at the end of these days spoken unto us in His Son, Whom He appointed heir of all things, through Whom also He made the worlds; Who being the effulgence of His glory, and the very image of His substance, and upholding all things by the word of His power, when He had made purification of sins, sat down on the right hand of the Majesty on high."

I go back to these men before the resurrection and see that gleams were upon the sky. To repeat my own figure of speech, the flush of the dawn was upon the sky, but it was twilight. They were not sure.

On the other side of the resurrection, the sun is in the heavens shining in full glory. Christ is horizoned as the Son of God with power by the resurrection of dead ones, not by His own resurrection only, but by the resurrection of dead ones.

Let us go back again to the period before His cross. I have three stories of His raising the dead. First, the widow's son. What effect did that miracle produce? The people glorified God; they said, God has visited His people. They had not come to final doctrinal understanding of the Person of the Man Who had wrought the work, but when He raised the dead they said, God has visited us.

The resurrection of the son of the widow of Nain was evidence to them of the Divine presence, the Divine visitation, and therefore of holiness. When He raised the widow's son, a great man was in prison; "Among them that are born of women there hath not arisen a greater than John the Baptist." He had changed all the inspiration of a great public ministry which made kings tremble—for Herod heard him gladly at one time—for the dungeon and loneliness and questioning. I cannot help feeling that he had come to wonder whether, after all that, Jesus of Nazareth Whom he had named, was the actual One; but when he heard this, that one was raised from the dead, he sent his disciples to ask, "Art Thou He that should come, or look we for another?" It was this supreme miracle of resurrection which renewed questioning, wonder, hope, in his mind. Then presently He raised the daughter of Jairus in that inimitable word spoken, thrilling with the power of Deity: "Little darling, arise." The parents were amazed. That is all, but that is much. Amazed, they had touched the consciousness of power beyond the reach of humanity. Once again, Lazarus is dead, and they bring Him the news. What is His own account of the fact that He did not hurry, that He permitted Lazarus to die? This is it. "That the Son of God might be glorified thereby." "Declared to be the Son of God, with power . . . by the resurrection of dead ones." That is the supreme revelation. That is the supreme miracle.

But what next? The cross. What did that mean? All the fitful gleams of light which had been shining through Judaea, Peraea and Galilee, all the flush of dawning upon the eastern sky which the eager watchers had seen, went out, and never a ray of light remained. The sun was eclipsed in blood. According to the flesh, oh yes, we knew Him well, "Born of the seed of David," the genealogy is complete. We hoped, when He raised the daughter of Jairus, and the widow's son, and Lazarus, that He was more, but He is dead. You know the rest. We celebrate it this morning. He arose from among the dead. Many infallible proofs for forty days. He is horizoned. Horizoned as the Son of God.

> Lo, our sun's eclipse is o'er.
> Hallelujah!
> Lo, He sets in blood no more!
> Hallelujah!

The resurrection was the vindication of every claim He made; the demonstration of His Sonship; the revelation of His holiness.

According to flesh, "born of the seed of David." We can be accurate. According to the spirit of holiness, Who is He? There is only one way in which it can be proven, and that is by the resurrection of the dead ones. The son of the widow of Nain, the daughter of Jairus, and Lazarus. Yes, but He died. But He is alive forevermore. Take that away from me, my masters, and I renounce your bastard Christianity.

I have no hope if that be not so. "If Christ hath not been raised, then is our preaching vain, your faith also is vain . . . ye are yet in your sins." Blessed be God, why such supposition? He arose, and is alive!

The final demonstration is not yet. I am not coming to the supreme value of the plural in my text. "Horizoned as the Son of God, marked out as the Son of God, with power . . . by the resurrection of dead ones." The final demonstration will never be until the Advent, when not only the first fruits, but all the company are with Him, "The resurrection of dead ones."

> Ten thousand times ten thousand,
>   In sparkling raiment bright,
> The armies of the ransomed saints
>   Throng up the steeps of light;
> 'Tis finished—all is finished
>   Their fight with death and sin!
> Fling open wide the golden gates,
>   And let the victors in.
>
> What rush of Hallelujahs
>   Fills all the earth and sky!
> What ringing of a thousand harps
>   Bespeaks the triumphs nigh!
> Oh, day, for which creation
>   And all its tribes were made!
> Oh, joy, for all its former woes
>   A thousandfold repaid!

The final demonstration will be in the resurrection of the saints. So that the resurrection of the saints is not the last thing, it is the beginning. Do not limit God and humanity by the end of this age, or by the millennium. Everything so far has been preparatory. Stretching away beyond me, I dream dreams of unborn ages and new creations, and marvellous processions out of the being of God, but through them all, the risen Christ and the risen saints will be the central revelations of holiness and of life.

That is the glory of the final resurrection. As so often, we leave the subject, not that it is exhausted. Suffer me this final word. The fact of His Divine Sonship demonstrated by the resurrection is the rock of our assurance. Said a man imperfectly knowing what he said, "Thou art the Christ, the Son of the living God." Answered Christ, "Upon this rock I will build My Church." The rock foundation of the Christian Church is this fact of His Divine Sonship, and so essential Deity lies beneath the Church, an impregnable rock. Thank God if we are built thereupon by sharing the very nature of this risen One.

Let us go away this morning rejoicing in the resurrection because it is the message of a great confidence. He is King, Priest, Warrior, and Builder, and all the great relationships are linked to His resurrection because He is demonstrated thereby as the Son of God.

His Kingship is an absolute monarchy. I have no anxiety about His reign. I believe in an absolute monarchy when we can find the right King. We have found Him.

As to His Prophetic mission, it is one of absolute authority. What He said is true. It cannot be gainsaid. All the words gathered from His tender lips, and printed here and preserved for us, are words which abide. "Heaven and earth shall pass away, but My word shall not pass away." I have no intellectual quarrel with anything He says.

As to His Priesthood, the resurrection demonstrates its absolute sufficiency. Do you really believe that? Then why do you grieve God by this perpetual grieving over sin, and the declaration that you cannot believe He can forgive you?

> Grace there is my every debt to pay,
> Blood to wash my every sin away.

I know it because the Priest rose and entered in.

As to His triumph, He hath broken in pieces the gates of brass. He hath cut the bars of iron asunder. He hath triumphed gloriously, and He will win His battle and build His city. Then so help me God, as He will permit me, I fain would share the travail that makes His Kingdom come, entering the fellowship of His sufferings, for all the while the light of His resurrection is upon the pathway, and I know that at the last the things which He has made me suffer will be the things of the unending triumph.

I greet you this morning in the name of the Father, and of the Son, and of the Holy Spirit! Seek not the living among the dead. He is risen, and because He is risen, we shall rise, and His victory and ours will be won.

CHAPTER XI

HOW TO SUCCEED IN LIFE

In all thy ways acknowledge Him, And He shall direct thy paths.

PROVERBS 3:6.

THIS TEXT HAS A PECULIAR PLACE IN MY HEART. IT HAS been with me day by day for three-and-thirty years. It was on the morning when I was first leaving home for school that my father said to me as his last word, I want to give you a text for school and for life; and this was the text. He gave it to me without note or comment, save the note and comment of his own godly life. "In all thy ways acknowledge Him, And He shall direct thy paths.

I have not always been obedient to the injunction. I have often forgotten Him, often failed in the acknowledgment commanded, but so far as I have been obedient, I have proved the promise true. He has directed my paths.

In order that we may understand the message of the text, let us first consider one or two simple facts. Within the consciousness of man there exists a dual sense; that of possibility, and that of limitation. Every man is conscious that he is able to do. Every man is conscious of limitation in that ability. Every youth and every maiden, in that golden age when the light is forever flashing upon the eastern sky, comes to this twofold consciousness. In youth, this dual consciousness causes perpetual delight. The limitation is opportunity. The possibility is equipment. In old age, when the life has been wasted, the dual consciousness abides, but it is that of despair. The limitation becomes everything, and the possibility is gone. Dreadful indeed is such old age. There is, however, an old age of the youthful heart, in which expectation is still busy painting pictures of coming victories. When life has been well and truly lived the dual consciousness abides, but the proportion is very different. The limitation is growing less with every passing hour, and the possibility is growing more.

I sat yesterday by the side of an old man whose years have reached four-score and five, and he said two things to me which profoundly impressed me. He said first: "As I lie here and think, and listen, that of the world which most profoundly impresses me is its sin." Then, with a new light in his eye, he said: "I want to be away, to be with Christ in God."

My brothers and sisters with the flush of youth upon your faces, and the light of hope in your eyes, I tell you his dreams were more wonderful than your visions; his expectations more wonderful than your hopes. The life well and truly lived has come to age, but the light that never was on land or sea is resting upon his brow. Limitation is growing less, and the consciousness of the possibilities of his own being is growing more.

It is out of my strong desire that your present hopefulness may never grow less, but burn more brightly when the long day's journey is done; and that when the sun goes westering and the shadows are flung across the landscape, new light may break upon you; thus I bring you the message of my text.

It is certainly a Divine arrangement that the young

should see visions; that they should build their castles in the air; that they should aspire after success.

Let no embittered and disappointed man check the enthusiasm of youth, and that for two reasons.

First, because my brother, embittered and disappointed though you be, I question whether you have any right so to be. I feel almost as though I would like to stay and preach to the old man for a moment. You tell me, looking back, that you dreamed your dreams, and built your castles in the air, and have failed. I ask you, How do you know you have failed? If according to your light, and in the measure of the opportunity which has come to you, you have been true to God, then just beyond the limit where the infinite sky kisses the finite earth, you will discover that the commonplaces of your life are transfigured into part of God's great whole of perfect work. I would hearten you, rather than that you should discourage others.

Also, because it is within the Divine intention for youth that it should dream dreams, and build castles, and see visions, and be ambitious to succeed, I say to you, never dishearten, never check, or attempt to kill the enthusiasm of youth.

> How beautiful is youth! how bright it gleams,
>   With its illusions, aspirations, dreams!
> Book of beginnings, story without end,
>   Each maid a heroine, and each man a friend!
>
> Aladdin's lamp, and Fortunatus' purse,
>   That holds the treasures of the universe!
> All possibilities are in its hands,
>   No danger daunts it, and no foe withstands;
>
> In its sublime audacity of faith,
>   "Be thou removed," it to the mountain saith,
> And with ambitious feet, secure and proud,
>   Ascends the ladder, leaning on the cloud.

Youth is forever looking to the distant. The vision is always of things ahead. The boy who stands by his mother, and tells her what he is going to be, is the symbol of all that of which I speak.

Sometimes the height is never reached, success is never achieved. The gleaming glory seen afar fades and passes, and there is nought but darkness and disappointment. The reason is that while the glory was true in possibility, the true path to the mountain heights has not been discovered. There in the distance is the alpine height, but if we do not know the way, the end will be in the valley, in the place of disaster, in the place of defeat. "In all thy ways acknowledge Him, And He shall direct thy paths."

That within us which makes us desire victory, the passion for perfection, the determination to achieve, is all of God; and if we can but discover His way, His plan, His thought, and follow His direction, then we shall come to fulfilment even though it be through battle and through strife, through conflict and through tears, through apparent disaster and defeat.

My appeal is made to those who have the goal insight, and it declares the abiding condition upon which the pathways which lead to the goal may be discovered. "In all thy ways acknowledge Him, And He shall direct thy paths." The whole text conditions life in the present, and so conditions it for progress to consummation.

Let us then take the text in these two parts; first, the injunction, "In all thy ways acknowledge Him," And secondly, the promise, "And He shall direct thy paths."

"In all thy ways acknowledge Him," are comprehensive words, recalling us at every point of our lives from atheism. I have used the word atheism quite carefully, in order that I may arrest your thought, that I may even startle you into consciousness of the insidious peril which threatens us every day and everywhere. There is a very practical and widespread atheism which would very much resent the term. There are a great many atheists who would be very angry if we called them such. What is an atheist? One who is without God. Atheism is not merely intellectual. There is a volitional atheism, which may recite the creed and imagine it believes it, while through all the busy days it violates and denies it. The Apostle Paul connects atheism with the death of that principle which is the supreme charm and value of youth. "Atheists and without hope." These two things are forever closely associated. The proportion in which a man is without God is the proportion in which light is fading from the sky, shadows are settling upon his way, darkness is overtaking him. Godlessness, I repeat, is infinitely more than intellectual disquietude, questioning, and unbelief. Godlessness is life lived without reference to God. That is the peril against which this text warns us. That is the danger from which it seeks to deliver us.

The first idea of the word "acknowledge" is that of vision. It is as though the Preacher had said, In all thy ways see God. It calls us to recognition of the fact of the presence of God at every point of our lives. It reminds us that in all our ways, God is. It denies the heresy that God is in the sanctuary, and not in the market place. It denies the heresy that God is interested in the central spiritual fact of human life, and has no relationship with the mental and the physical. See God everywhere. The word thus calls us to a recognition of His existence, which must produce fear, not slavish fear but that solemn awe of the soul which holds life in balance and proportion. That awe which the age lacks disastrously. It is absent largely from the life of today. Man is standing altogether too erect in the presence of high heaven; challenging the wisdom of God, or laughing at the ancient conceptions of His majesty; abandoning the figures of speech by which the prophets, seers, and psalmists of bygone generations attempted to bring men into subjection, and with the abandonment of the figures, forgetting the facts.

I am not pleading for a solemn and awful dread which will banish all brightness. I do desire to recall youth to that awe in the presence of the ever-present God which delivers from the flippancy and frivolity which curse, and spoil, and mar life.

Such recognition of His existence will issue in acceptance of His claim, and produce obedience.

Such obedience will strengthen belief in His interest, and issue in prayer.

Yet, I think there is another meaning in this word "acknowledge." To acknowledge Him, is to use His gifts in the sphere of His will, recognizing that they are His gifts, and that we are responsible to Him for them.

There are some words of Jesus which I think we often interpret altogether too narrowly, if not with absolute inaccuracy. In the Sermon on the Mount, that great Manifesto of the King, Christ said to His disciples, "Consider the lilies of the field, how they grow; they toil not, neither do they spin: yet I say unto you, that even Solomon in all his glory was not arrayed like one of these. But if God doth so clothe the grass of the field, which today is, and tomorrow is cast into the oven, shall he not much more clothe you, O ye of little faith?" And again, "Behold the birds of the heaven, that they sow not, neither do they reap, nor gather into barns; and your heavenly Father feedeth them. Are not ye of much more value than they?"

Our Lord did not for a single moment mean that as the lilies are clothed, without toiling and without spinning, we are to expect to be clothed without toiling. Neither did He mean, that if He provides for the birds of the air without their forethought, we are to neglect forethought. He meant rather that if the lilies of the field and the birds of the air, unable to plan and arrange, are cared for, how much more will God provide for those to whom He has given reason, and ability to plan.

Let no man think that he can come to the fulfilment of his life by prayer alone. Let him understand in this respect also that "faith without works is dead." We have another figure of Christ, that of the mountain removed by faith. We say mountains are never removed by faith today. Yet is this true? At this hour in different parts of the world, mountains are being removed and cast into the seas. We say, "That is a great engineering triumph." What lies behind the work of the engineer? The faith of the engineer. No mountain has ever been leveled or tunneled, and no highway has ever been flung up by humanity, save by works preceded by faith. There is first the vision of the possibility, and then the action which realizes the vision.

"In all thy ways acknowledge Him," does not merely mean see Him, believe Him, pray to Him, fear Him; it means also, take the forces which He has placed in your personality and use them under His government. Do not expect that He will ever bring you to the mountain height unless you climb. Do not imagine that you will ever come to fulfilment of your own life unless you toil. Do not for a moment think that to acknowledge God means that if you are a member of the Christian Church He will make your life full and beautiful and rich if you are lazy in the matter of your daily avocation.

I want to save young life in this age from the idea that godliness consists wholly in singing hymns and going to prayer-meetings. What is the capacity within you? Is it mechanical? Then you are not merely to pray, you are to work out to perfection the forces which God has placed within you. You are to neglect no single side of your nature which He has created. When you have discovered what your calling in life is to be, you are to remember that you can only come to fulfilment thereof by consecrated toil under the government of God.

"In all thy ways acknowledge Him." Let us take one or two illustrative applications of the principle.

In your home life. In the home in which for a while you sojourn, the home of your childhood which as yet it may be, you have not left. "In all thy ways acknowledge Him." Recognize His goodness, recognize the authority over you as representing His authority. Jesus went down and was subject unto his parents. He had first said, "I must be about My Father's business."

In your thinking about the homes which you will presently make for yourselves, in that whole sacred and wonderful matter of the birth of love within your nature, acknowledge Him. I may be allowed to say from this Christian pulpit, and as a Christian minister, that I am weary to death of a great deal of flippant, foolish joking on the subject of love between youth and maiden. Sacred, high, holy, and beautiful, is all such love when heaven born; but it tends to hell when it is not tested in the light of the love of God. I have seen the daughters of the King, the fairest and most beautiful, full of promise, robbed of their beauty by alliance with men who lack recognition of God. I have seen young manhood, enthusiastic for the Kingdom, full of force, paralyzed by alliance with those who have no such vision. "In all thy ways acknowledge Him." I pray you remember, that unless you can test your love by the light of heaven's pure love, it is going to be the most unutterable curse that ever came into your life.

Take another application at which I have already hinted, that of your business. What are you going to be in the world? Someone said to me but today, Are you going to make all your boys preachers? I said, God forbid. What did I mean? As God is my witness, nothing would gladden my heart more than to see all of them preachers, but I cannot make them preachers, and I have no intention of suggesting to one of them that such should be the work of his life. I take that illustration simply to lead me to say this. You have no right to choose what you will be. Seek Divine guidance. Pray about it, but do not end with praying. For remember this, in every human life there is some power which God needs, not merely for the supply of all that is necessary to the life possessing it, but for the commonwealth. It is for every man to discover in God's presence, and in fellowship with Him, what that power is; and then to take hold of it and develop, and use it, as in the will of God.

I would say to those of you who have already discovered the line of your life in this world; master it in every detail, be restless until you are able to do the thing you have set out to do, so that when done you can hold it up to God, and say, Here is this piece of work.

Very reverently I pause to illustrate that, from the wonderful carpenter's shop. Jesus Christ, as a carpenter, made yokes in which the oxen ploughed the plains of Bethshan. Jesus Christ as a carpenter constructed those single-share ploughs with which the farmer drove the furrow through his field. I affirm, without one moment's hesitation, that when Jesus Christ made a yoke it was one that heaven itself would have accepted. When He had finished the plough it was true to the measurement of eternity. Presently, He left the carpenter's shop and came to His preaching, and He borrowed the things of His toil to illustrate His preaching. "My yoke is easy." He knew what He was talking about. He had made yokes, and so made them that they never galled the neck of the oxen that wore them. "No man, having put his hand to the plough, and looking back, is fit for the Kingdom." Note the masterly assumption. He did not suggest that the furrow could be crooked because the plough was wrong. It is the man who must be wrong, when He has made the plough.

Put your godliness into your business. Let all your religion be seen in the letter you have to write for your employer, in the piece of work you have to do for him. "In all thy ways acknowledge Him."

In your recreations also, let this be true. What does that mean? That you can have no recreation which dulls your perception of God. However harmless it may be to you, if to me it raises a mist through which I cannot see clearly the face of my Father, then I must have none of it. However harmless it may be to me, if you, seeking recreation in the same way, lose your keenness of scent in the fear of the Lord, then you are to have no such recreation. That is the test.

I am told that today the question of amusements is a very difficult one. By no means. It is a very simple one. That is its test. "In all thy ways acknowledge Him." You say, I am very doubtful about———. That settles it forever! If you are doubtful, you dare not. "Whatsoever is not of faith is sin." "In all thy ways acknowledge Him." Remember, God is God not only of your life, but of your brother's life, and you cannot seek recreation in that which ministers harm to other people. I leave you to apply the principle. Any recreation, though it may not be harmful to me, which can only be gained by harming the man who provides it, I cannot, if I acknowledge God, indulge in.

Forgive the illustrations. I think sometimes illustrations do but minimise the value of the whole. Listen to the whole word of the preacher. "In all thy ways acknowledge Him." Not the ways of Sunday only, but of Monday, Tuesday, Wednesday, Thursday, Friday, Saturday. Not the days of the Lenten season only, but the three hundred and twenty-five days remaining after Lent is over. Not the ways that are public to the gaze of others, but the inner secret ways of which men can know nothing. Acknowledge Him, see Him, in the dark as well as in the light; in the shop as well as in the sanctuary; in the valley as well as on the mountain height; at play as well as at work. "In all thy ways acknowledge Him."

In a brief, concluding word hear the promise. "He shall direct thy paths." That promise calls for the exercise of faith. Our one responsibility is that of obedience to the condition of which I have been trying to speak. Yet let me say this, the truth of the promise is discoverable in all retrospection. Perhaps that is the most difficult thing for youth. It is so hard to look back. There is so little to look back at. Hear then the testimony of those who look back after long pilgrimages and arduous days. The testimony of the whole of them is that as they have acknowledged Him in all their ways, He has directed the paths.

He has many ways of directing. He directs by obstacles placed across the way which I cannot overcome, and which drive me into a new way. He directs by clearing obstacles away, which I thought could not be moved. He directs by delay, keeping me waiting long after I have heard His call to service. He directs by immediateness, flinging me out into a new position, wherein I must seek His guidance. He directs by opposition; the Spirit hindered Paul. He directs by encouragement, by whispers in the soul, which make a man dare, when all men tell him his daring is of no avail. He directs by disappointing, or by realizing our dreams. I state these contradictory things in order to throw you back upon this profound conviction; not from me nor from any man, must you take your rule of His direction. You must discover the rule for yourself in immediate relationship with Him. I say this now out of profound conviction, God help me to say it as it ought to be said. No youth or maiden has ever yet bared their soul to God, desiring to be led of Him and determined to follow, but that He has led, He has directed.

I love the personality suggested by the pronoun in the text: "*He* shall direct thy paths." Behind the "*He*" of the ancient preacher is the God of the Bible. Because that is so, the "*He*" trembles with the tenderness of the Father's love. No evil can baffle if He direct the path. No enemy can prevent the final realization of His purpose. No obstacles can hinder if He lead. No opposition can overcome if He direct. No exigencies can overwhelm the wisdom of God, no surprises prevent Him. Oh, the safety of being in the will of God. "He shall direct thy paths."

Not always in easy or pleasant paths, but always in right paths. Not always in those I would have chosen, but always in paths which lead to success. There may be the vastest difference between success and fame.

"He shall direct thy paths." The paths that He directs lead always, through mist and mystery, through battle and through bruising, to the fulfilment of the meaning of life.

How much that is called success is dire and disastrous failure. I believe that these conditions may put limitations upon material success. It may be you could make a far larger fortune if you forgot God. But that is a very material thing to say. I have used the word fortune in its debased sense. I have used it as though it only applied to those material things which you can grasp and state in figures. The man who would lay up treasure for eternity cannot forget God. The man who would make to himself friends by means of the mammon of unrighteousness must acknowledge God in all his ways.

The final test of life is beyond the things of time and sense. It will be a test of fire; only that which cannot be destroyed will remain. In the light of that final test if we would make our lives successful we must begin right. What is the first step. Surrender. What the plan of life, the pathway to the end? Obedience. Confronting everyone of us tonight, God in Christ asks for our lives.

I pray for you that you may realize your ambitions, and fulfil your dreamings. In order that when the eternal morning flushes the eastern sky, you may come to fulfilment. "In all thy ways acknowledge Him, and He shall direct thy paths."

CHAPTER XII

MY LAMBS—MY SHEEP

Feed My Lambs . . . Tend My sheep . . . Feed My sheep.
JOHN 21:15, 16, 17.

THESE WORDS CONSTITUTE OUR LORD'S FINAL COMMISSION TO Peter, and as Peter stands ever before us as the representative man, the words were spoken through him to the Church. We need to rescue these words from an altogether too narrow interpretation. It has been said that, on the shores of the lake in the flush of the early morning, Jesus handed Peter the crozier, the staff of the pastoral office, and thus entrusted to him the oversight of the saints of God. This is undoubtedly true, but the whole truth is more than this. That narrow view of our Lord's meaning is due largely to the fact that our minds are obsessed almost by one particular utterance of our Lord, in which He drew a clear and sharp distinction between sheep and goats. It is well to remember that Christ only once made such distinction.

If in that great chapter of Matthew, our Lord was referring to a final assize, when individuals will appear before Him for sentence, then we must recognize that He never makes the division until the day of final assize, never suggests that men are goats on the one hand, and sheep on the other, until the day of final destiny. I do not believe that our Lord even then had any such meaning in His speech. The picture of that chapter of Matthew is not that of the assembling before Him of individuals for individual sentence. It is, rather, the picture of the assembling before Him of nations for national sentence. When He makes His division as between sheep and goats, the division is not between individual men, but between nations. The prophecy had special reference to Israel.

The spaciousness of these words spoken to Peter on the shores of the lake can only be discovered as we adopt the usual line of teaching suggested by the figure of the shepherd and the sheep in the Scriptures. The seers and psalmists of the old economy, in moments of highest exaltation and clearest vision, saw that the supreme truth concerning the Kingship of Jehovah is that He is a Shepherd, and that the direst woe fallen upon the sons of men is that they are as sheep without a shepherd.

In that very brief paragraph, which I read from the Gospel of Matthew, we have something we need to attend to very carefully. Matthew tells us that Jesus went through all the cities and villages preaching, teaching and healing, and that when He saw the multitudes He was moved with compassion for them, because they were distressed and scattered, *as sheep not having a shepherd.*

In that matchless discourse recorded in the tenth chapter of John, Jesus said, "I am the good Shepherd . . . other sheep I have which are not of this fold: them also I must bring."

When Peter, who heard these words on the shore of the lake, came to write his letter afterward to Christian men and women, he said: "Ye were going astray like sheep, but are now returned unto the Shepherd and Bishop of your souls."

The words spoken to Peter must be interpreted in harmony with these uses of the figure of the sheep. When Jesus, looking into the eyes of Peter as He restored Him by challenge, confession and commission, said, "Feed My lambs . . . shepherd My sheep . . . feed My sheep," His holy, lovelit eyes were looking far beyond the first narrow circle of His own disciples, to the vast multitudes of all nations, all peoples and all tongues who were in His heart, because He was the good, the great and the chief Shepherd.

These words are suggestive, as they reveal to us the nature of the work committed to the Church. It is not my intention to deal with them now in that way. I ask only that you ponder, at your leisure, these simple facts. Of the lambs He said, Feed them, and there is profound significance in the fact. He did not suggest that our first work should be that of finding them. He spoke of the children as already His own. When He referred to the sheep, His first word was, shepherd them; that is, find them if they have gone astray, seek them if they are lost, then fold them and guard them. Then, beyond that, "Feed my sheep."

I desire now to direct attention first, to the assumptions of Christ which these words suggest, and, secondly, to what they reveal as to the preparation that is necessary for all such as seek to feed the lambs and shepherd the sheep.

First, let us listen to the words as revealing the assumptions of Jesus: "My lambs . . . My sheep." The note that first impresses the heart is that of infinite and tender compassion: "My lambs . . . My sheep."

Let me illuminate this by reference again to the passage in Matthew. When He saw the multitudes, what effect did the vision produce upon Him? As God is my witness, I hardly know how to cite these words to you. I am afraid of harshness of tone. Yet I am also afraid that if I attempt to do other than recite them with the natural harshness of tone, I may but libel the exquisite tenderness that ought to be heard in them. "*He was moved with compassion for them.*"

How familiar we are with the words. Would that in the quiet hush of this moment, they might come to us with all their infinite meaning. "He was moved with compassion." The final outcome of that compassion was the cross.

Why was He moved with compassion? Because He saw them "distressed and scattered." Take the words and let them be pictures, as they really are, and in a moment we discover their true significance. I do no violence to them if I say that our Lord saw the sheep harried by wolves, bruised, wounded, flung to the ground, faint and weary; and it was that vision of humanity in its degradation, spoiled and ruined, that moved His heart with compassion. "My lambs . . .My sheep." We cannot hear these words, interpreted by the declaration of the Gospel of Matthew, without discovering in them the note of infinite tenderness and compassion.

Yet, there is infinitely more in them than the note of compassion. There is that of supremacy. It was Homer who once said that kings are the shepherds of the people. Perhaps it would have been more correct to have said kings ought to be the shepherds of the people. It is at least perfectly true that the master figure of kingship in the Old Testament is that of the Shepherd. All God's chosen, ordained kings and leaders were of the shepherd heart. If Moses was to lead the people, he had to learn the art of leading them by being a shepherd for long years. If David was to come to the throne, he had to discover the secrets of victory by slaying the lion and the bear that came against the sheep of his father's flock. The idea of kingship in the economy of God is always that of the shepherd, who feeds rather than is fed, who guards rather than seeks to be guarded. It is the true ideal of kingship.

Ringing through this word of Jesus, coming up out of

the old Hebrew economy and ideal, is the note of supremacy, "MY lambs . . . MY sheep." Standing in the midst of humanity, speaking to His own disciples, He claimed absolute Lordship over all the race.

We have not yet touched the profoundest note. We go to the tenth chapter of John, and listen: "I am the Good Shepherd: the Good Shepherd layeth down His life for the sheep." Then, with a touch of fine scorn: "He that is a hireling and not a shepherd . . . fleeth because he is a hireling, and careth not for the sheep." The Good Shepherd enters into conflict with the wolf, and even though He die, He dies to slay the wolf. Jesus saw the sheep distressed and scattered as by wolves, and He was moved with compassion for them; and then, as King, He entered into conflict with the forces that spoil, and, though dying in the conflict, He despoiled and triumphed over the foe in His cross, making a show openly of such as were opposed.

There is yet another note, that of resurrection victory. Once again we go to the same chapter of John for exposition. He not only said, "The Good Shepherd layeth down His life for the sheep." He also said this strange, mysterious, overwhelming thing: "No one taketh it away from Me, but I lay it down of Myself. I have power to lay it down, and I have power to take it again." That was an empty and a vain boast, unless He rose from among the dead. I need not argue it. He rose. He took again the life laid down, and, standing there on the shores of the lake, He said: "My lambs, My sheep." I am the Good Shepherd. I lay down My life for them. They are Mine by virtue of life laid down. I am the Good Shepherd. I have taken My life again for them. They are Mine by virtue of resurrection.

We think of the Galilean lake, and, in imagination, see all humanity gathered around that central Person; the men of

His own age, of every successive age, this congregation, the whole of this city, all the nations of the world, and of them all He said: "My lambs . . . My sheep." In His voice there is the note of infinite compassion, the ring of absolute authority, the passion of the cross and the triumph of resurrection.

Now, in order that we may understand the commission itself, and our responsibility, let us inquire at what point in the life and history of this man, Peter, our Lord gave him the commission. In order to gain anything like a full and adequate answer to that inquiry we need the whole story of Peter. My comfort is that we know it. We are very familiar with it. I need therefore stay only to refer to the outstanding facts in Christ's method of preparing this man for the hearing of this commission. The work began when Jesus first met him. In that hour, and upon this alone I dwell, the glamour of Christ's personality fell upon Peter. He did not understand Him. He had no theory as to His Person, no doctrine as to His mission, but he felt the irresistible attraction of His personality. He was not yet ready for Christ to commission him to feed the lambs and gather the sheep, but the first stage in his preparation was accomplished.

What next? All the patient training of the weeks, months, years over which we pass, until we come to Caesarea Philippi, and again we have a familiar story. I need but refer to it for illustration. There at Caesarea Philippi this man looked back into the eyes of Christ, and said: "Thou art the Christ, the Son of the living God." The Christ, for Whose coming Jeremiah had watched, shedding bitter tears; Whose advent John had announced; for Whose work Elijah had sighed; the One to Whom all the prophets had given witness. Peter had reached the second stage in his preparation for hearing this commission when he uttered that confession. He had come to the hour in which he no longer placed Christ on the level of other teachers, but had discovered His absolute supremacy; knew that all the light that burned in others was derived from this one essential source of light; knew that all the aspirations, and hopes, and longings in the hearts of men were to be fulfilled in Him.

The third stage in preparation followed immediately, as for the first time he beheld the tragedy of the cross. I think sometimes that we are unfair to Peter and the rest of the disciples about that cross. We preach sermons upon their frailty and folly. Had we been among their number we would have shared their disappointment when Jesus spoke of the cross. It was absolutely revolutionary. There was nothing in human philosophy that could understand it. Who ever heard of a man coming to crowning by way of a cross? Who ever heard of a man winning universal victory by the way of disastrous defeat? "I will build My church, and the gates of Hades shall not prevail against it. I will give unto thee the keys of the Kingdom." These are the things to be desired. And immediately He declared He was going to Jerusalem to die, to be mauled by brutal hands, to suffer and be crucified. Ere we criticize Peter, let us get back into Peter's place. In that moment, he saw the tragedy of the cross, to use Paul's great word, the offence of the cross, the scandal of the cross, scandal in the true sense, the thing in the way that prevents progress. He had to see that, to feel the agony of it, before he was ready to feed the lambs and shepherd the sheep.

One final and revealing matter. When Jesus gave him this commission He was the risen Lord. It is so easy to say this, but can we put ourselves back into his place? What does Peter say about the resurrection? He declares we were begotten again "unto a living hope by the resurrection of Jesus Christ from the dead"—a most graphic and wonderful statement—by which he meant this: I saw Him die, and was certain that by that death all my hopes were put out in darkness, all the high and noble things I had hoped for Him and through Him were defeated; but when I saw Him alive beyond death, I was born again, I came to a new vision, a new understanding, and the very cross from which I had shrunk was transfigured with light, and became glorious with a glory that amazed my heart and soul. It was never until Peter had seen his risen Lord that the Lord commissioned him to feed the lambs and shepherd the sheep.

Mark the four stages. First, he felt the glamour of His personality. Second, he came to conviction of His absolute supremacy. Third, he came to the horror and tragedy of the cross. Finally, he came into the light of the resurrection, and saw that selfsame cross transfigured until it shone with a beauty and glory of which he had never dreamed. Never before was Peter ready for the great commission, for the great and sacred work.

These four experiences of Peter coincide exactly with the assumptions of Jesus. The first note is that of His compassion. Peter felt the glamour of His personality. The second note is that of His supremacy. Peter came to the confession of this at Caesarea Philippi. The third note is that of His cross. Peter had felt the offence of the cross. The fourth note is that of resurrection. Peter stood in the light of it.

Does not the meditation carry its own lessons? Christ still stands amid the multitudes of the world. The more I think of my Lord, the more I study His teaching; the more I strive to come into fellowship with Him; the more I recognize that in His presence there are no divisions. He will have none of our adjectives such as *home* and *foreign*. He stands in the midst of humanity, universal in His own humanity, whether it be east or west, a Man among men, standing in the midst of the multitudes of our own city, and of the far distant places of the world, moved with compassion for their sorrows and their sins.

If we are to fulfil His commission, we must pass through exactly the same experiences of spiritual life. No man can feed the lambs and shepherd the sheep until he himself has felt the mysterious attraction of the Person of Christ upon his own life. No man can feed the lambs and shepherd the sheep until he has put Christ in the place of final supremacy. If I am a mere discusser of comparative religions, if I put Christ's name by the side of that of Buddha, or Confucius, or any other, I cannot feed His lambs and shepherd His sheep. Until I see that He is above them all, that every gleam of light in their teaching, every touch of truth in the things they said were derived from Him, that He is the supreme, absolute, final Lord, I cannot do His work, neither can the Christain Church. If there be paralysis of missionary endeavour, that is the essential reason of it. We are not sure about His supremacy. We are not absolutely convinced that He is the one lonely Lord and Master of the race. We are trying to put others into comparison with Him, and to admit that perhaps other lords are better for other men than this Lord Christ of ours. All such comparison cuts the nerve of missionary endeavour, and paralyzes the possibility of obedience to this great and gracious commission.

We can never fulfil this commission until we ourselves have come to a sense of the horror of the cross. We must see the offence of it, or we cannot serve. I know that in the light of resurrection we see the glory and beauty of it, but let us be careful lest we miss all that lies behind—the offence, the scandal, the horror of the cross of Christ. That is the danger of the present moment. It is affirmed by some that the doctrine of the cross is vulgar. Hear me now patiently. The cross is vulgar; nothing in human history is so vulgar, nothing so dastardly, nothing so unholy. But what is the vulgarity? Listen to this awful word of Scripture. "He was made sin." There is the vulgarity. It is the vulgarity of the sin that made the cross necessary. Until I have felt it, the horror of it, the scandal of it, and have come to a sense of the shame of the sin that erected it, I cannot shepherd the sheep. We cannot heal humanity's wounds with rosewater. We cannot touch the sheep with their festering sores until we see the horror of the wounding. Who else saw the multitudes as Christ saw them? Not the disciples of those early days. Not the rulers of the people. Not the people themselves. But He knew the poison of sin, the awfulness of sin. That led Him to the cross. We must measure the ruin of humanity by that cross ere we can hope to help it, or serve it, or save it.

That is not the last word. We must know Christ as risen, and so understand the cross as infinitely more than the revelation of sin. It is the revelation of grace—triumphant grace, rich and spacious and overwhelming word of the Christian Church, altogether too lightly and too glibly used in these days. Grace, let the first Pentecostal preacher tell the story of the cross. He fixes your attention upon the Person of the Christ, and says: "Him, being delivered up by the determinate counsel and foreknowledge of God, ye by the hand of lawless men did crucify and slay." There is your sin: Lawless men mauled the Christ of God. There is God's grace, "Delivered up by the determinate counsel and foreknowledge of God." We never see the cross in that way until we see Christ risen from among the dead. We are not prepared to feed the lambs or shepherd the sheep until we know the risen Lord, and know Him for our very selves.

When He had prepared this man for the work, He brought him face to face with these four matters. Let us state them in sequence. "My sheep." That is the note of compassion. The first thing that Peter ever felt when he came to Jesus was the glamour of His personality. Now Christ begins there, "Lovest thou Me?" You know, of course, that the word Christ used for love is not the word that Peter used. The revisers in the margin have drawn attention to the fact that these words are not the same, and thus they have only made darkness visible by not distinguishing between them. The word of Jesus suggested love illuminated by intelligence. Peter dared not climb to it, and he said, using a simpler word which seemed a warmer one, "Thou knowest that I love Thee." Christ challenged him again—"Lovest thou Me?" —on this high level, with love governed by judgment and understanding, and Peter kept to his own word. Then Christ came down to Peter's level. That is why Peter was grieved, not because He asked three times, but that the third time He came down to his word. But the essential matter is love. The first condition of service is love. That is the first question, not do you love the heathen, but do you love me? If we go to the heathen because we love Him, we shall come to love the heathen also.

What next? He said to Him, "Feed My lambs . . . Shepherd My sheep." Mark the grace of this. What did He give them to do? His own shepherd work. We have been saying that the shepherd is king. Kingly work, then, is that of feeding lambs and shepherding sheep. He says to Peter: Prove your loyalty by sharing My royalty. I am King. You have crowned Me King. They are My lambs, My sheep. My work as Shepherd is to feed them and gather them. Share it with me. Do it by My side. Prove your loyalty by fellowship in the exercise of My royalty.

Then the cross. "When thou wast young thou girdedst thyself, and walkedst whither thou wouldest; but when thou shalt be old, thou shalt stretch forth thy hands, and another shall gird thee and carry thee whither thou wouldest not. Now this He spake, signifying by what manner of death he should glorify God." Jesus brought him back to the cross, and said to him: You can only feed My lambs and shepherd My sheep as you have fellowship with My cross. It is a very actual, definite word, believe me. In the case of Peter, it was an actual, positive cross to which he came. We say that has no application to us. No! And yet, think again. I have a newspaper clipping at home. I have had it for more than twenty years. I have read it scores of times for the discipline of my life. It was from the pen of Thomas Champness, and it is headed "Sheer Hard Work." He declared that no minister of Christ has any right to lay his head upon the pillow on any given day of the seven until he is worn out in work. What is true of the minister is true of every man who bears the name of Christ. We have not begun to touch the great business of salvation when we have sung "Rescue the perishing, care for the dying." We have not entered into the business of evangelizing the city or the world until we have put our own lives into the business, our own immediate physical endeavour, inspired by spiritual devotion. We must get to the cross in actual fellowship, in weariness and pain and suffering. When the Church of God gets there, we shall hear no more of decrease and languishing exchequers, the impossibility of raising funds for missionary work, no more of the necessity for calling home missionaries and closing doors. It is to go back to the cross, to individual toil and pain and suffering, that is our supreme need.

But there is one other thing. When Jesus said this final word to Peter about the cross, He did not finish there. He said, "Follow Me." That is to say: When I first named My cross you shunned it; you must come back to it, but "follow Me." You saw Me go to it; you lost hope. You have seen Me alive again. "Follow Me." The man who comes to the cross with Me comes to resurrection with Me. The man who comes along the pathway of suffering in fellowship for the doing of My work comes to the hour of absolute and assured victory with Me. The Lord challenges us still to follow Him to the cross, but to follow Him to the cross is to follow Him to resurrection and to triumph.

Now we must leave these words of His that are more than all the preacher has tried to say, infinitely more! As we scatter to our homes, those who bear His name and sign, let us listen to His voice, as He says, "My lamps . . . My sheep." Yes, those children you saw in the street, "My lambs." Yes, those bruised and broken men and women, those far distant peoples sighing and crying in desolation and darkness, "My sheep."

If we hear His own voice, we shall want to get very near to Him, and to obey Him, when He says: Feed them, shepherd them, feed them!

CHAPTER XIII

BUT!

I will follow Thee, Lord; but . . .
LUKE 9:51-62.

WHEN THE EVENTS TOOK PLACE WHICH ARE RECORDED IN the paragraph from which the text is taken, the face of Jesus was set toward Jerusalem, and the days were days of crisis and testing in the matter of all human relationships to Himself.

While He was a boy, a youth, and a young man in Nazareth, He was beloved, for Luke tells us that He grew in favour, not with God only, but with men also. In the early days of His public ministry. He was the center of attraction, and men of all grades and all classes crowded after Him to see and hear Him. In the process of that ministry, as He began to make clear to those who listened that His mission was a mission of right and truth and purity, the essential things of the Kingdom of God, men gradually fell away from Him; and in these last weeks or months prior to the cross there were great crises in many lives, and all human relationships passed through a time of severe testing.

His own disciples were busy reasoning among themselves as to their relative greatness, and He rebuked and corrected them by putting the child in the midst. John was disturbed because someone had been seen working in the name of

Christ, who was not following with the disciples. Mark carefully what John complained about. He was not able to say that the man was not following Christ, but he was not following *with the disciples.* Jesus quietly and firmly rebuked his exclusivism. The Samaritans refused to receive Him into one of their villages because His face was set evidently toward Jerusalem. Boanerges, sons of thunder, would have called down fire upon them, but Jesus rebuked them, and passed on to another village.

Somewhere on those journeys toward Jerusalem, while His face was set toward the city which He knew and which He loved—the city which He well knew at this time was so hostile to Him that it was only waiting for His arrival to arrest Him and kill Him; somewhere on these journeyings toward the city, the things happened which are chronicled in this brief paragraph.

One man, for some reason unexplained by the story, in the fulness of his heart, under sudden impulse as it would seem, said, "I will follow Thee whithersoever Thou goest." Another man, perchance a little farther on the way, Christ looked at, and called him to follow, saying, "Follow Me." Yet a third, with less impulsiveness than the first, and with more of hesitation, said: "I will follow thee, Lord; but first suffer me to bid farewell to them that are at my house."

Before the first of these men, who declared himself willing to follow the Lord wherever He went, He set a difficulty. It is as though He said to him: You say you are prepared to follow Me whithersoever I go. Do you really know what My lot in life is? "The foxes have holes, and the birds of the heaven have nests; but the Son of man hath not where to lay His head"—that is, does not possess as His own a resting-place for His head.

The second man, whom the Lord called to follow Him,

declined on the plea of filial duty; for when he said "Suffer me first to go and bury my father," his father in all probability was still living. It was not a case of asking to attend a funeral. I never understood that, until in conversation with Dr. George Adam Smith, he told me of what happened to himself when endeavouring to persuade a young Arab to accompany him into the interior. At last the Arab looked at him, and said, "Suffer me first to go and bury my father," in the very words of Scripture; and the old man was sitting by his side when he uttered them. What he meant was, I have a filial obligation that prevents my coming. To the man who raised that difficulty Christ said: "Leave the dead to bury their own dead; but go thou and publish abroad the Kingdom of God." That is the supreme matter, and its demands are more imperative even than such filial obligation.

Before the third, the man who suggested that he desired to follow, but would like first to bid farewell to those who were at his own house, Christ affirmed the superlativeness of His own claim: "No man, having put his hand to the plough, and looking back, is fit for the Kingdom of God."

Now, let me at once say to you, I do not propose to follow the incidents that are given here in any further detail. They constitute a background. I am far more anxious to discover the principles involved, and make application of them to the present hour and present congregation. Whether any of these men ultimately followed the Lord, we do not know. There is no reason to suppose they did not, although that has been very generally taken for granted. It has been our habit to consign all these doubtful cases to perdition. We have no right to do so. We know nothing about them. It may be that these men followed Christ at last. We do not know. It is not intended that we should know. The things of value are the revelations in this passage; first, of the call of Christ and of the supremacy of Christ as He calls men; second, of the fact that difficulties present themselves to the minds of many, which are very real and very definite; third and finally, the passage teaches us the urgency of immediate decision, that when we come to deal with Christ, counting the cost is out of place. He calls us to follow, to follow immediately, to follow whatever the cost may be.

Let us first spend two or three minutes with this word of Christ, this call of Christ to follow. On two occasions in the course of this paragraph men made use of the word. In the central one, Christ used it. The first man said, "I will follow Thee." The third man said, "I will follow Thee, Lord, but . . ." To the other man Christ said, "Follow Me."

I think it is quite fair to suppose that the word of the first man and of the third prove that they had heard Christ utter that call to someone. It was His favourite method of calling men after Himself, "Follow Me." There are other things that He said to other men when He dealt with them as to their spiritual needs, but all His other methods were incidental, and are not often repeated. For instance, He said "Ye must be born again" only to one man, never repeating it. Over and over again, to men when He would first attract them, to the disciples when He would call them into the fellowship of His work, to the apostles when He would call them to higher service, He made use of the same simple words, "Follow Me."

If we consider quietly the suggestiveness of the call of Christ, we shall discover in it a demand made for confidence and submission. Confronting a man sitting in the midst of his daily avocation, let us say, at the receipt of custom, He looked into his eyes and said, "Follow Me," and we at once see that

He meant: trust Me, trust yourself to Me, put confidence in Me, and obey Me. It is His claim of supremacy and His call to submission to that supremacy.

There is more in it than the claim of supremacy and the call to submission; there is inferentially the promise of guidance and of victory. The assumptions of this word of Jesus' are very great and gracious. He assumes His own knowledge of the way, His own ability to direct those who come after Him, His own ability so to guide and direct them that they shall come to the fulfilment of all that is highest and noblest in life.

"Follow Me" is still Christ's word to men. I say this out of my heart. I believe it is the one thing He would say to every man and woman in this house. A thousand things to a thousand of us, all different when dealing with particular and definite individual need, but one thing to all, "Follow Me."

It is His universal call to men, a call in which He claims authority, and assumes ability to guide, and lead, and deliver; a call in which He insists that those who come after Him must believe in Him and demonstrate their belief by obedience. Its simplicity is its sublimity. The very fact that the words are brief, and so natural that any little child can understand them, still does indicate the fact that when they are uttered there is nothing more to be said, "Follow Me." The first step in the Christian life is that of obedience to that word. The whole pathway of Christian experience is trodden in obedience to that ideal. The final triumph of the Christian life will be won when the trusting soul, in final confidence in Christ, passes over the threshold into the "other room"—to quote George Meredith's description of death. It will be but following Him.

But, there are difficulties in the way. There are those

who positively and definitely refuse to obey Him, those who reject His claim of Kingship. There are those who hear Him, but are not attracted; they neglect the wooing winsomeness of His call. To neither of these classes is my message tonight addressed. There is yet another class, made up of those who are attracted by Jesus Christ, who admire all they know concerning Him, who are supremely conscious of their own need of just that which He claims to be able to supply, who, in their deepest heart intend to follow Him, but . . . "I will follow Thee, Lord; but . . ."; men and women who can make use of the exact language of the last man in our paragraph. "I will follow Thee, *Lord*"; I recognize Thy supremacy; Thou art Lord; I confess my desire and determination to follow Thee; but . . . And the following never begins, the discipleship never commences. To such I desire to speak tonight.

I am constrained to do so by the fact that in my correspondence, and quite recently especially, I have heard from numbers, who perchance are sitting in this house tonight, who virtually have said that. Two weeks ago, in our after-meeting, God gave us great and gracious evidences of His power and His willingness to save, and since then message after message has reached me from someone who was present, saying: I want to be right with God; I fain would give myself to Him; but . . . And they have halted at that point. "I will follow Thee, Lord; but . . ."

My message tonight, if I may state it broadly before I proceed to deal with it and to illustrate it, is that the claims of Christ are such, and the power of Christ is such that everything which comes after the "but" needs to be resolutely put out of the life. There can be nothing after such a "but" as that, which warrants the halting of a soul. "I will follow Thee, Lord; but . . . !" You cannot add to that "but" anything which is justifiable in the light of the claims of Christ, in the light of your own deep need, in the light of the ability of Christ. Yet, how many and how varied are the things that are thus dealt with.

Many years ago I heard Margaret Bottome, the founder of the King's Daughters in America, speaking to a great gathering in Northfield, and her address consisted of a simple story in her own experience in travel, and of illustrations from it, in application to the young life which she was then confronting. She told us that when she first traveled in the Far East, there came an hour when the guide came to take possession of the party, and lead them through all their journeys. Three simple things happened which revealed to her the meaning of a guide. In the first place, the guide came to them and said: "Will you be good enough to give everything to me? I will take charge of everything." They handed over to him all their main articles of baggage—or luggage, whichever you choose—but they were retaining, she among the rest, those small handbags which ladies carry. The guide said: "You must give everything to me." They made their protest, saying there were in those bags things that would be necessary on the journey. Said the guide: "They will be far safer with me, and you will be far safer without them."

After a little while, they were waiting at a railway station for a train; the guide was attending to the baggage. A train came in, they selected a carriage, and the whole party entered it. As soon as they were seated, the guide returned, and said: "Will you be good enough to come out?" They came out, and then asked why he had required them to do so. He replied: "That is the wrong train. Will you be kind enough not to go before me, but after me?" She had learned her second lesson as to the necessity for a guide. In the course of the next day or two, on a long train journey, they were wondering what provision would be made for them on their arrival at their destination. Some stranger, coming from the place at which they were to stay, had told them there was no accommodation, and the guide was strangely silent. When they arrived everything was ready, and the guide said quietly: "Perhaps you will trust me to prepare for you ahead." Three things: Give everything to me. Follow me; but do not go before me. Trust me about the hidden things of the future.

Margaret Bottome has entered into rest, but I bring you that simple message tonight. Whatever your philosophy of life may be, whatever your intellectual difficulties, the whole suggestiveness of that simple story illuminates the thought in the word of Christ, "Follow Me."

"I will follow Thee, Lord; but . . ." Surely there is no need to give everything up to Thee; there are so many things I shall need on the way. Is it not enough to give myself to Thee and keep as for myself and under my own control some of these things that are so necessary—my money, my occupation, my affectional interests? May I not keep these things?

The answer of Christ to the soul that makes such inquiry is: "You will be far safer when I have charge of them, and they will be infinitely safer with Me." In other words, there are those who are holding back from Jesus Christ because they are not prepared to give to Him all—themselves and everything they have. They are not prepared to recognize that the moment in which they become the possession of Christ, their business belongs to Him, and must be under His control. They are not prepared to recognize that in the moment in which they hand themselves over to the Lord, all they have, as well as all they are, must be handed to Him; that in all things He may direct, control, suggest and master.

Is that the way with you, my brother? Would you have given yourself to Christ, but that, in the handing over of your life to the Kingship of the Lord Christ, He claims, and must have, authority over everything you possess?

If that be recognized, something else grows out of it. Perhaps you are saying, That is not quite the trouble, though you are approaching it. If I consent to hand over to Him all I possess, I know what will happen. There are things I possess which He will immediately destroy, and permit me to carry no further. In the case of some, there are actual evils in the life, evil habits, practices, friendships; in the case of others there are forces which are mere impedimenta, hindering progress—"weights," as the writer of the letter to the Hebrews calls them. These must be left, dropped, lost. It is all quite true. Let there be no mistake about it. There can be no discipleship, as the Lord Himself said, save as a man renounceth all that he hath. "I will follow Thee, Lord; but . . ."

How shall we answer? I answer in the exact words of the guide. You will be much safer without them. You will be much safer when you have handed them over to Christ, and they, so far as they are right, true, pure things—your possessions, your occupation, your affectional interests—will be far safer in His keeping and under His direction. The things which ruin apart from His control become the things which make and glorify when He guides and governs.

Again, "I will follow Thee, Lord; but . . ." I do not desire to give up entirely my own independence. My aim is to be right, but I rebel against being refused permission to think or plan, or initiate or arrange. There are so many things in which the way seems quite plain, and I cannot understand why I am asked to remit every decision to Christ. I am not imagining a case. Sitting in my vestry not long ago was a young lady of position and culture, who said to me: "I have never learnt to submit, and I do not think I can." It is the story of hundreds of people.

I am afraid the trouble is that some of us lead men to suppose that it is not necessary. I am here to affirm that it is absolutely necessary. I can undertake nothing concerning which I have not consulted Him. Discipleship means I cannot choose my own calling, or friends, or place of residence. I must consult. I am compelled to prayer. Everything must be remitted to Christ. Jesus Christ is not asking for that kind of submission to Him which means sentimental acquiescence in the glory of His ideal, or in the accuracy of His ethic, or in the beauty of His own person. He says, "Follow Me." He demands submission of the whole being, and, that from the moment when we begin to follow Him we shall consult Him. Again, to return to the simple figure of the guide, Christ says: "Come after Me; do not go before Me."

There are others who are saying: "All these things are not my difficulties. 'I will follow Thee, Lord; but . . .' I desire to follow. I desire to be a Christian, but there are difficulties ahead of me. There are great uncertainties in the future, and if I give myself to the Christ of Whom you speak, Whose call I have heard, I do not know what will happen. I am afraid to follow in the direction He indicates. Discipleship with me," says such an one, "means in all probability absolute change in my vocation, the passing out of my life of things essential to my material being. I am afraid to follow because I cannot see how the way is to be made clear, or what I am going to do." I hope I am not stating this too indefinitely. Someone says: "I shall have to resign the position I hold in life, and face possible beggary." I do not think that is so very often, but it certainly is so sometimes. I have seen, in the course of the ministry here, more than once, cession to Christ, which meant loss of all the living. It may mean it to someone else. We halt for fear of the uncertain tomorrow. We see the immediate, and the immediate is that of obedience and sacrifice. What lies beyond it?

How am I to answer that statement of difficulty? I might answer it theoretically. If I did so, I would do it by citation from the Scriptures of the Old and New Testament. I would remind you of the one who in olden days spoke of a "covenant ordered in all things and sure." I would remind you of one who, in the New Testament, declared that the saints walk in works foreordained of God. I would remind you of that great song of the leader of Israel, who, looking back over the way, told them that God had ever moved before them, choosing them out a place in which to pitch their tents, even when they marched through what he himself described as that "great and terrible wilderness." God was always ahead of them. When at eventide the moving pillar halted, and they pitched their tents for the night, they pitched them in the place which God had chosen.

Such is the ancient picture. Do you say, It is full of poetry? Then let me answer you no longer by citation of Scripture, but in the voice of the experience of the saints of God. No man has ever yet committed his way to this Christ and followed Him, but that, although mists hung immediately in front of him, they dispersed. He leads us surely onward, and we have never missed our way, as we have followed Him. Though all those things in which our trust reposes have to be abandoned for the following, He is equal to all the way; and when at eventide we reach the place of our abode, we shall find everything prepared, the bread given and the water sure, and shelter provided and secure, and out of every place of temptation the door of escape provided. Such is our final answer to all objections. It is the universal testimony of trusting souls.

Those are but illustrations. Add to my suggestions other difficulties which suggest themselves to you. Nay, rather put in after the "but" the word you yourselves are saying, the thing you have allowed to hinder your following: "I will follow Thee whithersoever Thou goest," but—what?

Christ will halt the impulsive man, not to check him entirely, but to show him what following means. "The foxes have holes, and the birds of the heaven have nests; but the Son of man hath not where to lay His head." What shall we say in answer to that? That it were better to be His companion in the loneliness of the longest night than to be homed and housed without Him. It is such an easy thing to say, yet so absolutely impossible to say it as one knows it to be. Does not your heart agree that it would be better, far better for the sake of the joy of life, of the victory of life, to be the comrade of the poor and lonely Christ, though He never comes to wealth, though He never comes to victory? In other words, the heart of the man who has ever looked into the face of this Christ is compelled to own it, were better to be defeated and die with Him, than being apart from Him to win any passing triumph. "I will follow Thee, Lord!"

Let me urge upon you the importance of definite decision, in view of these very words of Christ. If the following be admittedly costly, then remember this also. The things I have been supposing are not the final things. To follow Him means to go with Him by the way of the Cross, but do you remember the last time He said "Follow Me" to Peter? It was by the shore of the Galilean Lake, in the tender, gracious light of the morning hour, when He Himself, the risen Lord, was bringing Peter face to face with the necessity for his own cross, telling him that at last even he should stretch out his hands and die by the death of the cross. He led Peter to the cross by saying "Follow Me." Being Himself the risen Lord, the light of His resurrection flashed back upon the cross and transfigured it. If it be by the cross, you must follow Him, remember that whoever shares the shame of His cross enters into the glory of His resurrection; and that not merely in God's great tomorrow, not merely in that life which lies beyond; but here and now, in the midst of the present life, the way of the cross is the way of resurrection.

The Lord insisted that the supreme duty of life is to follow him. "Leave the dead to bury their own dead, but go thou and publish abroad the Kingdom of God." He thus set up a claim upon human life which is absolutely supreme. Neither father nor mother, husband nor wife, child nor lover, must be permitted to stand between the soul and Himself. He calls us to follow Him with all the heart. Following Christ means finding the highest, truest wealth, whatever it may be that we abandon; the highest service, however sacred, we have to leave in order to follow Him; the fullest, most glorious realization of life, however, for the moment we may seem to be impoverished in obedience to His command.

The Master waits for our answer, "I will follow Thee." Now, can we not be away from all theory to the actual business of this. In the quiet hush of this Sabbath evening, I appeal to you once again. How is it that you are not following Him? I do not ask that answer to be given to me. I ask you to remember that the answer is given. You cannot escape it. You are now making reply to that inquiry in the very presence of God. You have declared the reason already. That is a thing that I say with all confidence and with all earnestness. I find men today are trying to persuade themselves that they are not sure of the reason. If you will be perfectly honest with your own heart and with the God in Whose presence you are in this evening hour, you know why you are not following. "I will follow Thee, Lord; but . . ." But what?

That which comes after that "but" is that against which you must fling all the force of your resolve; for the ending of it, the putting away of it, you must bring to bear your own will and choice, and henceforth say to Him: "I will follow Thee, Lord," though there be no place where I can rest my head. I will follow Thee though I have to abandon all that seems most dear to me. I will follow Thee in order to find my way into that fellowship with Thee whereby Thy name shall be glorified, my life shall be realized, and I shall be at Thy disposal for helpfulness to others in the publication of the Kingdom of God.

CHAPTER XIV

GOD IN CHRIST

God was in Christ reconciling the world unto Himself.
2 CORINTHIANS 5:19.

THE HOUR OF THE BIRTH OF JESUS OF NAZARETH WAS THAT in which the Light that lighteth every man came into the world. To describe the event in terms which suggest its value in the economy of God, I should be inclined to speak of it as the last crisis in the Divine procedure. By *last*, I do not mean to suggest that there will be no other, but rather that there has been none since.

Every student of the Bible will recognize that God's methods with man have been ever those of process and of crisis. Long periods of preparation have led up to some moment when, by a new and independent activity on His part, a new departure in human history has been made.

Without staying to argue that, at any length we must recognize, if we read the Scriptures carefully, that this has been the method of God in all human history and in all creation. Just as in the poetry and accuracy of the first chapters in our Bible we see some Divine act that we cannot perfectly understand, leading on to processes which we can follow, until we reach another crisis, when there is another act full of mystery followed by succeeding processes, so not only in creation, but also through all God's dealings with men, this process is discoverable. And so far as Scripture has revealed anything of the future, it clearly leads us to expect that the next crisis will be that of the second advent of our Lord. Today, we are living in that period of process which lies between the last crisis, that of the first advent, and the next crisis, that of the second advent.

If I were asked for the briefest declaration of Scripture, setting forth the meaning of the Christian economy, including these advents and all that lies between them, both as to its method and its purpose, I should not hesitate to quote this text: "God was in Christ reconciling the world unto Himself."

While not dealing in detail with the mystery of the method of the first advent, while not describing in detail the processes of the life of Jesus, while not describing in detail the processes of the years multiplying themselves into centuries, and the centuries into millenniums following that advent, and while not dealing in detail with the mystery of the method of the second advent, it gathers the whole fact into one brief and comprehensive declaration, "God was in Christ" —that is the method; "reconciling the world unto Himself" —that is the purpose.

Our purpose in this meditation is to dwell upon the method, referring only to that purpose of reconciliation so far as is necessary for our interpretation and full understanding of the method.

"God was in Christ." That is the initial and supreme wonder of our holy religion. I am anxious, that I may be able by the Spirit of God, to lead you a little beyond the first and simplest things, to the profounder sublimities of the first advent. We speak of the birth of Jesus of Nazareth, and that alone is a wonderful story. But I am anxious that we should recognize that in the birth of Jesus of Nazareth there was something far more wonderful than the birth of a man, far more remarkable than the coming into human life of another human being. That assuredly did happen, infinite though the mystery may be, and forevermore transcending our comprehension of how He was human, and yet more. Nevertheless, the fact abides that the birth of Jesus was much more than the birth of a man.

While our eyes are fixed in meditation, and in adoration, upon the Child held in His mother's arms in helplessness, having gold, and frankincense, and myrrh offered to Him by the Persian Magi, which He at the moment, in His simple humanity, did not understand the value of, yet, let us recognize that we are gazing upon One in Whom God is beginning a new movement and a new method. Our eyes are allowed to rest for a moment in imagination upon the Person of a little Child, of Whom the deepest and profoundest truth is declared in the words of my text, "God was in Christ."

Let us first think, in a few brief and quiet moments, of a preliminary matter. What was the position of the world without that Christ? What did men know of God, or what could they know of Him apart from Christ? Secondly, we will turn to the more positive consideration of this declaration, "God was in Christ." Finally, in one word of application, we will consider the declared purpose of the mystery, "reconciling the world unto Himself."

Our first consideration then, which is preliminary, and of the nature of background to the foreground of consideration, is that of human thought about God, apart from Christ. Theologians have told us that man's thoughts of God are necessarily anthropomorphic. May I put that into another sentence? Man's thoughts of God are necessarily the result of man's consciousness of himself. Man does—and now I use the word *man* in its generic and broadest sense—man does think of God; and, thinking of God, he does so upon the basis of his own personality and consciousness. There can be no escape from this; man can only argue of God from what he is in himself, and every idea of Deity that possesses the mind of men—and will you allow that word *possesses* now to be a perpetually present tense, having application to past and present conceptions—results from this one line of activity. Man projects into immensity the fact of his own personality, and calls the result God. I do not care for the moment whether you think of the most depraved or degraded form of religion, using the terms of our usual speech, or whether you think of your own religion; the same thing is true.

All our conceptions of God, to go back to the word of the theologians, are anthropomorphic. I am not speaking, of course, of a man as he appears to his brother men. I am not speaking of that which is external, and physical, and material, and unimportant—transient, and therefore not important, and only in that sense unimportant. I am speaking of man in the essential facts of his personality. And man does necessarily take these essential facts, when he thinks of another Being, and project them into immensity. His conception of that other Being, greater than himself, is that, nevertheless, of his own nature, it is created on the pattern of his own personality.

Think of the essentials of human life, and I am going to take the very simplest—the essentials of which every child is conscious. The first word of human consciousness is "I am," and when that word of human consciousness is analyzed, these are the terms of its expression: "I know," that is mind; "I will," that is choice; "I can," that is force. These are the simplest things of human consciousness. Man takes these ideas of experience, and projects them into immensity, and so constructs his idea of God. Mind, infinite knowledge; will, supreme choice and consequent government; force, absolute ability. These things underlie all streams of religious thinking. Wherever religion has placed at its center, personality as Deity, it has been because man has taken of himself, and has imagined something of the same pattern, the same nature, the same kind, but vaster and greater.

Now mark what man has been doing. In every case, apart from Christ and apart from His ministry, man has projected himself into immensity, and consequently, he has projected into immensity all that is in himself. In every case, therefore, there has been an amplification of failure. Self-centered life flung out into immensity postulates a self-centered God. All the things of human limitation, resulting from human sin, abide in human conceptions of God, apart from that which has come into the world through Christ. An enlarged conception of mind, an enlarged conception of knowledge, based upon man's own consciousness of knowledge, which is limited, creates an imperfect conception of knowledge. Man has never come, apart from Christ, to a consciousness of full and final and perfect knowledge of God and consequently, man persists in his attempts to deceive God. When man attempts to deceive God, he, by that very action, reveals the fact that he does not believe that God knows all and perfectly.

The whole system of sacrificial worship in other religions is that of attempting to persuade God to change His mind, and alter the method of His procedure.

Or, if man thinks of will, his will is capricious and revengeful, and he flings that out into immensity, and his conception of God is upon the pattern of what he is in himself.

Consequently, in all religions other than the Christian, through all the ages, the deities postulated are grotesque representations of humanity. The underlying ideals revealed in the deities referred to in the Old Testament—Moloch, Baal and Mammon—continue this statement; the deification of the emotional in Moloch, of the intellectual in Baal, of force and power in Mammon. In every case, at the back is a human being, and the monster that is worshiped is but the projection into infinity of the failure of the human being.

The gods of ancient Greece and Rome, or the gods men worship today—sensuous gods, vindictive gods, lazy gods, trivial gods—prove the same truth. We only know these things because we see them in another light. We see these gods by comparison with the one God Who has been revealed to us.

But when, apart from revelation, man seeks a deity, he evolves his conception of deity from himself; he must think of that being upon the pattern of what he is in himself. And so, to make the illustration simple, given a man trying to think of God, he thinks of himself, and then of someone as himself, but vaster; but the things he sees in himself, his evil as well as his good, the wrong as well as the right, the meanness as well as the nobility, are all present in his god, and the visions of men apart from the Christian religion are filled with deities, grotesque and enlarged limitations of man in his failure and in his sin.

My youngest friend will allow me a simple illustration, and the older ones will be patient. You have but to think of a magic lantern. Here you have a small picture, and you look at it, and on it is the figure of a man. You put it in the lens, and away yonder on the sheet is the same man, magnified. But it is the same man, it is the same picture, and if here in the lens the picture be that of a man twisted and distorted and grotesque, the picture there on the sheet is twisted and distorted and grotesque. That is exactly what men have done in their creation of gods. Take all the gods of the heathen world and trace the lines, and you will find they are focused in the men who imagined them.

But, you tell me we have grown away from these ideas; you tell me there are a great many men in the world today who do not claim to be Christian, who yet have a wonderfully true and accurate idea of God, of His uprightness, and beneficence, and tenderness, and holiness; you tell me there are men who will not accept the Christian doctrine of incarnation, who yet have a beautiful ideal of God. I know it, but whence came it? Every advance in man's conceptions of deity is Christian, even though the men who hold the new and higher view do not name themselves Christian.

It is almost a grotesque way to state it, and yet you will catch my meaning, when I say that I am perpetually inclined to say to the men who have these high and noble ideals of Deity, but who deny my Christ, what Samson said to the Philistines: "If ye had not plowed with my heifer, Ye had not found out my riddle."

In the light of these considerations, we turn to the declaration of the text, "God was in Christ." This, then, is the meaning of incarnation. God answers the human necessity; enshrines Himself in humanity; thinks, speaks, chooses, acts through human channels; comes into the very midst of human history, after man had begun to write that history; and thus gave humanity the one and only Man from Whom the lines flung out into immensity include God as He really is.

All that was found in the perfect manhood of Jesus may be projected, and the result will be the truth about God. Fall back if you will upon my simple illustration of the camera. See in this same picture of your New Testament that which you put into the lens, and when the light shining through it projects the figure full of truth and unsullied splendour on the canvas, I see God. Every line is a line of beauty, and every expression of the face is full of beneficence, and yet of righteousness. I come back to this Man of the New Testament, and I follow Him and watch Him, and I take the things I see and fling them out, and I find God. I will take, for illustration, these self-same things to which I have made reference —the mind, and the will, and the force. Now I must leave you to wander at will, through these gospel stories, and I hope some of you may, and watch the working of the mind of the Master, anywhere and anytime; and when you do so, let the lines pass out until they fill the infinite spaces, and you will have found the working of the mind of God. Observe Him in the hour of His choices, anywhere and anytime, and then fling the lines out into immensity, and you have discovered the good and perfect and acceptable will of God. Mark every effort of Jesus, every putting forth of strength. See it in its purpose, watch it in its method, observe it in its victory, and fling the lines out, and you will find that He is vindicated in what He said. "My Father worketh even until now, and I work." There is perfect harmony between the two.

Mark well the mind of Jesus in its essence by observing its activities; it encompassed vast eternities, and compressed him into the simple speech of childhood. I have taken up an old sea-shell, and have put it to my ear, being told when I was a boy that if I would I could hear the ocean. Of course I heard it; the shell was made by the ocean, fashioned by the ocean, was of the ocean, and the ocean of the atmosphere repeated the action of the atmosphere of the ocean, and I heard the sweep and the music of the sea in the shell. Quite reverently —the figure is an imperfect one, I know—I put my ear and listen when this Man speaks, and He speaks in little words, all human language: "Come unto Me all ye that labour and are heavy laden, and I will give you rest. Take my yoke upon you and learn of Me, for I am meek and lowly in heart, and ye shall find rest unto your souls." Oh, my masters, put that shell to your ear this morning, and the infinite speech of eternity is singing itself through your soul, and as you obey you find rest.

So there came into human history two thousand years ago, a Man through Whose personality, whether of mind, or of will, or of force, I fling the lines out into immensity, and the result is God. A new revelation of man has resulted in a new revelation of God.

At the back of all the activity of this Man, love was the motive. The expression of His activity was service rendered to others, and all the way I see Him flaming in white hot anger against everything that bruises and hurts; and whether I watch Him taking children in His arms and blessing them, or watch Him when in quiet dignity He pronounces the eight woes upon a guilty city, it is ever the vision of God that is breaking on my life. "God was in Christ," and what is the result? We have found God, and He is a God of joy and a God of sorrow, a God intimately interested in all the details of human life, a God forever active; and all these things I have come to know through the Child, and Boy, and Youth, and Man of Nazareth.

Did I say that God answered man's method, that man's method is that of projecting man into immensity, and God adopted it? And did the way in which I said that make it appear as though God were turning from His own first purpose, and accommodating Himself to human failure? By no means. That is God's return to first purpose. He made man in His own image and after His own likeness. And man, true to himself, might have flung out upon the canvas of eternity his own image, and have found God. The most intimate relationship existed between man and God in the Divine economy. But, when man shut his eyes to the farflung vision, and began to live as though that upon the earth which was material was the whole of himself, then he became distorted, iniquitous—exactly the same meaning is in the two words—sinful, sensual; and then, lifting his eyes to the heavens, were shadows indeed, and all his knowledge of God was based upon the knowledge of his fallen self, and was evil. But in Christ, we have the very effulgence of His brightness, and when all that He is in humanity is seen and enlarged, we have found God.

And one final word as to the purpose, "reconciling the world unto Himself." Man's misconceptions of God have resulted in man's hatred of God. I want you, if you will, to think of that, and think of it carefully. You tell me that the carnal mind is enmity against God, and I agree with you. But I ask you, Why is the carnal mind at enmity against God? And from the very letter of Paul that declares that the carnal mind is enmity against God, I make another quotation. The carnal mind does not know God, nor can it. It is at enmity against God. Yea, verily, I need not argue it; I need not argue it in London. But whence the enmity? The enmity is the outcome of ignorance. You say we are far away from the idolatry of our Hebrew Bible, with its Baal and Moloch and Mammon. I am not sure, but I will not press that. We are far away from the idolatries of ancient Greece and Rome. Again I am not sure, but I will not argue it. But you are not far away, or humanity is not far away from its hatred of God. It does not express itself in brutal and vulgar language always. It expresses itself in the West End in the fact that the name of God is tabooed, and you must not mention Him. Men do not love God. Why not? They do not know Him. The old German sang well and truly, and you remember Wesley's magnificent translation:—

> O God, of good the unfathomed sea,
> Who would not give his heart to Thee?

And whenever a man gets that vision of God, he gives his heart and everything else to Him.

But though humanity has had a revelation of God in incarnation, the incarnation as revelation does not reconcile men to God, neither can it. The birth of Jesus was the birth of a Man perfect in Himself, but other men will not be reconciled by that birth. The old prophet saw far beyond his own age, and I quote you his language: "When we see Him there is no beauty that we should desire Him." Do you imagine for a single moment that the prophet meant that there would be no beauty in the Servant of God when He came? I do not so read the prophecy. There was no beauty that would appeal to men. Why not? Because they are blind and cannot see. And here is the root of the trouble with the world.

"God was in Christ" is a great word, the meaning of which is not exhausted by the birth and life of Jesus. We must go on, and include the cross. The cradle demands the cross; or else I have seen a Man, strangely other than I am, and I shall hate Him because His purity rebukes my impurity, and His spacious, spiritual and eternal conceptions are a perpetual rebuke to my clinging to the dust of my materialism and the devilish sin that I love. Such hatred was the cause of His crucifixion. That is why they crucified Him.

And then, to face another mystery as infinite as the first, God in man suffered, as man apart from God suffers. And out of that came the fulfilment of all that began on the morning of the birth of Jesus. And when at last, by the infinite mystery of that dying, the life of that self-same Christ is communicated to men, they see Him as they had never seen Him, and they find God as they had never found Him, and in the vision there is at once illumination and energy.

So that brethren—let us remember this also—while we sing our carols at Christmastide and rejoice in the presence of the Child, not by His coming, not by the beauty of His Babyhood, the strength of His Manhood, the glory of His moral character are we saved, but by that final mystery to which this all led, the mystery of His cross; and by the way of His death I find my way back into His life for illumination and for energy. It is thus that we find God, and not only find Him intelligently, but find Him in victorious relationship and fellowship; and, to use the daring and marvelous and awe-inspiring language of Peter, we are made "partakers of the Divine nature."

And so we have attempted to look a little beneath the surface, and have been compelled ultimately to look at something infinitely beyond the birth and life of Jesus. We know God through Jesus. No other interpretation is correct. How important then that we should know the Christ and know Him intimately. And to do it, brethren, we must begin at His cross. He is known, not by outward contemplation, but by inward revelation; and that inward revelation comes to the men who meet Him at the one trysting-place He has provided—His cross. And so I leave you at the cross, for there we must begin, and by the mystery of its cleansing tide and its regenerating forces we come into sympathy with Jesus, the Man of Nazareth, and find our God, and so our peace.

CHAPTER XV

THE SET TIME

Thou wilt arise, and have mercy upon Zion: For it is time to have pity upon her: yea, the set time is come. For Thy servants take pleasure in her stones, And have pity upon her dust.

PSALM 102:13, 14.

THIS PSALM IS PECULIAR, IN THAT IN THE INSCRIPTION TO be found at its head we have a declaration of its character, and a revelation of the circumstances under which it may be used. That inscription reads thus:

> A prayer of the afflicted, when he is overwhelmed, and poureth out his complaint before the Lord.

It is a prayer of the afflicted when he is overwhelmed. It is a prayer that is to be used when the afflicted and overwhelmed soul is in the presence of Jehovah. It is a psalm, therefore, which sets affliction in the light of the government of God.

It is impossible and unnecessary to find the date of the writing of this psalm. Hengstenberg earnestly maintained that it was Davidic, whereas Perowne shares the general opinion that it was written in exile, and that the *set time* referred to the end of Jeremiah's seventy years, when the exiled people were hoping for the dawn of a better day.

These are opinions only. The far more interesting fact is that the author of the letter to the Hebrews ignores altogether the question of human dating and human authorship, and ascribes some of the words of the psalm to Jehovah Himself. In the opening chapter of that letter he declares that God says of His Son,

> Of old hast Thou laid the foundation of the earth,
> And the heavens are the work of Thy hands:
> They shall perish, but Thou shalt endure,

all of which is direct quotation from the latter part of this psalm.

Consequently, the New Testament would lead us to understand that the fulfilment of the psalm—that is, the filling to the full of its spiritual significance—is only discovered as it is interpreted by the experiences of our blessed Lord Himself. According to the writer of the letter to the Hebrews, the psalm is pre-eminently and finally Messianic.

If that be accepted, let us at least pause long enough to notice the fact that it falls into three parts. In the first eleven verses we have nothing but the expression of overwhelming and desolating sorrow. At verse twenty-three the strain, broken in upon at verse eleven, is taken up again: "He weakened my strength in the way; He shortened my days. I said: O, my God, take me not away in the midst of my days." Again it is the plaintive note of an overwhelming grief. In the middle of that verse the tone changes, and we read, "Thy years are throughout all generations"; and we should certainly have read that as though it were still the appeal of the suffering one to God, were it not that the writer of the letter to the Hebrews says that these are words in which God answers the cry of His suffering servant. When out of the midst of sorrow he cries, the answer of the Father is this: "Thy years are throughout all generations. Of old hast Thou laid the foundation of the earth." Therein, we have revealed the secret of the Messiah's strength and victory.

But in the paragraph which I have omitted, verses twelve to twenty-two, we have the great song of Zion—Zion personified, Zion afflicted, Zion expecting deliverance. And the text that I have chosen this morning lies at the center of that central section of this wonderful psalm. Its immediate application is to Zion:

> Thou wilt arise, and have mercy upon Zion:
> For it is time to have pity upon her: yea, the set time is come.
> Because thy servants take pleasure in her stones,
> And have pity upon her dust.

That is, upon her very rubbish.

But if the immediate application, when the singer wrote his song, was an application to Zion, its principles are of much wider application. There is no solution suggested here of the problem of pain, or, to use the larger word, which indicates both cause and effect, there is no solution here of the universal problem of evil; but there is a revelation of the place of affliction in the economy of God for the men of faith. I am quite conscious that all about this text there is the atmosphere of Hebrew hope and expectation. I am quite conscious of how much there is in it that seems to belong wholly to the past; but I propose to turn aside from such things in order that we may discover two or three matters of supreme importance as they cast their light upon the afflictions of the men of faith. There is, I repeat therefore, a revelation here of the place of affliction in the economy of God. And I crave your patience while I tarry a moment longer, by way of introduction, to speak of the word affliction. I am not speaking here, neither is this the thought of the psalm, or the common thought of that word affliction, of certain phases of personal grief and sorrow, for the coming of which there is no responsibility resting upon the sufferers. That is an entirely different matter. Affliction here is chastisement, the dealing of God with a sinning people. Whether individually or nationally, or in a Church application, the principles are the same. And so I repeat, that in these wonderful verses of the ancient psalm, light is flung upon the economy of God in His method of afflicting His people on account of their sin.

I will first of all summarize these matters in three statements, which I shall then endeavor to lay before you by way of illustration and application.

These words, in the song of the psalmist, remind us first of all that there is a *set time*, a set time for deliverance out of affliction. "Thou wilt arise, and have mercy upon Zion: For it is time to have pity upon her: yea, the set time is come."

In the second place, this quotation from the song of the psalmist makes it perfectly evident that the set time for deliverance arrives when God arises. "Thou shalt arise, and have mercy upon Zion."

Finally, the song teaches us that the attitude of His people in affliction determines the set time of His arising to deliver. The set time is come because, "Thy servants take pleasure in her stones, And have pity upon her dust."

Let me repeat even more briefly the threefold thought. First, there is a set time in the economy of God for deliverance out of affliction. Secondly, the set time arrives when God arises. Finally, God arises when His people have gained the value of affliction.

Perhaps now I ought to pause long enough to say, in the presence of this congregation, that which is especially upon my heart. During the past week, I have been present at a very remarkable meeting in London. On Friday evening last, it was my privilege to speak at St. James's Hall in company with Canon Hay Aitken and Mr. John McNeill at a meeting called for the purpose of praise and thanksgiving for the Revival of

Religion fifty years ago. And I am bound to say to you this morning, speaking as I now do to my own people, and in the home of my own service, that I was variously impressed by that gathering. That it was a very remarkable one, no one who was present can possibly deny. To sit surrounded by so many of these men was to feel glad that so many of them tarried until this hour. To hear the story of what God then wrought was to fill the soul, even at this distance, with a great joy and a great gladness. But to be in that meeting was to be conscious of a grave peril, a peril that I think characterizes this hour peculiarly—the peril of persistent looking back instead of confident looking up. And growing out of that is another peril—that of desiring to imitate the methods of the past, to adopt the phrasing of the past, to compel this age to forgetfulness of the freedom and the freshness of the Spirit's activity, and to crowd it back into the methods of fifty years ago.

I was impressed, moreover, with the more insidious and graver peril of an undue haste to be away from the time of affliction. That this is a time of affliction in spiritual things, I suppose we are all ready to admit. There is a sense in which we do sigh for manifestations of bygone days, a sense in which we cannot help being appalled, first of all, at the apparent carelessness and overwhelming indifference of the masses of the people to spiritual things; and, secondly, at the growing selfishness of the most spiritually minded people in the Christian Church. First, I say at the carelessness and indifference of vast multitudes of men and women by whom we are surrounded. We need look no further afield than our own city. We need take in no wider period than that of this morning's service. We have but to remind ourselves of facts with which we are so familiar that they fail to appeal to us, that at this very hour the vast mass of London's population has no thought of God and no care for religion.

We have also to confess that there is a grave danger in this hour, that we should be guilty of that which James described, as asking in order that we may spend upon our own lusts. Remember, brethren, that passage has an application to us, and its profoundest application is not that which we usually make. The lust of spiritual selfishness is more devilish than the animal lust of the street. When a Christian man foreever prays that God will bless him, and loses his passion for the lost and the ruined, he is denying Christ far more forcibly than the man who profanes openly upon the public highway; and the peril of all our Bible conferences and conventions is this, that vast crowds come together for their own spiritual enrichment.

I know that this is a day of dearth, a day of drought, a day of affliction; but I am growingly convinced that the thing we need to do is to discover, and yield to the principle revealed in this passage in the Psalms, the principle revealed through all the teaching of the Bible. We need to come to an understanding of the fact, that when we pray that God will end this state of things we may be very sincere; but we may be making a profound mistake, and God may be saying to us, in answer to our praying: "Wherefore criest thou unto Me? Speak unto the children of Israel that they go forward." While we may be absolutely sincere as we cry, "Awake, awake; put on strength, O arm of the Lord," He may answer us as He answered His people in the ancient days: "Awake, awake; put on thy strength, O Zion; put on thy beautiful garments, O Jerusalem." It is as though, in answer to our cry to God for revival, He should say to us, I have never slept or slumbered. It is you who have slept and slumbered. In order that we may understand this matter, let us here consider these things in quiet and solemn meditation. I bring you this morning the message which God has spoken to my heart, a message not to you, beloved, first, but to me; and to be shared with you, because I believe it is the thing we need to hear in the presence of the widespread drought in spiritual things that characterizes our outlook.

Let us, then, remember that there is a set time, and mark the significance of the word—an appointed time, a set time for deliverance out of affliction. This is in itself a message full of comfort, full of encouragement. We must, however, consider it in its relationship to the other things to be said; but let us dwell upon the simple fact itself for two or three minutes. The people of God in the day of affliction are not abandoned by God. The verse preceding that which I have chosen as text has these words: "But Thou, O Lord, shalt abide forever." The marginal reading of the Revision surely helps us here. "But Thou, O Jehovah, sittest as King forever, And Thy memorial unto all generations." This was the consciousness out of which the song of the psalmist's confidence was born. God has not abandoned His people in the day that seems to be a day of drought, and a day of darkness, and a day of affliction. He is nigh when He seems absent. He is watching when He seems blind. He is active when He seems idle. Said Habbakuk, mystified by the drought and darkness, and the dread of the day in which he lived: "What is God doing? 'I cry out unto Thee of violence, and Thou wilt not save.'" He complained because of the sin of his age, and God seemed to make no response. In answer to that complaint, Jehovah declared: "I work a work in your days, which ye will not believe though it be told you." And then He told him—told him that He was girding Cyrus, a man outside the covenant, to do the work which was not being done by the people within the covenant. And Habbakuk, more amazed than ever, said: "I will stand upon my watch, and set me upon the tower, and will look forth to see what He will speak with me;" and the result of that patient waiting for God was that the prophecy ended with a great song:

> For though the fig tree shall not blossom,
> Neither shall fruit be in the vines;
> The labour of the olive shall fail,
> And the fields shall yield no meat;
> The flocks shall be cut off from the fold,
> And there shall be no herd in the stalls;
> Yet I will rejoice in the Lord.

That is the true attitude of faith today. In the midst of the drought, in the midst of the failure, we dishonour God when we allow ourselves to give way to panic: "Thou, O Lord, sittest as King forever."

We are to remember also that deliverance is always closely related to affliction in the economy of God. Deliverance is the reason of affliction. He doth not willingly afflict. And wherever affliction comes, His purpose is deliverance; not from the affliction, but from that which was the reason of the coming of the affliction. Why does God afflict, withhold the evidences of His power, suffer the deadly drought to settle upon His people, until there is no flower and no fruit, and no realization of spiritual things? In order to correct some underlying evil, and therefore deliverance is the reason of the affliction. He afflicts in order to bring a deeper and profounder deliverance. We cry too often to be delivered from the punishment, instead of the sin that lies behind it. We are anxious to escape from the things that cause us pain rather than from the things that cause God pain. Deliverance is the reason of affliction, and deliverance, therefore, is the issue of affliction. And when it comes, it is the explanation of affliction. The Church of God has never yet passed through a period of affliction, but that, looking back, it has seen the reason of it; and the wonderful deliverance wrought has explained all the process of chastisement and of darkness.

And once again, therefore, affliction in the economy of God is beneficent. Read the song of Zion in this central paragraph to the end, and what do you find? "That men may declare the name of the Lord in Zion, And His praise in Jerusalem." The result, then, of affliction in the experience of the men of faith is the blessing of others.

All the days of darkness are in His economy. These principles have application to the individual; they have application to the nation; they have application to the Church of God.

I turn over in this wonderful Book of Psalms to the one hundred and nineteenth, and I find the value of affliction in the life of the individual recognized in these words. In verse sixty-seven: "Before I was afflicted I went astray; But now I observe Thy word." In verse seventy-one: "It is good for me that I have been afflicted That I may learn Thy statutes." In verse seventy-five: "I know, O Lord, that Thy judgments are righteous, And that in faithfulness Thou hast afflicted me." How many saints there are in this congregation this morning who could add their testimony to the truth of these words! Delivered from affliction we see its infinite value, and we are able to say, It was good for us that we have been afflicted.

That also is true in national life. Without turning to it now, I pray you read most carefully at your leisure that awe-inspiring passage, the first chapter of Isaiah, in which all the bruising and wounding and affliction of Israel is revealed to be God's necessary method of restoring the nation to Himself.

Or, in illustration of the application of the principle to

the Church, remember the words of the writer of the letter to the Hebrews, which we read in our lesson: "All chastening seemeth for the present to be not joyous, but grievous: yet *afterward* it yieldeth peaceable fruit unto them that have been exercised thereby, even the fruit of righteousness."

By so much as the present darkness and the present drought is the act of God—and it must be His act, for He withholds—it is part of a process by which He is preparing for a great deliverance. Decreases! I am weary of the lament over them. They may most assuredly be evidences that God is at work, sifting among His people. I pick up all kinds of religious newspapers, and I read of decrease and of consequent lamentation. Nay, rather thank God if He will but sift our ranks, and make our numbers less, in order to make our forces greater, for then deliverance is at the doors. All the afflictions of God, if we set affliction in the light of His Throne of government, are beneficent.

But now mark the second thought. The set time of deliverance arrives when God arises. "Thou wilt arise, and have mercy upon Zion," and that takes us back to the initial word, "But Thou, O Lord, sittest as King forever." There is no limitation of His knowledge. He understands the causes, watches the processes, and proceeds toward the issues. There is no limitation of His power, and mark how the psalmist explains this: "Thy memorial, Thy remembrance unto all generations." That is to declare that God's attitude always takes posterity into account; that whatever He does today, He is doing not only in the interest of today, but in the interest of tomorrow. His remembrance of the generations is a principle that we often forget when we revolt against Divine judgments; that when God visits in judgment it is not merely the moment of His visitation which is within His own infinite mind, but the next moment, and the following day, and the years that lie ahead, and the centuries and millenniums and ages of the future. The King Who sitteth enthroned forever is not acting in your life in the interest of the half-hour in which He acts, but in the interest of all the generations that lie ahead. Why should we attempt to hasten His movements? Why should we pray as though He had forgotten? Why should we express the agony of our hearts in the presence of present failure as though the blame of it lay upon God? He will arise, said the psalmist. When? At the right moment, at the set time, when trouble has done its work He ends it. When wrath has praised Him, He restrains it. When the forsaking for a season has resulted in a sense of need, He returns. Nothing can prevent Him; His remembrance never fails. It is not necessary that we should remind Him. His purpose never changes. It is useless that we should attempt to change it. His throne never trembles. It is not necessary that we should endeavor to hold it up. I speak out of my own heart when I say to you that I am convinced that what we need is a new vision of God and a new vision of His throne, in order to be delivered from the panic that fills our hearts within the Church about spiritual things, and within the nation about national things. These restless, feverish, godless, narrow thoughts sweeping over us are born of a dim vision of the throne of God, and of the God Who sits upon it.

> Thou, O Jehovah, sittest as King forever,
> And Thy memorial unto all generations.
> Thou shalt arise, and have mercy upon Zion;

and the heart that comes to consciousness of this twofold fact is delivered from panic, and is kept firm and steady.

But once again and finally, and this is the point of importance to us. The attitude of God's own people determines the set time of His arising to deliver.

> Thou wilt arise, and have mercy upon Zion:
> For it is time to have pity upon her: yea, the set time
>   is come.
> Because Thy servants take pleasure in her stones,
> And have pity upon her dust.

Place the psalm where you will in the history of the ancient people, it matters not: the principle is the same. Jerusalem in ruins, her stones in heeps, her beauteous places piles of rubbish; and the people have been careless and indifferent. But at last there comes a sense of shame and a sense of repentance and contrition, and they begin to mourn over the ruin. In that hour the set time is come. Not when amid the ruin the nation flings the blame of it upon God, but when amid the ruin the nation takes the shame of it into its own heart, and gets down in humiliation before God; that is the hour of hope. These are the tears which He gilds with the glory of a new day. This is the hour for God's arising. When the lesson is learned, and the wayward heart weeps over the ruin, the set time for deliverance has come. When—it may be through blood and desolation—the nation learns the value of righteousness, then the set time for deliverance is come.

Or, finally—and that is the main point of application now—when within the Christian Church the ineffectiveness of everything in the absence of God makes us pity the dust of Zion, the day of revival is dawning. The interpretation of that thought is to be found in the words of Christ to Laodicea. What Laodicea said, the Church is in danger of saying today: "I am rich, and have gotten riches, and have need of nothing." The Divine estimate is otherwise: "Thou art the wretched one, and miserable and poor and blind and naked." When the Church realizes the truth of that, and comes to the realization of the ineffectiveness of all she has, while Christ is excluded, having to seek admission to His own home, then the day is dawning, and the first breath of the wind of renewal may be felt sweeping over the garden of God.

I say to you solemnly this morning, it is utterly useless to meet and pray for revival. Let us rather humble ourselves before God, repent in dust and ashes, confess that numbers and wealth and statistics are nothing, that what we supremely need to recognize is our ruin and our rubbish. When we pity these, God will pity us. The set time of deliverance is determined by the attitude of His people.

This meditation, beloved, should produce two results. It should cure all panic, if our hearts are right with God. "He sitteth as King forever," and He will arise. And, strange and contradictory as this affirmation may seem, a paradox indeed, if this meditation should issue in the cure of panic, it will also become the inspiration of anxiety—anxiety to learn the lessons of our affliction, and anxiety to right the wrongs that exist within our own borders. We must be patient with God because He is patient with us. We must be impatient, not with Him, but with ourselves. The day of revival, the day of visitation, the day of new blessing, manifested perchance in a new way, entirely different from anything the past has ever seen, comes to the individual, to the nation, to the Church in that hour when he or it or she has learned the lessons of affliction.

> We wait beneath the furnace blast
>   The pangs of transformation;
> Not painlessly doth God recast,
>   And mould anew the nation
> Where wrongs expire;
>   Nor spares the hand
>   That from the land
> Uproots the ancient evil.
>
> Then let the selfish lips be dumb,
>   And hushed the breath of sighing;

>   Before the joy of peace must come
>   The pains of purifying.
>   God give us grace, each in his place
>   To bear his lot;
>   And, murmuring not,
>   Endure and wait the labour.

In the midst of affliction, therefore, let us remember that God needs no persuasion to act, and that our anxiety should be that we come to such an attitude as will enable Him to do so.

CHAPTER XVI

GOD'S FIGHTING FORCES

By the three hundred men that lapped will I save you.
JUDGES 7:7.

IN HIS ADDRESS FROM THE CHAIR OF THE CONGREGATIONAL Union last month, Mr. J. D. Jones, of Bournemouth, uttered these words:

> Numbers are not the first consideration with the Christian Church. We need to be delivered from the tyranny of schedules and from the craven fear of comparative tables and statistics. It is possible for churches to lose in numbers, as Gideon did, and to gain in strength.

These were courageous words in an hour when the passion for figures is paramount, and when the mention of decrease breeds panic in the heart of the people of God. They were timely words because on every hand we hear of decreases. The returns of church membership come in at this season of the year in many cases, and if one note has impressed me in the meetings of this year which we now designate May meetings, it has been the note of depression consequent upon statistics which declare decrease in church membership. I have not the ear of all the Christian Church, but I have the ear of those who gather here, and I desire to utter a solemn and at the same time, I trust, a sympathetic and courteous protest against this whole business of lamentation.

Yet, we are compelled to recognize the absence of many things which even our eyes have seen in other days and under other conditions, the absence of many things of which our fathers have spoken, and of which we have read in the history of the Church. There does seem to be just now a widespread indifference among multitudes of our people to spiritual things, and an almost appalling lack of enthusiasm within the Church of God. If we are not to be depressed by the story of decrease, we are to be anxious as to our own personal, individual responsibility, not for the decreases, but for the halt which seems to have come in the march of those enterprises of our Lord and Master which are, or ought to be, the supreme things in our thinking, in our life, and in our serving.

I am not interested in the causes of decrease. I believe that the *cause*—and I draw the distinction carefully between the singular and the plural—is that God is sifting our ranks, revealing weakness as prerequisite to the creation of strength. It is not against the sense that we have been halted, and that there is a lack of spiritual consciousness, that I make my protest. It is rather against the way in which men deal with this sense. It is against the prevalent idea that decrease itself is a sign of the absence of the working of God. Not that we are to be less careful concerning the matters of His Kingdom, but that we should interpret the signs of the times in the light of God's perpetual method with His people. So far as I read my Bible, so far as I am able to read the doings of God in the history of the Church for nineteen centuries, I affirm that sifting and decrease are but evidences of His activity. Let us understand that activity. I have read these words from the address of my dear and honoured friend Mr. Jones, and my business this evening is to take the illustration which he gave in less than half a sentence, and make it the basis upon which we may illustrate and enforce the principle that he laid down in the course of the brief paragraph I read to you.

Let us remind ourselves again of this old story of Gideon. Seven and forty years had passed since Deborah had sung her song. After the singing of that song, and the deliverance wrought through the inspiration of the prophetess and the leadership of Barak, the land had rest for forty years. There succeeded to the forty years of rest seven years of Midianitish oppression. It is not for me this evening to tell the story of that oppression. It is written in the Book of Judges, and you may turn to it for yourselves if you are not already familiar with it. Suffice it to say that perhaps at no period in the earlier history of the people of God was oppression so severe, and suffering so great, and the sense of defeat so overwhelming as during those seven years of Midian's oppression. One instance will suffice. The people were so cruelly treated, so oppressed by Midian that in multitudes they had left their homes and made dwellings for themselves in dens and caves of the earth, hardly daring to show their faces. Then there came the hour, the "set time." The "set time" arrived when the people became conscious that the visitation was a visitation of chastisement and judgment, and affliction of God intended to teach them lessons of profound importance. With the coming of the "set time" there came, as there always does, the providential man. Gideon was discovered, not by Israel, but by God. God almost invariably discovers the man of the hour where no one else is looking for him. He found Gideon, and there were two qualifications in the character of Gideon which fitted him for service. First, that of his personal faith in God; and secondly, that of his fidelity to his own business. With reluctance almost amounting to fear, he shrank from the work to which he was called, and asked tests of God. We may criticize him for so doing. We might be inclined to say that it was evidence of faltering and feebleness of faith, and

I think such criticism would be perfectly true; but while we criticize, let us remember that God gave him the tests he asked.

Gideon sent his call through the tribes, and in response there gathered to him thirty-two thousand men. As I watch them gathering out of the different tribes around the standard of Gideon, two thoughts occur to me. First, it is a very wonderful response, seeing the terrible condition of the people. Second, it is an utterly inadequate response, if the vast hosts of Midian are to be engaged in battle and overcome. These, I say, would be the impressions made upon my own mind if I watched the movement with perfect naturalness, as one unacquainted with the deeper secrets of the Divine procedure. A leader has arisen, he cries for helpers, and thirty-two thousand marshal to him from among the oppressed people. Only thirty-two thousand! If you can put yourselves back for a moment in imagination in the place of Gideon, and look at these hosts of Midian encamped along the valleys, holding all the strategic positions, hemming in the people of God, and then look at the army of thirty-two thousand as against the unnumbered hosts of Midian, you will discover how hopeless the task must have seemed, to engage Midian's trained, disciplined hosts with only thirty-two thousand oppressed, and broken, and degraded people.

Then the voice of God, speaking in the soul of the man, declared to him that the people were too many. Too many! A very simple test is given. He is to proclaim to the company that all who are—mark the words—fearful and trembling shall return to their tents. Almost immediately we see twenty-two thousand passing back because they are fearful and trembling. Now Gideon has only ten thousand left. Again the voice of God, speaking within the soul of the man, declares to him that the number is too great, and a new test is imposed.

The essential need of the physical life of these men is water. Let them now be tested in the presence of necessities. I watch the procedure. It is purely Eastern, and as such we must look upon it. Of the ten thousand, nine thousand seven hundred kneel, bending over the water in order to obtain that which is a necessity of life; but there are three hundred men who stand, and, bending over, catch the water in their hands and lap it. Three hundred men taking necessary things, but in the evident expectation of the work they had to do. Nine thousand, seven hundred men taking unnecessary time with necessary things. It was a severe ordeal. Nine thousand, seven hundred men go back. Then the words of my text are heard: "By the three hundred men that lapped will I save you." That is a story of decrease. It is the story of God's method of sifting a people.

Look over the actual story again. The whole nation is conscious of the oppression under which it suffers. The whole nation desires deliverance, but when the call is given, of the nation thirty-two thousand rise a little higher than the nation, thirty-two thousand are prepared to make some venture, and to gather around the standard that is being raised. Among the thirty-two thousand there are twenty-two thousand who are not quite sure, twenty-two thousand who feel the tremor of fear shaking them, and they are sent home; ten thousand are left who have moved to a higher level. Of that ten thousand, there are nine thousand seven hundred who will take unnecessary time for the supply of the necessities of life. Let them be sent home. There are three hundred only out of the whole nation for God's fight.

There is no more radiant revelation of God's method of sifting His people in the whole Bible. It is a revelation of the fact that with God quality is infinitely more than quantity. It is an explanation out of the Old Testament of the reason of the severity of the terms of Jesus as we read them in the New. It explains that constant habit of our Lord and Master, strange habit that has so often surprised and startled us, of scattering crowds by the severity of His terms. I venture to affirm that there are words of Jesus in the New Testament which if I read in this congregation at this late hour of the Christian era, men would shrink from them as from the touch of fire. This severity of terms was due to the fact that always quality counts with God for more than quantity. That is a beneficent movement, therefore, which sifts the ranks and gets rid of certain classes of men, always because, in order to accomplish any great, mighty work, God must have men upon whom He can depend.

There are two lines of thought that I shall ask you to follow briefly. First, the story as it reveals the men with whom God cannot move to victory. Second, the story on the positive side, as it reveals to us the character of the forces with which God is able to win His triumphs.

I am not discussing the subject of personal salvation, but that of service. There is no weak, faltering, failing, cowardly heart that God refuses to receive for salvation. Let no man imagine that God demands that any man who is seeking His grace and favor shall be courageous. He may come with all his trembling and all his weakness, meanness, cowardice, and God will make him a new man.

There are two classes with which God cannot proceed to victory—the fearful and the trembling. Who are the men who are fearful—the men in whose vision the foe bulks bigger than God? That is always a cause of fear. It is a perfectly natural thing. I see those massed, mighty hosts of Midian encamped in all the valleys, and I feel that it was a perfectly natural thing that men looking at those hosts, continuing to look at them, beginning to count them, should be filled with fear. The natural outlook in the great conflict of right with wrong is always a depressing outlook. It always has been; it is yet. It is possible for us today to count the forces against us, and gaze upon them until the heart is filled with fear. These twenty-two thousand men who were fearful were men who were looking at the foe. Is there not a deeper reason why they were fearful when they looked at the foe? I think the second word in the ancient record helps us, trembling. Why trembling? They were men who thought more of their own safety than of the great cause. They looked at the hosts, and said: "If this means battle we shall be slain; we cannot win." That was the inspiration of panic. They were not prepared for suffering and death. They were fearful because they looked at the foe, trembling because they were more anxious about their own safety and ease than they were concerning the great victory of the Kingdom of God.

Why is it that God declines to move with such men for the accomplishment of His enterprises? First, because such men create panic in a crisis; fear is contagious. Lead thirty-two thousand men to fight, twenty-two thousand of whom are fearful, and the ten thousand will be afraid in the clash of the conflict and in the hour of battle. Second, because men who are fearful and trembling cannot strike any heavy blow in the hour of battle. Trembling is always weakness.

I am inclined to think the application need not be made in any word of mine. Are we afraid of the issue? Then God cannot work with us. Are we so busy in these days, looking at the foe and counting the forces against the Lord, that in our heart there is the tremor of fear? Then we are not the men God can depend upon. In the day of battle our fear will spread to others; it is contagious. In the day of dire conflict we cannot place any heavy blow upon the foe. Fear paralyzes the arm because it unnerves the heart. All such fear is born of gazing upon the foe. The fearful and trembling man God cannot use. I know the word is a severe one, but it is the word of this story and of the whole Bible. The trouble today is that the fearful and trembling man insists upon remaining in the army. A decrease that sifts the ranks of the Church of men who fear and tremble is a great, a gracious and a glorious gain.

Mark the second type of man revealed. I have twice described this man as one who takes unnecessary time over necessary things. To do that is always to lack a keen sense of the urgency of the mission in hand. This is one of the causes of weakness and failure today, and perhaps a more prolific and widespread cause than any other. Is not this true of many men who have no fear of the ultimate issue, the ultimate victory, who have no panic as regards God's ability; but while they name the name of Christ, and profess to be His crusaders, they take unnecessary time over necessary things? There are things necessary to the physical life, if I may begin on the lowest level, such as eating, sleeping, dressing. There is a vast amount of time wasted by men who name the name of Christ on all these. Or take the mental level. Unnecessary time is spent over reading, unnecessary time over study and investigation. I have in my own mind now a man, finely, wonderfully equipped in mind, who has spent all his life in preparation, and has done nothing—no blow struck, no brick laid in the great building, no serious work put into the business of cooperation with God. Unnecessary time is taken over the most necessary business of personal spiritual culture, reading and study of the Bible, with no application of its teaching in the warfare against sin, seeking for personal enrichment in the spiritual realm, and no output in sacrifice and strenuous endeavor. Unnecessary time is taken over recreation. I think I need not say one single word here to defend myself from misunderstanding. I believe in the necessity for recreation, but how much time we are wasting! Unnecessary time in the matters of the daily calling, the amassing of wealth.

There is no sense of urgency. The idea of Christianity with too many has become that of an opportunity for their own worship and their own ultimate salvation, and they forget that there is a great battle on, and that God is seeking for warriors, and that He does—account for it how you will or leave it unaccounted for, a mystery of His own gracious and perfect will—He does limit Himself by the method of seeking the cooperation of men. He must, as His own economy has arranged, strike the blow for His victory through men. There is no instance in all the history of the centuries of God acting entirely as apart from His own. All this is lost sight of, and we name the Name, and sing the songs, and wear the uniform of the army, but we take unnecessary time over these necessary things.

The urgency of this business of Christ's campaign in the world, His battle against evil, His compassionate regard for men, and His desire to deliver them, His passion for the Kingdom of God; these things are not recognized as urgent. Such attitude is not the attitude of conflict. Such repletion of necessary things unfits for campaigning. If it be that in these days He is sifting, sifting, sifting; and those departing are those who are fearful and afraid, or such as are not prepared to make His business the one overwhelming master passion of all their life, then we gain by the decreases. Even though the numbers be reduced until they be but three hundred out of every thirty-two thousand, God's word to us, as it was to Gideon of old, is this: "By the three hundred men that lapped will I save you."

Who, then, are the men who constitute God's fighting

force in the world? They are courageous men. That is to say, they were men who saw the vision of God, who saw God at the back of national life, and who saw God in the movement to which they were called. They were men who were prepared to venture something in the great enterprise of the moment, men with such a lack of consciousness of their own importance that they were prepared to die. A man never can say this kind of thing in this day without being rebuked for it. I made a reference of this kind in a recent sermon here, and have had several letters protesting against my saying that it is necessary today for a man to die for Christ. I am perfectly aware that every man must be true to the laws of God about his own health in the interest of the war; but all of this lack of conviction about the supreme importance of the things of the Kingdom of God breeds ease and softness, and unfits men for the fight. God does want men today who have such a clear vision of Himself as to have no panic in their hearts and such abandonment of themselves that they have no trembling as they go forth to the war. Such men inspire confidence. Thank God He has many such today, more than three hundred. Such men do exploits; they are winning their victories even in a day when we hear of decrease. He has those upon whom He can depend. They are men of courage, courage born of their vision of God and of their conviction of the supremacy in all life of the matters of His Kingdom.

They are also consecrated men. Consecration means discipline, the ability to do without. Consecration means ability to take necessary things in necessary quantity and in necessary time. This is the practical expression of consecration. Men who realize the urgency, and "use the world as not abusing it." God seeks such men because with such men He can fight, for such men are ready for the fight, and are not seeking merely for parade; and because such men are ready for the fight, they can "endure hardness as good soldiers of Jesus Christ."

Turning, finally, from the story itself, and with its teaching in our hearts, let us apply God's tests and act. Are we fearful, are we trembling? How shall we cure this tremor of the spirit, this fear in the heart? Only as we see God. Unless the vision of God be clear to us, it is better for ourselves and for the world, and better for the Kingdom of God, that we retire out of the fighting line. What does the vision of God do for a man? It reveals two things to him invariably. First, his own utter, absolute unworthiness and uselessness. Secondly, God's infinite ability, and his own usefulness to God when once he yields himself to Him.

Mark the stories of your Old Testament. The vision of God was granted to the prophet, and he said: "Woe is me, for I am undone." When a vision of God came, the patriarch who had argued at length against all the philosophy of his friends said: "Behold, I am of small account." Daniel, in the light of that vision, exclaimed: "My righteousness is become as filthy rags." No man ever comes to vision of God without feeling the sense of his own unworthiness and the overwhelming conviction of his own inability. That is the first condition for fitness for fighting. I know how easily it is said, and I know also how hardly the lesson is learned. I speak tonight in the presence of those whose experience in life and warfare has been longer than mine, but I am perfectly sure, if my appeal might be made to them, and their answer given to this congregation, they would all agree that the hour of victorious fighting in the enterprises of God dawned when they found their own weakness and inability. It is out of the "I am unable" that there comes the great "I can do all things through Christ which strengtheneth me." Gideon saw God, and saw that he could do nothing apart from God, and therein was the first stage in preparation for doing everything. He shrank from his work. Therein was evidence of the commencement of God's making him fit for the doing of his work. Over against the panic to which I have made reference, over against this complaining lament which has run like a minor monotone through the meetings of the past month, there is another tone even more perilous, the tone that affirms our ability to do anything. The courage that can endure fighting and conquer is always generated in a sense of unworthiness and unfitness born of the flaming vision of God. There Gideon began. There Isaiah, Job and Daniel began. There all the men of the past began, and there we must begin. We shrink from it and hold back from it. We will not look toward the glory that breaks upon our lives, will not submit ourselves to the fiery, searching test of the eyes of flame. Hence our weakness and hence our fear. False fear can only be cast out by the birth of the new fear, the fear of God and the fear of our own inability.

Our first business is to inquire in His presence as to whether we are fearful and trembling, and, if so, then what is left to us? I put the whole thing into this brief word. See God, or else retire from the fighting line.

To make application of the second truth both in its negative and positive aspects. Are we kneeling at some stream of personal satisfaction? I am afraid, as I almost invariably am today, to begin to illustrate that question, and apply it. I would infinitely rather leave the question to be answered alone in the presence of God.

Suffer me an impossible supposition. If Christ is to be defeated, how much will you lose when He is bankrupt? That is the test of whether we are ready for God's fight or not. What have we put into this business of time, of toil and serving? When that question is asked, we begin to see where we are, kneeling at some stream simply desiring to satisfy ourselves. Up, men, lap and march, or fall behind! The Christian Church devoted to the Christ of God, having seen the vision that rebukes and heals, having observed the glory that burns and renews; the Christian Church, placing all her resources, the resources of her individual membership at the disposal of Christ; and the Christian Church, conscious that the first business of every believer, not on one day in seven, but on seven days in seven, not in fulfiling the service of the sanctuary, but in all the duties of the hurrying days, is the business of waging Christ's warfare and winning Christ's victory; that Church will immediately produce the very results that we long to see, arousing the attention of the multitudes, affirming the reality of spiritual things, compelling men—or, if you will take the more tender word, constraining men—to the Lord Christ. All dearth and all death are to be blamed upon our own failure and not upon the withholdings of God. The Midianitish hosts are in all the valleys; the forces against God and His Christ are marshaled, perchance, as they never were before. We are not to be oblivious of the forces of the foe, but in God's name, we are not to look at them so long that we fail to see God Himself.

The true outlook is that of the man who wrote the Roman epistle, who began by looking with such intrepid courage into the heart of the world's corruption as he wrote the third chapter of the Romans. If you want to know what are the massed forces of sensualism and evil, read that chapter again and again, and yet again. Paul began there. He looked straight into the heart of it, but he did not end there. He moved on in argument and appeal until I see him climbing the height, surveying all the field, and saying: "If God is for us, who is against us?" There is a note of laughter in the question, a ring of triumph in the challenge! He saw the forces massed against Christ and His Church—things present, things to come, angels, principalities, powers, all the massed forces of spiritual and material evil—and he said: "If God is for us, who is against us?"

A man with such a vision of God is such a one as Paul, who for at least three and thirty years of Christian service never halted, never wavered, never took unnecessary time even for necessary things, was forevermore a warrior and a pilgrim, a builder and a toiler, in perils oft by land and sea.

We lack this vision, therefore we lack this consecration. Now God is sifting the ranks. Let us be reverent and let us wait, and let us have done with our lamentation over falling statistics; but in God's name let Him have His way with us. Let us at least remit our own lives to Him, and beseech Him to banish the fear and end the trembling by giving us a clearer vision of Himself. Let us beseech Him that He will so reveal to us the urgency of the enterprise that we never again shall bend over a stream and take unnecessary time over even necessary things. Then we shall be among the number of those of whom he will say today, as he said of old: "By the three hundred that lapped will I save you."

CHAPTER XVII

THE SECRET OF THE LORD

*The secret of the Lord is with them that fear Him;
And He will shew them His covenant.*

PSALM 25:14.

THE SOB OF A GREAT SORROW SOUNDS THROUGHOUT THIS psalm. The circumstances in which it was written are most evidently revealed by the words which occur through its process; desolation, affliction, distress, travail.

These and other kindred words, sobbing in sorrow, vibrant with pain, are the outstanding words of the psalm. Yet, its main message is not a message of despair, but rather of hope, of confidence. If at your leisure you will read this psalm again, you may discover that with which one cannot stay to deal at all, particularly now. The singer depressed by sorrow, yet perpetually rises above it; profoundly conscious of the overwhelming and crushing pressure that rests upon him, nevertheless spreads his wings and, rising, the sob becomes a song. The sorrow is made the occasion of the psalm. It opens and closes with prayer. The first seven verses constitute a prayer, and the last seven verses constitute a prayer; or, rather, and more accurately, the first paragraph and the last paragraph constitute one great prayer; and between these two paragraphs is the central one, beginning at the eighth verse and ending with the fifteenth. That central paragraph is occupied almost wholly with the contemplation and declaration of the goodness of God; not that these things are confined to that central paragraph; they run like a major note throughout all the minor wailing of the sorrowful experience, which created the necessity for, and found expression in, the psalmist's prayer.

Out of the central song of contemplation and declaration, we have taken this one verse, because it is the secret of the song in the midst of sorrow, the explanation of the reason why this man was able, even in the day of darkness, to lift a face radiant with light. It is impossible to escape the conviction, if the psalm be carefully studied, that in this declaration we have found the secret of this man's triumph over pain. "The secret of the Lord is with them that fear Him; And He will shew them His covenant."

My message tonight is to those who are sorrowful, a message to which I am constrained for a reason which I cannot give. I am content to answer the call, and attempt to lead such of you as are in sorrow, stress, strain, difficulty of any kind to an examination of this wonderful word of the psalmist of old, very familiar to all of us who have known anything of our Bibles from childhood, and full of wonderful suggestiveness. "The secret of the Lord is with them that fear Him; And He will shew them His covenant."

First, let us quietly meditate upon the blessing that is here referred to, "The secret of the Lord." Second, let us solemnly consider the condition upon which we may enter into the experience of the blessing described, "Them that fear Him." In conclusion, let us notice one result of the blessing which the psalmist describes, "He will shew them His covenant."

"The secret of the Lord." We need to be careful with this word. There comes to mind another of the great verses of the Bible, "The secret things belong unto the Lord our God; but the things that are revealed belong unto us and to our children forever." I cite it only that I may ask you to remember that the word "secret" in that verse is an entirely different one from the word "secret" in our text. "Secret things"; that is, quite literally, veiled things, hidden things, things that cannot be discovered, things that cannot be revealed. There are always such, even for the saints, to the end of the journey; the secret, veiled, hidden mysteries of life and of government. But the word here is quite other, and I propose this evening to adopt a method of interpretation, wholly Biblical. I am going to illuminate my text by four other texts in which the same Hebrew word occurs, but in which it is used with a slight variation of application and of intention. If we can gather from these four the thoughts which they suggest, I believe we shall find something of the wealth and comfort that lie in this old and familiar declaration of the psalmist, "The secret of Jehovah is with them that fear Him." Let me be understood. The verses to which I shall now refer do not, in the whole of their statements, throw any light upon this passage; but the occurrence in them of the same word will help us to understand the richness of suggestion in our text.

I turn first of all to Psalm 111:1, and I find these words: "Praise ye Jehovah. I will give thanks unto Jehovah with my whole heart, In the *council* of the upright and in the congregation." We may therefore, with perfect accuracy, say that "The council of the Lord is with them that fear Him."

Let us turn to Psalm 55:14: "We took sweet *counsel* together; We walked in the house of God and with the throng." The word of my previous reference was "council"; "Counsel" is yet another word with a slightly different suggestion.

We should be perfectly justified in reading, "The counsel of Jehovah is with them that fear Him."

Let us turn to the Book of Proverbs 3:32, and we have the word of our text translated in the same way, but another suggestion is made by its use in the light of the context: "The perverse is an abomination to the Lord: But His friendship is with the upright." With the suggestion of the word there we shall deal presently.

One other reference, again from the Book of Proverbs 11:13: "He that goeth about as a talebearer revealeth *secrets:* But he that is of a faithful spirit concealeth the matter." Let us now examine these four verses, not for their own statements, but for their use of our word, in order that we may find out what the psalmist meant in all fulness and richness when he said, "The secret of the Lord is with them that fear Him."

When the psalmist said, "In the council of the upright," he used the word in its very simplest sense, a sense more truly in harmony with its root idea than that of any other of the verses we have read. The idea is that of a company of persons sitting together, of one mind, of one heart; of a company of people separated from the heathen and from strangers, unified, of one heart, with single purpose, at absolute agreement with each other. It is a very beautiful idea, rarely realized in the experience of any company of men and women. The poetic and beautiful idea of the psalmist is that of the gathering together of such as have no controversy as between themselves—a perfect company. Once in the history of humanity, so far as I know, there has been such a gathering. It was on the day of Pentecost, when they were all together of one mind, and of one heart, and of one spirit, under the dominion of one Lord; with one master passion in their heart, that of obedience to Him. It was soon lost, and we have never regained it. That, however, is the idea of the Hebrew word; perfect union because of no discord; perfect harmony therefore. "The secret of Jehovah is with them that fear Him." Jehovah sits in council—that is, in perfect union, in perfect harmony—with such as fear Him. There is no controversy between them and Himself, no controversy between Him and such.

The word suggests the consciousness of perfect friendship, though no word be spoken. It suggests that friendship which is equal to absolute silence. Not the friendship—let me carefully safeguard this—that must be silent, but the friendship that can be silent. Turn the thought back for a moment, for the sake of illustration, to the simplest things of love and friendship in your lives. You have not many friends in the world. Mark that well. Just a few friends; many acquaintances, thank God for them all; but not many people that you can be absolutely safe in being silent with. I sometimes think that in all human relationships the last sign of friendship is this ability to be quiet. The acquaintance will entertain the stranger, and weary him by talking to him; but the friend will sit by his side silently, knowing that there is no need for speech; in mutual understanding, with no controversy, no conflict, nothing that has to be hidden. There are children of God who know this secret in its height and depth. We know that they know by the serenity and calmness and dignity of their friendship with God. That is the first thought, the council of the upright, the assembly, the meeting, the sitting together. The idea of speech is not in the word in this connection. "The *secret* of the Lord is with them that fear Him."

In Psalm 55:14, the word, as its context shows, has a slightly different meaning, or, rather, shall I say a slightly different suggestion? Let us hear it: "We took sweet *counsel* together." Here the silence is broken; here is speech, but it is the speech of familiar conversation. It is a step in advance of the last. The word in its use in this psalm suggests the freedom in speech that comes when friends understand each other well enough to be silent. I am afraid that that is awkwardly stated. Yet some of you know at once what I mean. When friendship can afford to be silent, then speech is the speech of friendship. I never can make such a reference as this without there coming to my mind a passage from a book written by Mrs. Craik. Many of you are familiar with it, and those who know it best will least object to hearing it again. She says: "Oh, the joy, the inexpressible delight of being alone with your friend, when you can pour out everything that is in your soul, all you think, wheat and chaff together, knowing that your listening friend will with the breath of kindness blow away the chaff and keep only the grain." That is the kind of speech that comes out of the capacity for silence. "We took sweet counsel together." We talked to each other by the way, amid the busy throng, in the courts of the temple. We talked, and each said to the other all that was in the heart. This is the freedom that comes when friends understand each other. "The secret of the Lord is with them that fear Him." The secret of the Lord is with the man who has no secret from Him. Who pours out before Him all the things that are in his own heart, God can talk too of the things that are in His heart, and in His purpose, and in His will.

Can God speak freely to me? I make the question personal. I had rather do it than put the question to you. I do not propose a public answer, but a private investigation. Can God speak freely to me? This age often affirms that God does not speak to men now as He used to do. I will not argue it save to say that the measure in which that seems to be true is the measure in which men have ceased to talk to Him. If I have a secret from Him, then He cannot have His secret with me. When I have learned friendship with God so as to be able to pour out everything before Him, then He can speak freely and unreservedly to me.

I turn to the use of the word in Proverbs 3:32: "The perverse is an abomination to the Lord: But His *secret* is with the upright." The setting of the word there suggests another phase of the same great and gracious and wonderful fact. Not now the silence; not now that familiar and confidential speech in which each pours out to each the deepest and truest things of the life. Here the thought is rather that of advice and guidance. "The secret of the Lord is with them that fear Him." To such He can give advice, can guide, can say behind them as they walk the path all wrapped in mystery, "This is the way: walk ye in it."

Once again, while the verse seems to have least to do with our theme, the word is used in its fullest sense in Proverbs 11:13: "He that goeth about as a talebearer revealeth secrets." Secrets—what are they? Particular confidences, the last and most intimate demonstrations of friendship. As we grow older we do not talk so much about secrets. Take two children, especially girls, who are friends—close friends in the sweet, bonnie days of their winsome childhood, and the last proof of friendship is that one tells the other a secret! You smile at it. You have lost something since the days in which you were young enough to have secrets, and to tell them. Why do we cease talking about secrets as we get older? Because we are afraid someone will betray us. Why? Because we have so often betrayed someone else.

When Jesus Christ took the child, and put him in the midst, He was right. The child is nearer the ideal of the Kingdom of heaven than anyone in this house tonight. So we get back to the children, and their secrets constitute the last seal of their friendship. God help us all to see the beauty of it, when two children have secrets between each other.

"The secret of the Lord is with the upright." We do not want any exposition of it if we will thus get back to childhood and look at the children. God can tell His secrets to some people. "Shall I hide from Abraham that which I do? For I have known him." And He did not hide it from Abraham. Lot, the successful, progressive, business man knew nothing; but the old-fashioned man of faith got the secret of the Lord. Do not tell me that is old history. It is as fresh as the morning. There are men to whom God can tell His secrets still, the deep confidences of His own heart, of His own economy, of His own purposes. They cannot tell them to other people. Do not misunderstand me. The secrets of the Lord are not for publication. "I knew a man in Christ, fourteen years ago (whether in the body, I know not; or whether out of the body, I know not; God knoweth such a one caught up even to the third heaven . . . and heard unspeakable words, which it is not lawful for a man to utter." God told Paul secrets, and you have never found out what they were. They were secrets that drove him and made him, and the revelation of the secret is not the telling of it, but the manifestation of the changed and glorified life resulting from it.

Mark the four things, then. I will but name them. The first thought is that of sitting in restful silence because there is no controversy. The second is that of mutual conversation. Just two, telling and listening. Then counsel, advice, guidance, and finally special confidences. The secret of the Lord.

Oh, sorrowful heart, God comfort you with this tonight. This is to be able to do what this man did in this psalm, say everything, the thing of sorrow, of desolation, of travail. The man who knows this will never play the hypocrite in the presence of God. He will never pretend resignation when he feels rebellion. He will pour out the rebellion in the listening ear of heaven, and God is never angry with that. To know this is to have found the light that turns the tear of sorrow into the medium of the rainbow of hope. "The secret of the Lord." Who does not desire it, long for it? To be able to sit in silence with God; to talk to Him and to hear Him talk to me; to know that when I talk He hears, and that if I listen He will speak; to have immediately and directly, not as the result of any mechanical contrivance or priestly intervention, his guidance, His counsel; some day, perhaps, to have Him tell me some secret.

Ere we pass from the brief meditation on the blessing itself, I must ask you to notice another word. Those of you who followed my reading of the psalm, perhaps wondered why, when it *says* Lord, I said *Jehovah*. Simply because it is the actual word. Every occasion in this psalm where the word Lord appears, the Hebrew word is Jehovah. I emphasize it because it is a significant word. This psalm, which is a sob of sorrow merging into a song of salvation, the psalm which has at its center this revealing verse that we are trying to think about, through all its process refers to God as Jehovah; not Elohim, which suggests His might, not the secret of the Mighty One; not Adonahy, which suggests His sovereignty, but Jehovah, which suggests His adaptability, His adaptation to the capacity of men and the needs of men. "The secret of Jehovah" the becoming One, the One Who becomes in all circumstances, to all men, the thing necessary to their succour and for their salvation.

Let us think for a brief moment of the condition. "The secret of the Lord is *with them that fear Him*." Though the distinction has often been made, at this moment we must make it again. Let us understand what fear really is. There are two kinds of fear. They have been defined as servile and filial. I sometimes define them thus. There is a fear which is fear lest God should hurt me. There is a fear which is fear lest I should grieve God. This last is the fear referred to in my text. They are utterly opposed. Servile fear dreads God, and issues in hatred, in deceit and in ultimate ruin. But this fear, how does it issue? Note the first fruit of this fear. I am certainly in the humor tonight for Bible definition. Let me go back to one of the wisdom books of the Old Testament, to Proverbs 8:13, "The fear of the Lord is to hate evil." From that, turn over to chapter 16:6, "By the fear of the Lord men depart from evil." I am content with these two passages for our present purpose. "The secret of the Lord is with them that fear Him." What is it to fear Him? To hate evil and to depart from evil. The secret of Jehovah cannot be with a man who loves his sin. The secret of Jehovah cannot be with a man who, conscious of sin, hating it, yet refuses to abandon it. Is it true that we know nothing of being able to sit in silent fellowship with God? Is it true that we know nothing of holding familiar intercourse with God? Is it true that we know nothing of what it is to hear God directly, immediately, counseling, advising, guiding? Is it true that He cannot tell us a secret? Why not? There is only one reason. It is that our sin is shutting us out from God. The old prophetic word is a living word; it is the whole truth in a sentence for this hour. Hear me with patience. Have you been reverently, but decidedly, amused by the meditation of this hour? Have you said this is all a preacher's dreaming about the secret of the Lord? I can call witnesses in this house if it be necessary that the thing I have said is a thing of sober and immediate truth. There are men and women here who know the secret of the Lord. I charge you remember if you know nothing of these things, if the language is foreign to you, then it is because of your own sin. Your sin—not your father's sin, God has dealt with that in the economy of His grace, and can break its power—your sin, your persistence in some way of evil, your definite decision and determination not to depart from evil. The crookedness of your business methods! The dishonesty between yourself and other men! Some sin of which friend and neighbour nothing know until this moment, but in which you still indulge. Your sins are the things that shut God out of your consciousness. I pray you pause and consider carefully before you affirm that the religious affirmations of past generations and the religious declarations of living men are false. Inquire whether it be not that you have eyes and see not, ears and hear not, that the spiritual sense is so blunted by your own sin that it is impossible for you to discover the very things in the midst of which you live. "The secret of Jehovah," the friendship of God, living, actual, personal, positive, is with them that fear Him; with such as hate evil and depart from evil. God will not give Himself to such as love evil and persist in evil. "The secret of the Lord is with them that fear Him."

One final word. The psalmist gives us one result of the great and wonderful blessing. "He will show them His covenant." What is a covenant? An engagement entered into. The covenant of Jehovah with His people is an engagement into which He has entered with them, and I may add today, for I speak under the shadow of the cross, the engagement which Jehovah enters into with His people through His Son. The old prophet of lamentations and tears foresaw and most wonderfully described the great and gracious covenant. "This is the covenant that I will make with the house of Israel. I will put my law in their inward parts, and in their heart will I write it; and I will be their God, and they shall be My people; and they shall teach no more every man his neighbour, and every man his brother, saying, Know the Lord; for they shall all know Me, from the least of them unto the greatest of them, saith the Lord; for I will forgive their iniquity, and their sin will I remember no more." The first application was to the house of Israel, and will be fulfilled to the letter. The principle within it is the principle of the covenant, an engagement entered into between God and His people. He enters into an engagement with all such as hate evil and, desiring to depart from evil, find their way to Him through the Man anointed, appointed to be Saviour and Judge.

"He will show them His covenant." The thought is not that He will make plain to them the terms of the covenant, but that they shall see the ratification of it in the experience of their life.

The fear of the Lord is to have His secret; with what result? We shall watch through all the processes, and disciplines, and trials, and sorrows of life, God's faithfulness to His covenant with us. There will be many a day when, by reason of our own frailty, our own fearful and trembling hearts, we shall wonder whether or not God has forgotten; but before many hours have passed we shall be ashamed of our wonder. Has it not been so? Look back, dear sorrowing heart, tonight if it be possible; look back out of the midst of the present stress and strain and difficulty. There are other days in the past—dark, mysterious days—when everything seemed to be failing, when we were foolish enough to say with Jacob, "All these things are against me." Then come a little way forward from that place at which you have been looking, and you had to say with Jacob again, "The God of the covenant has been with me all my days." Is it not so? The showing of the covenant is not wholly postponed to the life beyond. Then it will be perfectly shown. Then—ah, then —and we know it well, who know anything of the secret of Jehovah, then we shall look back over all the way, and we shall sing, "Right was the pathway leading to this." But we sing it already in measure. The music is already being wrought out into clearness to our astonished ears. He is showing us His covenant.

Those who have been in His fear longest, and know His secret most profoundly, can trace the meaning of this text in its last declaration. There are men listening to me tonight, and women also, who look back over a pilgrimage of faith far longer than that of which I have had experience, and it is good sometimes to take a backward glance. There lie the strange, devious paths of life; hours of agony and hours of deliverance; strange, perplexing phantoms of the night that came gliding over the storm-tossed seas, and then the voice, "It is I, be not afraid." He is ever showing us the covenant. That He will continue to do, until if our Lord shall tarry and we pass through the valley of the shadow, then there will be light in the valley, and the gloaming and the glooming will merge into the gleaming glory of the unveiled face of God. "He will show them His covenant."

We are sure of the last anthem because "The secret of the Lord" is already ours. Then may we learn to set the sorrows of the hour in the light of the present consciousness of God, and the sob of sorrow shall become the song of salvation.

CHAPTER XVIII

THE MIND OF CHRIST

Have this mind in you, which was also in Christ Jesus.
PHILIPPIANS 2:5.

THE LETTER TO THE PHILIPPIANS IS PRE-EMINENTLY THE letter of Christian experience. It is most difficult to analyze, because it is so largely personal, and almost exclusively a love-letter, the letter of Paul the prisoner to his children in the faith.

Among the most remarkable facts concerning it is that of the omission of certain words with which we are very familiar in our study of the writings of Paul. The word sin never occurs. The flesh is mentioned only to be dismissed. There are no disputes referred to, except, perhaps, a friendly rivalry between Euodia and Syntyche. The dominant words are "mind"; and "joy" or its equivalents.

This is the more remarkable when we remember that this letter was written from prison, from the midst of circumstances the most depressing that it is possible to imagine. It is, nevertheless, a letter which triumphs gloriously over all opposing circumstances, and sings its perpetual song of victory.

Just as surely as that, the life of Paul may be summed up in one brief sentence from this letter, that, namely, "To me to live is Christ," so the whole purpose of the teaching of Paul, so far as Christian people are concerned, is contained in the brief injunction of this text, "Have this mind in you, which was also in Christ Jesus."

It is indeed a great injunction. It declares the philosophy of the Christian life. If we can understand the mind of Christ, then we shall come to see what is the ultimate purpose of God for His children. "Have this mind in you, which was also in Christ Jesus."

In another of his letters the apostle says, "We have the mind of Christ," but the two words must not be confused. They are not the same in the actual text. When, in writing to the Corinthian Christians, he said, "We have the mind of Christ," he used a word which might be translated, the intellect of Christ, the knowledge of Christ. By that he meant to say that all the wealth of Christ's knowledge is at our disposal. A writer of the ancient economy had declared:

> Things which eye saw not, and ear heard not,
> And which entered not into the heart of man,
> Whatsoever things God prepared for them that love Him.

This Paul quoted, and then continued: "But unto us God revealed them through the Spirit: for the Spirit searcheth all things, yea, the deep things of God"; and he ended by declaring, "We have the mind of Christ"—that is, His knowledge is at our disposal.

The word here used for mind is one that indicates activity, or, rather, that out of which activity grows. It is a word which might be translated: "Have this disposition in you, which was also in Christ Jesus."

Wherever it be possible in human life to obey that injunction, Christianity passes from the theoretical to the practical, becomes an experience against which no argument, advanced by those who are in opposition to the dogmas or doctrines of Christianity, can prevail. The final argument for

Christianity is the mind of Christ reproduced in His people. "Have this mind in you, which was also in Christ Jesus."

The force of the text can only be felt by a study of the context, in which the apostle immediately proceeded to unveil for us the mind of Christ by that which is, perhaps, the sublimest statement found in the word of God upon this subject.

"Who, being in the form of God, counted it not a prize to be on an equality with God, but emptied Himself, taking the form of a servant, being made in the likeness of men; and being found in fashion as a man, He humbled Himself, becoming obedient even unto death, yea, the death of the cross."

Let us, then, attempt to discover the meaning of the injunction in the light of the context.

First, the revelation of the essence of the mind of Christ. Second, the revelation of the master principle of the mind of Christ. Third, the revelation of the activity of the mind of Christ. Finally, the revelation of the issue of the mind of Christ.

In essence it is love. Its master principle is that of infinite, unerring wisdom. Its activity is that of absolute and prevailing strength. Its issue is that of the throne of empire, and ultimate triumph.

The essence of the mind here revealed is that of love. "As a man thinketh in himself, so is he." If that be true, it is also true that when you know what the man is thinking you know what the man is. The true thought of a man always finds expression in the activity of his life. As one gets a general view of life, the thing that lies at the back of it, which is the reason of it, the inspiration of it, the driving force of it, becomes apparent.

What is true of every man is also true of the one Lord and Master of us all. The profoundest truth concerning Him is revealed in this passage. What is the explanation of that marvelous story which Paul tells? Is there any explanation of it possible other than that of love? Think, so far as the human mind is able to think, of the vast, the stupendous stoop indicated in this wonderful word, "Who, being in the form of God . . . emptied Himself, taking the form of a servant." Remember, in your contemplation of this passage, that the thought must be kept, from beginning to end, upon one Person, "Who, being in the form of God, counted it not a prize to be snatched at for personal enrichment this equality with God, but emptied Himself." The Person remained the same. He did not empty Himself of His essential personality, Whomsoever He may be. He emptied Himself, and took the form of a servant, but the Person remained the same. I state this as simply as I know how, because it has been affirmed that the doctrine of Paul here is that in the mystery of the Triune Deity the second Person emptied Himself of Deity. There is no such declaration made. He remained the same Person. He emptied Himself of one form of manifestation, the form of manifestation fitted to the eternities and to the abiding spiritual realities; and He took a form of manifestation suited to the mind of finite man. He took the form of a servant. I do not attempt to measure the amazing stoop. I stand in the presence of it, overwhelmed by the marvelous mystery, and I watch the processes of the passing of this Person from the height of the throne of all creation and all power to the depth of the position of a servant and of submission.

Then the process comes more within the possibility of our observation. He was made man, passing by the ranks of the angels, made a little lower than the angels; He took the very form of humanity.

"Being found in fashion as a man, He humbled Himself." The whole story of His life must come back to you to illustrate that; the humility, the loneliness, the meekness, the inspiration of all which is expressed in His own wonderful words, "The Son of man came not to be ministered unto, but to minister." The Son of man came not to be served, but to serve; not to receive, but to give. All the story of the life of Jesus, as we have it in the gospels, is true to that note of music.

"He humbled Himself, becoming obedient even unto death, yea, the death of the cross."

What explanation can there be of such action? There can be no explanation other than this: All the facts which Paul here groups in remarkable language demonstrate the profounder fact that behind all is the infinite, eternal, unfathomable love of God. Perhaps the great proof of love in this passage is that love is never mentioned. The word does not occur. "Love vaunteth not itself." Yet the thought is present. Every word is smitten through and through with its light and glory. The mind of Christ in essence is the mind of love, and the love is the love of God; disinterested love, self-sacrificing love; love stronger than death, mightier than the grave; love that can stay at nothing in order to express itself and to accomplish its purpose. The mind of Christ in essence is a mind of love.

Think once again of the passage, and mark the principle as revealed, the supremacy of the Divine wisdom. I am quite conscious that in saying that, I am saying something which does not at first appear, something that might be immediately challenged. It may be said that there is no mention of wisdom, no evidence of wisdom. It may be said, indeed, that the story is a story of unutterable foolishness, for the cross of Christ was indeed foolishness to the Greek, and the wisdom of the world, until this moment, has never agreed to the wisdom of the cross. The supremacy of wisdom is here manifest because the activity of love compasses human well-being. The wisdom of love is demonstrated by the result which is produced. If love be the inspiration, light is the law of the activity, and the mind of Christ was a mind in perfect harmony with the will of God. How men sought to prove the folly of His proposition when He mentioned the cross. When, in the language of time, speaking to men of eternal things, He declared that the Son of man "must go unto Jerusalem, and suffer many things of the elders and chief priests and scribes, and be killed," men sought to persuade Him of the unutterable folly of hoping to accomplish any great purpose by the way of death. He knew the wisdom of God. He Himself was the very wisdom of God. The mind of Christ as to its master principle was a mind in harmony with that wisdom.

All the things of humiliation and suffering and death, in order to gain victory, are things of unutterable foolishness according to human philosophy. No philosophy of man has ever been able to accept the evangel of Jesus Christ. The moment you attempt to arrange your theology within the compass of human philosophy, either one or the other must break down. Paul, writing to the Corinthians upon another occasion, said: "We speak wisdom among the perfect: yet a wisdom not of this world, nor of the rulers of this world, which are coming to nought; but we speak God's wisdom"; and he said also: "Christ Jesus, Who was made unto us wisdom from God, and righteousness, and sanctification, and redemption." As I watch this process of the self-emptying of the Son of God, the descent from the height to the depth, stage by stage, until I see Him a spectacle for men and angels in the brutal agony of the cross; I see that, which remains even until this century to the Greek unutterable folly, but I see Him in that which is the very wisdom of God. The demonstration of the wisdom is discovered in the victories which that cross has won in the reconstruction of human character and the remaking of human lives. The master principle of the mind of Christ, then, is that of co-operation with the wisdom of God, in spite of all human misunderstanding and human inability to comprehend.

Once again. We ask what is the activity of this mind of Christ? It is that of strength. It is that of strength created by the fact that persistently the mind of Christ compelled Christ to co-operation with the will of God. In the things which are referred to in this great passage, Christ was not passive; He was active. By that I mean active as against opposition. There was perpetual response in the whole ministry of Jesus to the will of God, but it was response as against opposition. The mind of Christ was not a mind resigned to the will of God. It was a mind acquiescing in the will of God. But it was a mind proceeding through opposition of all kinds and from all sources. There is one brief word in the Gospel of Luke, which we may read quite carelessly, but which reveals the strength of the mind of Christ: "He steadfastly set His face to go unto Jerusalem." Listen again to the declaration in the conversation on the mount of transfiguration with Moses and Elijah. What was the subject? They "spake of His decease which He was about to accomplish at Jerusalem." Whenever I read that, I am reminded of two things. First of all, they did not speak of His death as though it were something from which there could be no escape; they spoke of it rather as of a *decessus*, an *exodos*, a going out, a triumph. Second, they spoke of that going out in triumph as of something which had to be accomplished. The most infinite mystery of the strength of Christ is suggested in His words: "I lay down My life that I may take it again. No one taketh it away from Me, but I lay it down of myself. I have power to lay it down, and I have power to take it again." It was an accomplished decessus, an accomplished exodos; something wrought by persistent activity as against opposition. He proceeded forevermore against the question of personal rights, against the suggestion of ease or pleasantness. The cross was the supreme expression of the campaign in which the active mind of Christ cooperated with the will of God against all forces which were opposed to the will of God. The enemy suggested to Him, in the temptation in the wilderness, that He should reach the kingdoms of the world by a short and easy method; and He declined, and accepted His Father's way of the cross. His own disciples at Cæsarea Philippi protested against His declaration that the cross was necessary: "Spare Thyself that!" In stern rebuke He denounced the false conception, "Get thee behind me, Satan: thou art a stumbling-block unto Me: for thou mindest not the things of God, but the things of men." So against the opposition of foes, against the mistaken views of friends, the mind of Christ moved with unwavering strength, submitting itself forevermore, in spite of all the forces that were opposed, to the will of God.

Of that mind, the essence was love; its master principle was conviction of the wisdom of God; its activity was that of strength that perpetually yielded itself to the good and perfect and acceptable will of God.

We come, finally, to the last thought, the issue of the mind of Christ. "Wherefore"—that includes everything that has preceded it, from that first incomprehensible step from the form of God in the mystic far-flung splendours of eternity to the form of a servant in fashion as a man; and thence humbling Himself in human life, even to the death on the cross. Because of these things, "Wherefore also God highly exalted Him, and gave unto Him the name which is above every name: that in the name of Jesus every knee shall bow, of things in heaven and things on earth and things under the earth, and that every tongue should confess that Jesus Christ is Lord, to the glory of God the Father." The crowning is the issue. The triumph of God is the result. The glory of God is the ultimate of the mind of Christ. The all-conquering royalty is that of love, which acts in conviction of the wisdom of God, and with unfailing persistence bows to the will of God. That mind surely and absolutely ascends the throne, and comes to the place of universal power. All other purple fades. All other gold tarnishes. It is love that, through battle and smoke, through torture and martyrdom, climbs to the throne.

That is the picture of the mind of Christ. Love, its inspiration; acceptance of the wisdom of God as the only wisdom, its master principle; persistent and unyielding abandonment to the will of God, its strength; the throne of empire and the crowning, its issue.

Now let us hear the injunction. We must hear it in solemnity. We must hear it for our own rebuke. We may hear it, and God grant it may be so, for our inspiration and correction and encouragement. "Have this mind in you, which was also in Christ Jesus."

Love is to be the master of our life. To have the mind of Christ is to have love as the ultimate reason for everything said, and everything done, and everything desired.

The master-principle of the mind is belief in and acceptation of the wisdom of God. Perhaps that is the point where one is inclined to lay the principal emphasis, not wholly, but for the sake of the hour in which we live. I pray you be very suspicious of your own doubt about the wisdom of the cross as the method of salvation. Be very suspicious of anything in your thinking which constrains you to imagine that the evangel of the cross of Christ is a mistake, or that the necessity for your own dying and suffering does not exist.

We must accept the wisdom of God, which is foolishness according to the thinking of man. Unless that be the master-principle, we have not the mind of Christ. The mind of Christ was one that set the cross as the goal of His ministry. It is not for me to stay to prove it, but I make this affirmation, that not in the last few weeks alone, but from the very beginning of His public ministry, He most certainly saw the cross and moved toward it. He knew full well that the cross was the ultimate of His ministry. The wisdom of God, that infinite wisdom which apprehended the whole fact of human sin, and did not treat it as though it were a slight surface wound; that wisdom which understood that human sin can only be dealt with by that which is symbolized in the awfulness of bloodshedding; that infinite wisdom which knew full well that the deep wound of humanity could only be healed by the mystery of sacrifice, and suffering, and death; the wisdom of God, still foolishness with men; until we accept that as the master principle of our living and of all our service, we lack the mind of Christ.

Then the activity of our mind must be that of persistent yielding, in spite of opposition, to the call of love and to the wisdom which declares the cross to be necessary. We need not accept merely the doctrine of the love of God, not accept merely the doctrine of the cross of Christ, but to give ourselves to such identification with that cross as is the only sufficient expression of our identification with the love of God. We may sing of the mystery of love in the sweet and wonderful words of Whittier, or in the words of Faber, or of any of the great singers who have sung it most perfectly, and yet never come into fellowship with it; for to enter into fellowship with love is to come into fellowship with the cross, to make up that which is behind in the sufferings of Christ, to have an actual share in the suffering by which the world is to be won. We can only enter into such fellowship by a mind set to obedience against all opposition, the opposition of foe and the opposition of friend; the opposition of foe, that suggests there are easier methods for victory and the healing of humanity's need; the opposition of the friend, who declares that we should take care of ourselves and spare ourselves. The most subtle opposition that Christ set Himself against was the opposition of His own mother, who took a journey from Nazareth to Capernaum to persuade Him, out of very love for Him, to spare Himself, to return home to rest. In the hour of that subtle opposition, well intentioned but utterly mistaken, He said, in the hearing of men: "Who is My mother and My brethren? . . . Whosoever shall do the will of God, the same is My brother, and sister, and mother."

The mind of Christ, if in essence a mind of love, in its master principle a mind that accepts the wisdom of God as against all the opinions of humanity, is also a mind resolutely, definitely persisting in obedience as against every form of opposition.

Do not let us, however, forget that the way of darkness that seemed to culminate with the cross did not culminate in the cross. Beyond the cross is Easter morning; the resurrection life and the reign of power; the force of victory and the triumph of the throne. "Wherefore also God highly exalted Him." All those of us who, desiring to have this in mind, are yielding ourselves to His love, accepting His estimate of necessity as the height of wisdom, persistently compelling ourselves to obedience; are treading the way of sorrow, but we are treading the way to triumph. It is only out of such yielding to the mind of Christ that we can ever come to His triumph. It is a great prophecy, this word spoken concerning Jesus, of the issue that awaits all those who obey the injunction and have His mind.

So the last word becomes a personal word. Would I share His coming triumph? Then I must have His mind. Now let us observe the force of the apostolic injunction. I like the Authorized Version in this connection. It is quite as accurate, and to me at least a little more forceful. "Let this mind be in you." It is exactly the same thought, "Have this mind in you." The suggestiveness of the other translation is that it shows that if we name the name of Christ and lack His mind, we are in some way hindering what would be a natural process. To whom were these words spoken? Not to the promiscuous crowd of the men of the world. This was a letter written to saints in Christ Jesus. These are words spoken not to men in the world who have never yet submitted themselves to Christ for their own personal salvation. They are words written to those already in Him, who have given themselves to Him; who name His name, bear His sign, wear His livery, and profess to be His disciples. Thus, the great word has its signification. If we are in Christ Jesus, all the resources of His grace are at our disposal, and if instead of attempting to imitate the mind of Christ, we will let the mind of Christ have its way in us, we shall share it; not by our own effort, but by the effort of Christ. Not by imitation and struggling shall we ever come to this mind of Christ, but by yielding ourselves to the Indweller, by allowing Christ, Who is in us and in Whom we are, if we are His, to have His own way.

Do we lack the mind, the essential love? It is because we have closed some part of our being against Christ, have never yielded ourselves to the love impulse, have checked it, hindered it, quenched it. Is not this practically, absolutely true in the case of all of us? Find me a boy or girl, youth or maiden, man or woman yielding to Christ, and immediately, without any exception, in any country or in any age, the first consciousness of the yielded life is the consciousness of love

—love going out after someone else. The first movement of the life of God in the soul of a man is a missionary movement. If in this evening hour, in this church, some man yields himself to Christ before he leaves his pew, he will feel in his heart a desire that wife or child, brother or sister, may come to this same Christ. It is the life of God which is moving within him. We check and we thwart it, because this love struggling within us calls us to the cross, to sacrifice, to service. We check it, hinder it, quench it, because it beckons us along a path of sacrifice.

Mark the emphasis of my text. "Let this mind be in you." Do not quench it; let it burn. Do not thwart it; follow it. If in this hour, the life of God in your soul inspires love for child such as you have never known, love that desires your child shall always be Christ's, speak to your child. Take out of the way of your child the things that hinder, even though the taking of them away make you poor in this world's goods. "Let this mind be in you." It is in you if you are Christ's. In the moment in which you yield yourself to Him, His life within you is the love life, and it speaks of life in the terms of love, and suggests the sacrifice of love. "Let this mind be in you." We sing in the assembly of the saints: "Where is the blessedness I knew When first I found the Lord?" What was the blessedness? It was that of love springing up, running over, prompting to sacrifice, driving us out to a path of sacrifice in order to help other people.

Take the man who wrote this letter as an illustration of the great truth. When the love of God was shed abroad in his heart, he never quenched it, he never thwarted it. He let it drive him. If you want to know what it cost him, read his own second Corinthian letter; read the perils through which he passed, the sufferings which he endured, the buffetings which came to him, scourgings, shipwrecks, perils, scoffing, shame. Hear him as He says, "I bear in my body the stigmata of Christ." What does it mean? That he let the mind of Christ dwell in Him.

This is the trouble with all of us. I have spoken—how imperfectly no man knows more than myself, because the vision appals me—of the mind of Christ. We have heard it theoretically. We say, How can it be? Let the mind of Christ dwell in you. Answer its call. Have done with your prudent calculations. Be ashamed of the advice of Peter at Cæsarea Philippi. Abandon yourself to the call of the mind of Christ.

There let us leave it. In our leisure and in quietness let us take the passage again, and try to see the mind behind the mystery of the condescending, sacrificial Servant.

Then let us understand that if we are His, He has given us His life, and as we yield ourselves thereto His mind shall be ours and His victory shall be ours.

CHAPTER XIX

"KEEP YOURSELVES IN THE LOVE OF GOD"

Keep yourselves in the love of God.
JUDE 21.

THESE WORDS ARE MOST REMARKABLE IN THE LIGHT OF their context. Taken apart therefrom, it would be the easiest thing in the world to misunderstand and misinterpret them. Let us, therefore, be patient while we remind ourselves of all that which we have read as a lesson. The words of this text may be said to be the center of Jude's advice in view of danger; danger, let it be carefully observed, threatening the called, beloved, kept, for so in the opening words he addressed those to whom he wrote, "them that are called, beloved in God the Father, and kept for Jesus Christ."

To such he said, "Keep yourselves in the love of God."

It has often been pointed out that the theme on which Jude desired to write was that of our common salvation. While he gave all diligence to the great subject, preparing for his work; he was turned aside from his purpose by the Holy Spirit of God, and constrained to write words of exhortation in view of perils threatening the called; the beloved of the Father, those kept for Jesus Christ.

He first described the perils, "There are certain men crept in privily, even they who were of old set forth unto this condemnation, ungodly men, turning the grace of our

God into lasciviousness, and denying our only Master and Lord, Jesus Christ." He did not enter into any fuller description of these men. We may be left very largely to speculation as to what the teaching was which they were advancing, or what the habits of life in which they were living. Having referred to the perils, he proceeded to remind those to whom he wrote by three instances that those once saved might by their own wrongdoing be fearfully punished. The Isrealites delivered from Egypt, sinning in the wilderness, failing in faith, were destroyed. Angels who kept not their proper habitation, but left the appointed orbit of their being and service, were cast down from the heights, and reserved in darkness to the final assize. Sodom and Gomorrah, cities of the well-watered plain, having all the advantages of that wonderful country; failing to discover the Creator through the creation, and giving themselves over to all manner of uncleanness, were destroyed. Then, referring again to the evil workers, he compared them to Cain, the hater of God, who reddened his hands in the blood of his brother; to Balaam, who constrained and compelled of the Spirit to the uttering of truth in prophecy, did nevertheless, eventually seduce the people of God to idolatry, and hopelessly perished; and to Korah, who rebelled against the government of God, and was destroyed. Then follows that passage which we have so often read, and yet of which, as we read it together tonight, we felt the almost appalling force, showing the evil of lust and pronouncing judgment upon it. Then having referred to Israel, and illustrated his master thought, that privilege does not in itself ensure ultimate blessing, but brings grave responsibility to those who share it; he came to the positive part of his letter, "But ye, beloved, remember ye the words which have been spoken before by the apostles of our Lord Jesus Christ; how that they said to you, in the last time there shall be mockers, walking after their own ungodly lusts. These are they who make separations, sensual, having not the Spirit. But ye, beloved, building up yourselves on your most holy faith, praying in the Holy Spirit, *keep yourselves in the love of God*, looking for the mercy of our Lord Jesus Christ unto eternal life."

I bring you the message of that injunction. I bring it to those of you in this assembly who are "called, beloved of the Father, and kept for Jesus Christ." While we shall not have time in the course of one evening meditation to go back over this ground and consider it in all its detail, let us recognize that this injunction is one born of a consciousness of peril, filling the heart of a man who turned aside from what might have appeared to him would have been a greater, more important work—that of writing of our common salvation—in order to write this one brief page of exhortation. The final message of it, that to which all the rest lends force, is contained in these words, "Keep yourselves in the love of God."

I want to lead you in meditation; first on the plain meaning of this injunction; second, on its importance; and finally on the method which Jude reveals, by which we shall be able to obey the injunction.

Be patient with me if I take two or three moments to ask you to remember what this text does not mean. We are not told to keep ourselves in such a state as to make God love us. I think a recognition of that at the very beginning will help us in the consideration which is to follow. I am not called upon to bring myself to a condition of life which will compel or constrain the love of God toward me. I am not called upon in my life as a child of God to maintain a certain attitude in order to make God continue to love me. Let us start with the recognition of the fact, that God's love is unsought, undeserved and unconditional. We cannot, in this life, put ourselves outside the love of God. It is a great, fundamental truth of the Christian religion that "God so loved the world." The world did not seek His love. The world as He saw it in its sin did not deserve His love, and He did not impose upon the world, conditions fulfilling which, He would love them. He loved the world. I can never think of this for myself, without there coming back to me these lines full of simplicity, full of beauty, written by Charles Wesley.

> He came from above our curse to remove,
> He hath loved, He hath loved us because He would love.
> Love moved Him to die, and on this we rely,
> He hath loved, He hath loved, though we cannot tell why.

Said a boy in a Sunday School class to his teacher many years ago: "Teacher, does God love naughty boys?" The teacher said, "No, certainly not!" It was terrible blasphemy. Of course He does. There is a man somewhere in this congregation who has been disappointed within the first five minutes of my message, and is saying, This message is not for me; if it is to the called, the beloved, the kept for Jesus Christ; it is not for me. There are certain senses in which you are quite right; but remember this; God loves men, not upon any condition, not because they seek His love; but, I dare to put it even more forcefully as the idea is suggested in Wesley's hymn, because He would love; nay, He could no other, for His is love. However far you may have wandered, however far, the far country may be; you may have wounded Him, and grieved His Holy Spirit, but you have not made Him cease to love you. You may have forgotten Him, but God has never ceased to love you.

If that be admitted, then we may proceed. What then did Jude mean when he said, "Keep yourselves in the love of God"? Quite simply he meant this. Being in the love of God; keep yourselves from all that which is unlike Him; from all that which violates love and grieves the heart of God; or to use the actual word of Paul, that which causes sorrow to the Spirit of God.

Mark again the introductory word of this brief letter; you are "called, beloved in God the Father, kept for Jesus Christ"; therefore, seeing that you are loved, that you are dwelling in love, that love encompasses you, is set upon your perfecting, "keep yourselves in the love of God." Correspond to that in which you dwell. Answer the love of God.

Therein is the point of our personal responsibility; if indeed we are called of God, if indeed we are beloved of God, if indeed we are being kept for Jesus Christ, then to us the word applies, "Keep yourselves in the love of God."

Go back to the illustration of the earlier part of the letter; What was the sin of Cain? It was that of hatred, which expressed itself in murder. What was the sin of Balaam? The sin of greed, of covetousness, which expressed itself in the wickedness by which he seduced the people of God from their allegiance, and brought them into evil relationships with idolatrous peoples. What was the sin of Korah? Envy in the heart against the arrangements and the government of God, which expressed itself in rebellion against Him. I refer to these again only to ask you to notice that in each case that love is violated. In each case the action is contrary to love. Cain; hatred, murder; impossible to love. Balaam; greed, seduction; impossible to love. Korah; envy, rebellion; impossible to love. These illustrations, used to show the evil of the men against whom Jude is warning us, serve also to illuminate the meaning of this great charge, "Keep yourselves in the love of God." Being in His love, do not become careless, but remember that you are responsible. The atmosphere in which you dwell creates responsibility. The great and gracious fact of the unsought, unconditional, love of

God, into which you have been specially brought as you have been called, creates grave responsibility.

Last Sunday evening, we were speaking here of that great word of Paul, "Let this mind be in you, which was also in Christ Jesus," and the final message I brought you in that consideration was this, that the love of God shed abroad in the heart of the child of God if allowed to have its own way and master the life will express itself in the attitudes of the life. Paul's injunction is "Let this mind be in you." Answer the movement of the Divine life by bowing to the inward impulse of that life.

There is the same thought here. In speaking on that theme last Sunday night, I dwelt upon it as a great inspiration and gospel of hope to the child of God. Tonight, I come back to it, and listen to the emphasis of solemn warning. "Keep yourselves in the love of God."

Mark the importance of the injunction. We are surrounded by seductive influences. We are in the love of God; and yet we live in an atmosphere in which, unless we learn the art of watchfulness, unless we discover our responsibility, and answer it in the economy of God, we shall wander, not away from His love, for He will still love, but from the possibility of realization and manifestation; we shall fail to fulfil its purpose, and to answer its great and gracious impulse.

Take again these three illustrations. Let us take them in all their bare and naked horror. What are the dangers threatening those upon whom God's love is set; threatening those who live and move and have their being within the very love of God? The dangers are suggested by these illustrations; murder; Cain hated his brother; enticement of other men to actual evil; Balaam seduced the people of God; rebellion against the actual and established government of God in the midst of Whose love we live; Korah led such a rebellion. When I say these things in this assembly, speaking to Christian people, I can quite believe that there are those who object and say, We cannot commit murder; we shall surely never be guilty of deliberately seducing the people of God from allegiance, and leading them into the practice of evil; we never can be guilty of leading a rebellion against God. In answer to that objection, I pray you to remember one or two simple things. First, Cain immediately prefaced the murder of his brother by bringing an offering to the Lord. Balaam, compelled by the Spirit of God, uttered a prophecy concerning Israel more wonderful than any other in certain respects. Korah led a popular movement, and was a man of the people. All the things that are things of horror as we look back at these illustrations, were prefaced by others we are compelled to admire. Let the conceptions of Jesus fall upon these ancient illustrations. Cain murdered his brother. We say, We shall never do so. The answer of Christ is this, "everyone who is angry with his brother shall be in danger of the judgment." The actual crime is not the worst sin. The capacity for it, the tendency toward it, the willingness in certain circumstances to harm another. We are nearer to vulgar sin than we know oftentimes. The man who in the presence of so solemn a warning as this epistle brings, says: "These things have no application to me, I cannot commit murder, I cannot be guilty of the sin of Balaam, I can never be guilty of the sin of Korah," may be by his own self-satisfaction on the very margin of those very sins. "Keep yourselves in the love of God."

The warning is needed, for we lose, ere we know it, the graces and glories of the Christian character. Before we know it, these things which result from His love, and which are full of beauty according to His will, have lost their bloom, lost their freshness, the withering process has begun. I am afraid—I would not utter it as a word of censorious criticism, I associate myself with the statement—I am afraid the Church of God is full of men and women who belong to God, who are not in the love of God as to their own character, as to their own conceptions. The forces that are about us are full of peril. Ere we know it, we have fallen—not out of His love—but from such correspondence thereto, as fulfils His will, and manifests His purpose, and accomplishes His work in the world.

Then we need to take one step further most solemnly, and to remember that our age-abiding and ultimate safety depends upon our correspondence to God. We are not to think our salvation is the result of grace, independently of our response thereto. We are not to imagine that at last He will present us as faultless before the throne of the glory of God unless we are faultless. Christ will not introduce us into heaven's fellowship unless there be correspondence to God. Unless there be that love of God shed abroad in our hearts, mastering the life, which expresses itself in holiness, compassion and sacrificial service, He will never present us before the throne of God. There is a grave and awful responsibility resting upon us. Let us remember it.

These thoughts are enforced by the illustrations of the earlier part of the letter. Israelites delivered from Egypt were destroyed in the wilderness. Angels who kept not the orbit of their high and holy service were cast into darkness. Cities dowered with all the values of the fairest valleys and the well-watered plain, were destroyed by fire.

Privilege is not enough. It creates responsibility; and responsibility not responded to, unanswered, not yielded to, issues in destruction. "Keep yourselves in the love of God." It is necessary that over and over again those of us who name

"KEEP YOURSELVES IN THE LOVE OF GOD" 251

His name should bring ourselves back to the measurement of His requirements, and test ourselves as by His love.

If the word of the living God is searching and trying you, do not forget that He loves you still. You are in His love; answer it, respond to it, yield to it. All that in you is contrary to that love; all of bitterness, of hatred, of injustice, of impurity, all that violates the perfect law of the universe which is love; all these things are to be put away. So, we are to keep ourselves in the love of God, responding to it, allowing it to be the perpetual test of our thinking, the criterion of our conduct. We are responsible in these matters.

How may we obey the injunction. The answer is given in the words lying immediately around our text. It may be remembered by the remembrance of three simple words, *building, praying, looking*. "Building up yourselves on your most holy faith, praying in the Holy Spirit . . . looking for the mercy of our Lord Jesus Christ unto eternal life." These are the laws of fulfilment.

Building on faith. We hear a great deal today, I sometimes think too much, on the subject of character building, yet there is great value in the idea if it be rightly apprehended. How is character built? Character is built by thought and by action. Or, if I may take three words indicating a sequence: There is first the conception; then the conduct arising out of the conception; and finally there is the character resulting from the conduct. That is the whole process of character building, as I understand it. The matter of first importance is that of the conception, for "as a man thinketh in his heart so is he." According to our thinking, will be our doing; and according to our doing, resulting from our thinking, will be our being.

The foundation of the building is that of our most holy faith. When Jude used the term, he used it as expressive of truths which center in Christ. Enumerate, if you so will, the facts of the one great faith of Christ. "Christ; God incarnate. Christ; perfect, ideal Man, living a sinless life. Christ of the cross; God in Christ, reconciling the world unto Himself." Christ; "Declared to be the Son of God with power, according to the Spirit of holiness, by the resurrection of the dead" Christ; sitting at the right hand of the Father. Christ; coming again to receive His people and to administer the affairs of the world. Are these the cardinal truths? The central thought is that of Christ Himself. He is the object of faith. The Lord Christ; of the sinless life, of the atoning death, of the triumphant resurrection; is the object of faith. We are to build on that foundation. That is to say, that all the activities of our life must harmonize with the faith which we exercised in Christ, and by which we entered into that inner circle of the love of God.

Let us apply the principle to the illustrations of the earlier part of the letter. Is it possible for any man to slay his brother while he is building up on that faith? Can there be harmony between murder and obedience to the ideals of Christ? Is it possible for a man to build on that faith, and seduce the people of God, or rebel against the rule of God? Let that faith be the master passion of the life, let that Christ be not merely the object upon which faith fastens for its first realization of life, but let the Christ be Lord of the life. Faith on Jesus Christ as an act of twenty years ago is useless for the present moment. Faith in Jesus Christ must be the maintained attitude of the life; so that all the habits of the life, the thinking, planning, and doing, shall forevermore be tested thereby. To build on that faith is to keep in the love of God. To be true to Christ in thinking, loving, willing, and doing, is to abide in the love of God. That is the first condition.

Are some of you saying in your hearts, "All this is so patent?" I know it. I know also how easily we forget and how constantly we disobey, and how insidiously there creep into our lives wrong motives, and we fail to build on our faith. We, who in the sanctuary hear the message and feel its force, drift into the world, and ere we know it, we have denied the faith, not by open word that affirms disbelief, but by answering impulses that were born in hell rather than in heaven. "Keep yourselves in the love of God." Keep yourselves by building on the faith.

Take the next word; "Praying in the Holy Spirit." Then even the building on the faith is not to be an action wholly of my own will and in my own strength. If it were so, I should be hopeless. I should know the truth and be unable to do it. I am to pray in the Spirit. The testing of my desires is to be that of the Holy Spirit of God. I am to pray in the light of His interpretation of Christ. The sacred office of the Holy Spirit is to make real to the consciousness of the believer the truth about Christ. Some newborn child of God may say to me, "you have charged us to build on this faith, to test all our living by Christ, how are we to know?" The Spirit of God is given for constant, direct, immediate interpretation of Christ. We are not to imitate the example of a Leader separated from us by two millenniums. We are to walk in the will of God interpreted in the inner life of each of us by the indwelling Spirit of God. "Praying in the Holy Spirit." All the desires of the life are to be submitted to His purification, to the fire of His presence, which burns up the dross of base desires. So am I to build.

Do not let us forget the last word of the three; "looking for the mercy of our Lord Jesus Christ unto eternal life." The reference of Jude, without any doubt, is to that advent of our Lord for which we are bidden to look. I am convinced that the Church of God has lost, and is losing immeasurably because she has ceased to look for the coming One. When Paul was writing one of his earliest epistles, that to the Thessalonians, he described the new attitude of Christian men in these words, "Ye turned unto God from idols, to serve a living and true God, and to wait for His Son from heaven." We still insist on men turning from idols to the true God. We insist today as perhaps never before upon serving the living God. Remember, the perfecting word is the last, "to wait for His Son from heaven." In our Lord and Saviour Jesus Christ we have justification, sanctification, glorification. I know the words are old, but how full they are of value and meaning. I look back and say, "There and then I was saved." I think of the present process and say, "Today I am being saved." I look on and up and say, "Now is our salvation nearer than when we believed." The completion of the work will be at His coming. If we would keep ourselves in the love of God, we must be watchers for that morning. To remember that He may come and disturb me at my work, or in my play; will have wonderful effect upon my work, and on my play. I am so to live and toil and speak, that if the life were perfected, the toil ended, and the speech checked, by the flaming glory of His advent, I should not be ashamed from Him at His coming. "Keep yourselves in the love of God," by looking for the mercy.

Let our last thought be that suggested by the closing ascription of praise. "Now unto Him that is able to guard you from stumbling, and to set you before the presence of His glory without blemish in exceeding joy, to the only God, our Saviour, through Jesus Christ our Lord, be glory, majesty, dominon and power before all time, and now and forevermore."

Mark the beginning of the brief letter. Mark its central

injunction. Listen to its final doxology. How did it begin? "To them that are called, beloved in God the Father, and *kept* for Jesus Christ." How does it end? "Now unto Him that is able to *guard* you from stumbling." Between these two the charge, "Keep yourselves in the love of God."

Let us test ourselves, whether we be in the faith or not, by asking ourselves whether we are in the love. Is there bitterness in the heart, anger in the soul against some other man? Is there the making of murder in you, greed, covetousness, a spirit of envy? While God still loves you, you are not keeping yourselves in the love of God. I pray you with Jude, remember Israel delivered from Egypt, perishing in the wilderness; angels keeping not their first estate, cast into darkness; the cities of the plain desolated. May He help us to understand and to keep ourselves in His love.

CHAPTER XX

DIVINE SELECTION

Of a truth I perceive that God is no respecter of persons: but in every nation he that feareth Him, and worketh righteousness, is acceptable to Him.

ACTS 10:34, 35.

THE TRAINING OF THE APOSTLE PETER FOR THE FULFILment of his work in the world may be said to have consisted of a series of revelations of God in Christ, each successive one growing in value and in breadth. When our Lord first met him, he was apprehended by the Personality of Christ. Then, after a period of following Him as one of His disciples; listening to His teaching, watching His work, becoming more and more familiar with the marvel of His Personality; at Cæsarea Philippi he made his great confession. Finally, by the way of the resurrection, he came to full apprehension of the truth concerning his Lord; as he himself said in one of his letters, he was born again unto a lively hope by the resurrection of Jesus Christ. Through that resurrection and all the glory that followed it, he discovered that Jesus was not only Messiah, according to his interpretation of that word, but that He was the Saviour of His people.

In the story which is told at length in the chapter from which our text is taken, we have the account of how he came to a still larger conception of God through the ministry of

Jesus Christ. In the actual words of our text, we have his declaration: "I perceive that God is no respecter of persons."

His first meeting with Christ brought him no conscious vision of God. As he followed his Lord, heard His teaching, watched the wonder of His working, and at last saw that strange cross from which he had shrunk in dismay, transfigured by the glory and triumph of the resurrection, all the old, narrow prejudice concerning men vanished, by reason of the fact that he came to fuller, profounder understanding of the truth about God.

In the house of Cornelius he made still wider discovery, as his own words show. We need to study the declaration with solemnity, for while it breathes the very spirit of hope, it, nevertheless, utters a warning full of solemnity.

Let us hear the simple terms once more, "I perceive that God is no respecter of persons." That is the first matter. The second is: "In every nation, he that feareth Him, and worketh righteousness, is acceptable to Him." The first declaration sweeps away prejudices and barriers; the second sets up the severest of all tests. "No respecter of persons"; Cornelius the Gentile is to be received; but a respecter of character for the Hebrew by blood and ceremonial who does not fear Him, and does not work righteousness, is not acceptable with Him. The text, then, has its negative and positive values.

If the text were all, it is not characterized by comfort. While it seems as though barriers which we have erected are being swept away by its great and gracious declarations, we suddenly find that it is erecting another barrier. While the standards by which men receive other men are set aside, a new standard is erected, the standard by which God receives men; and while our hearts may at first be filled with comfort as we remember that God is no respecter of persons, if we look carefully at the second part of the declaration, we shall need something else, or we shall go away without comfort and without help. Therefore, let me immediately draw attention to the fact that the text without the context is not the gospel, is not the evangel. There is no good news in it if we remove it from its context. If we follow on, remembering that this declaration of perception on the part of Peter prepared the way for his declaration of the evangel, then we shall see the final value of our text.

Let us first notice particularly what is here revealed concerning the principle of Divine selection; God is "No respecter of persons," but He is the accepter of a certain type of character. Let us secondly consider what this text reveals incidentally concerning human rejection, that where that type of character is lacking, because God is no respecter of persons, He rejects. Finally, let us hear what Peter called the gospel of peace.

We begin, then, with the declaration of the text concerning the principle of the Divine selection. All that is necessary in this connection is emphasis and illustration of the declaration which the apostle made. First: "God is no respecter of persons." Second: "In every nation he that feareth Him, and worketh righteousness, is acceptable to Him."

"God is no respecter of persons." This we have heard affirmed over and over again. In some senses we believe it; yet it is indeed the most startling and most gracious assertion. God is not a capricious selecter of men upon the basis of anything accidental in their circumstances. Things which appeal to men, make no appeal to God. God is not interested in any man because of his wealth. It is equally true that the poverty of the poor man makes no appeal to Him. No man of wealth is loved by God on account of his wealth. No poor man is more welcome in the presence of God than is the rich man. The morality of the moral—using these words in their commonly accepted sense—makes no appeal to God. Morality in the estimate of heaven is the application of spiritual convictions to everyday life. A great deal of the morality in which men make their boast is simply that habit of life which makes it possible for them to escape the grasp of the policeman. That morality makes no appeal to God. Neither, on the other hand, does the sin of the sinful make appeal to Him. I think that also needs emphasis. I have sometimes felt as though, especially in evangelistic preaching, we are in danger of so preaching the gospel as to lead men to think that it is the man who is steeped in vulgar pollution that makes especial appeal to God. It is not so. The status of the privileged, the destitution of the despised, make no appeal to Him. He does not select persons on the basis of any of the things that are accidental. God has no favourites among men. Temperament, capacity, tendencies, temptations; none of these creates a claim upon the Divine attention. God does not select men of given capacities; poets, artists, students, workers. He knows all these things. He is profoundly interested in them; they are His own creations in the lives of men. God is interested in every man because he is a man. Perhaps here, as everywhere, we may be helped by thinking of our Lord because He revealed the Father. In a certain sense, He never saw the garments that men wore. He was not attracted to a man because upon his brow and around the borders of his garment there were phylacteries of breadth and bulk. He was not repelled by the rags of a beggar. He saw neither the phylacteries nor the rags. The clothing was nothing, the man wearing the clothing was everything.

No man is acceptable to God by reason of any accidental thing. Some of you were born into such circumstances that it has been possible for you to become educated men and women. Some never had that opportunity. God is not attracted by the culture of the educated man. He is not attracted by the ignorance of the ignorant man. He is interested in the man.

He is no respecter of persons. He has no one nation that He loves more than the rest. That was the thing Peter had to learn. It was a surprising thing to Peter. Peter had believed that God loved Israel and no other nation. Upon the rock of that false conception, Israel went to pieces. Today, we often subconsciously imagine that God loves an Englishman better than any other man. Of course we know that it is not true. When the preacher refers to it we smile at it. Then let us remember it. God profoundly loves man because he is man. He is interested in man as man. Incidentals are not noticed. The essential is not only noticed, it is known, watched, dealt with. He is no respecter of persons.

Why all this emphasis? Because we err perpetually, both in thinking of other men and in thinking of ourselves, through interpreting the attitude of God toward humanity by our own attitude toward our fellow men. If you see coming into your assembly, said the practical and ethical writer of the New Testament, a man wearing goodly apparel, and shall hasten to find him the chief seat, you are violating the Christian principle. We still respect persons. If I may say this without being misunderstood, all the method by which the Church is specializing in its work in the homeland is illustration. Special missions for special kinds of men. I will not criticize you if you feel led that way, but I have very little use for the method. Find me a man, apart from the incidentals, of temperament, or birth, or calling in life, or capacity, and I will preach to him, I care not whether he be rich or poor, high or low, learned or illiterate, moral or debased. "God is no respecter of persons." He is interested in man as man; for He sees in every man, despite the purple or the rags, notwithstanding the culture or the vulgarity, His own image, His own likeness. He sees in every human life possibilities which if set in right relation to Himself will be for His glory. He knows that in the life of the man whom we hold in supreme contempt there are vast forces, which if they are rescued, redeemed, remade, will make heaven richer and all the ages more glorious.

Now let us take the second part of this declaration. If we left it there we might be inclined to imagine that the apostle meant that God receives men into fellowship with Himself, in spite of what they are in themselves. It might seem as though God looks at human life in all its incidentals as though the incidentals did not exist, dealing with humanity ideally, and not actually and practically. But that is not the declaration of my text. He selects. I am quite willing to use the other word; He elects. He does accept some, and reject others. There is a condition of life which He respects though He respects no person. There is a condition of life for which He has no respect.

What, then, is the condition that He respects, selects, elects? The apostle tells us. "He that feareth Him, and worketh righteousness, is acceptable to Him." Simple words, but as I bring my soul to their test, as I compel my spirit to their measurement, I am appalled. "He that feareth Him." Let me take you back to definitions found in the Old Testament of what that means: "The fear of the Lord is to hate evil." "By the fear of the Lord men depart from evil." The fear of the Lord is a condition of the inward life, producing conduct in the outward life. The condition of the inward life is that of hating evil. The condition of the outward life is that of departing from evil. To fear the Lord is to be pure in heart. To fear the Lord is to be pure in conduct. If a man shall declare that he fear the Lord and love sin, he lies and the truth is not in him. If a man shall declare that he fear the Lord and shall continue in sin, persistently walking in the ways of evil, he is deceiving himself; he never deceives God. "He that feareth the Lord" is he upon whose spirit there forever rests the consciousness of God, in holiness, in truth, in absolute rectitude; a man in whose spirit there is perfect harmony with God. He loves the pure, the noble, the holy, and because of these things, hates the evil. As a result of this inward purity of heart, he departs from evil. Immediately, the second part of the definition follows, he that "worketh righteousness." The man who hates wrong departs from wrong, and does right.

How many of us are acceptable with God on the basis of that conception? All barriers of nationality, position, colour, sex capacity, are swept away, but this is erected. Character is supreme, character according to pattern; and the pattern is that of heart purity expressing itself in the life that departs from evil and does right. God is no respecter of persons, and no accident of birth or environment or temperament can exclude us from His attention, or prevent us from being received. Of whatever nation or people, or tongue or position in society—using the word in our degraded sense of it—we may come to Him; and as we come, the barriers men erect are gone; but a flaming sword is before us, we are halted; only those are acceptable who fear God, and do right. How many of us dare go on?

That leads me immediately to the second thought. In the light of the text, I am brought face to face with the appalling fact of human unfitness and consequent rejection. These are hard and fast lines of Divine requirement. No pity can overlook them. We cannot plead our weakness and folly, or our foolhardiness in the past, as excuse for the things which unfit us for the company and fellowship of God. I would put this case as superlatively as I can, and declare that if God can receive into fellowship with Himself, and hold in respect the impure, the vulgar, the demoralized, then He must be the Author of eternal disorder. It is because He is love, and His love is holiness and rectitude; and because His love is set upon the establishment of high and abiding conditions of life that this standard must be maintained. He cannot admit into His heaven the man in whose heart sin reigns supreme. Where is His heaven? Where He is. In London for the men and women who know Him and live in fellowship with Him. He cannot admit you thereto while evil reigns in your heart and sin is permitted, condoned, excused, persisted in. God help us not to hear this as a theory. It is a flaming fire. The thing in your life, in my life, permitted to remain, which we know is sinful; the evil that we do not hate, but love; the impure thing that we will not depart from, but give room to within the chambers of our personality; these are the things that shut us out from God. I affirm, therefore, that there is no comfort in this text if there be no more than the text.

That once again prompts me to go forward. This is not all that Peter said in the house of Cornelius. The background brings into living relief the gospel message. The sweeping simoon is followed by the gentle wind of God with healing in its every breath. If you think my language is overdrawn, or that there is over-emphasis in it, when I speak of the sweeping simoon, I can only say that that is how I feel. I speak with you more than to you. I will speak alone if you so will. In the sight of heaven I say if that text is all, then I am undone; I am excluded from the company and fellowship of God. I thought I was coming nearer when the Gentile might come as well as the Jew, I thought perchance there was an opportunity for me when I discovered that neither wealth nor poverty make appeal to Him. I was rejoiced to think that perchance I might be admitted to His fellowship when I discovered that it was not the man of special capacity whom He receives; and as I was coming, the light shone, and the word said, "He that feareth Him and worketh right." I am a sinning man, I have done the wrong. I will not waste your time or my own discussing and blaming my environment. I have done the wrong when I need not have done it. I have loved the evil and refused to depart from it. The stain and scar and paralysis of it are with me still. How am I to come? To me the declaration is a sweeping simoon, no song in it, no deliverance in it. It is awful with the awfulness of unsullied holiness, and unbending righteousness; and all I can do is put my hand upon my lip and cry unclean, unclean. I am a sinning man.

Let us hear the apostle finish. What is the next thing that he says? "The Word which He sent unto the children of Israel, preaching good tidings of peace by Jesus Christ"; and then the parenthesis which was necessary, because the word was said to Israel, and he was speaking in the house of Cornelius, "He is Lord of all"; no respecter of persons, rich or poor, bond or free, high or low, He is Lord of all, "That saying ye yourselves know, which was published throughout all Judæa, beginning from Galilee, after the baptism which John preached; even Jesus of Nazareth." Why the introduction of that word "even"? Because Jesus of Nazareth is the Word of the gospel.

The declaration already made revealed distance and the necessity for reconciliation between God and man. Peter knew full well that such a declaration would halt the soul, and create a sense of conflict, distance, difficulty, estrangement, and therefore he went on: "the Word which He sent." I wonder sometimes why they have not capitalized that initial letter all through the Acts of the Apostles, "the Word which He sent." What is that? "In the beginning was the Word, and the Word was with God, and the Word was God . . . and the Word became flesh." The Word that was sent.

Let us group the things he said about the Word. He was perfect Man. He was anointed with the Holy Ghost and with power, and went about doing good. He was crucified. He was raised from the dead. He is appointed to judge. The perfect One, Who died, rose, and is Judge. And all this for what purpose? To grant unto men remission of sins. That is the gospel.

Let us see what it means in the light of the declaration of our text. God is no respecter of persons, but He does accept the man who fears Him and works righteousness. Now behold the Man. Here is the Type, the Pattern, the Revelation. This Man went about doing good. He feared God and hated evil; He departed from evil, and wrought righteousness. Mark, I pray you first of all, this great fact, that in the Person of Jesus presented by Peter upon this occasion you have the fulfilment of the ideal suggested in our text. He feared God and wrought righteousness. Do I need to stay to prove it? Surely not! I need hardly stay to illustrate it. Think of the life of Christ and see how true it is. He feared God and hated evil. He was "tempted in all points like as we are, sin apart." "Which of you convicteth Me of sin?" Such was the negative challenge which His purity made. Here is its positive challenge. "I do always the things that are pleasing to Him." He "went about doing good and healing all that were oppressed by the devil." Doing good, when? Always. That means He wrought miracles? Oh no, that is specifically stated afterwards. He went about doing good, all the time, everywhere, and in the records I challenge you to find me a single picture of Him when He was not doing good. Look through the window that Mark has opened for us, and see Him during the long years in Nazareth making yokes and ploughs and building houses, for the carpenter in Nazareth was the builder also; He was doing good as surely there, as when presently in the midst of the crowds He spoke and devils fled; He touched, and diseases vanished; He whispered, and the dead woke; doing good, doing right. A human life in the midst of my circumstances, in the midst of my temptations; but adjusted to the measurements of eternity, taking into account the infinite and eternal. That is the Pattern, and if that is all, I am more than ever filled with fear. The abstract terminology of my text appals me. The living revelation of that ideal paralyzes me with panic. I cannot so live. Oh my masters, you who tell me in this day that all I need to do is to preach Christ as an Example, you have never seen Him. I say that without any apology or reserve. The man who tells me that all I have to do is to follow Him, imitate Him, has never seen His glory. The perfection of the Son of God captures my mind, compels my admiration, and paralyzes my hope!

Is there anything else? Yes, there is another thing. They slew Him. But, there is still something more. God raised Him. The light of the resurrection flashes back upon the cross. I do not understand it. There is an awful, appalling mystery in the cross. I see more and more of its shame. I feel more and more the profundity of its agony. But there are depths I cannot fathom, heights I cannot reach, mysteries that overwhelm me. God raised Him. The light of resurrection is flashed upon the cross, the cruel, rugged, bloody cross has become beautiful with the promise of new life. I, rejected by the severity of God's holiness, see myself in the mystery of that dying; but I see my salvation in the triumph of that rising.

Preaching peace, this is the great evangel. Peace by the way of the cross. That risen One is demonstration of the fact that the cross is infinitely more than we can encompass by human measurement. It is a transaction with God, and of God; and God's final act is the resurrection, and in the words of Peter, the risen One is made "Judge of the quick and dead."

Oh trembling heart, affrighted by the severity of God's holiness, behold your Judge! He is wounded in hands and feet and side. I come to Him and look into His face, the face awful with the awfulness of holiness, and that shames me; yet I look at Him again and say, "Who loved me, and gave Himself for me"; and I am loosed from my sins through the mystery of what He is, and what He has done.

At that point 1 may begin my new life. Now I dare go back to my text. That is the character, and God has not abandoned it; He is still seeking it, but He has provided the force that will realize it in men who lack it.

Would God that the truth might take possession of your heart. You listen to me patiently, reverently, and say, I am with the preacher, I also have sinned. Then hear the preacher to the end, as he declares the whole message of the text. You can be all God demands through Jesus Christ the Lord. He will give you first of all in the deepest of your life the fear of God which will make you hate evil. Is it not so? Are there not hundreds of men and women who hate evil? The struggle is not over; the conflict is going forward; the battle is often fierce against the allurements and temptations of the world; but in the deepest of them there is the masterprinciple of the hatred of evil. Already they are beginning to depart from it. The principle of goodness is there, because Christ is there. Let Him have possession and He will never end until He lead you, and lead me, hopeless, helpless people;

and present us in the unsullied and awful light of the holiness of God, without spot or blemish.

Let us submit to His measurement, and we shall be ashamed and condemned. Let us yield to Him, and we shall be remade and shall triumph.

CHAPTER XXI

FINAL WORDS

The Lord be with thy spirit. Grace be with you.
2 TIMOTHY, 4:22.

Grow in the grace and in the knowledge of our Lord and Saviour Jesus Christ. To Him be glory both now and forever. Amen.
PETER 3:18.

The grace of the Lord Jesus be with the saints. Amen.
REVELATION 22:21.

LET ME SAY IMMEDIATELY THAT THE TEXTS ARE CHOSEN for a definite purpose, which has only a secondary association with what they say. It is not my intention to deal with them from the standpoint of their particular teaching. My interest is rather in the fact that in each case they are the last recorded words of the men who wrote them: of Paul, of Peter, and of John. The systematic history of the New Testament ends with the last chapter of the Acts of the Apostles. That history gathers round a company of witnesses, martyrs, confessors of Jesus Christ the Lord. It covers a period probably of about three and thirty years, and gives some account of the journeyings, doings, and teachings of these persons. Among them, the three outstanding personalities are those of Peter, John, and Paul. John does not appear often in the

Acts, and only in association with Peter. The last definite reference to him therein has to do with his journey through Samaria with Peter. It is possible that he was at the Council called to consider the Gentile question about fifteen years later, but it is not definitely so stated. Peter is the most prominent figure in all the earlier part of that history, but he passes completely out of sight after the Council. Paul is the central figure in all the later part of that history, which is occupied with his missionary journeyings up to the time of his first imprisonment in Rome.

Beyond that, we have no authentic history. There are many traditions and legends of the Church, some of them undoubtedly well founded, but many of them quite unreliable. In the group of writings which complete the New Testament we have certain references which carry us a little further than the Book of Acts. These, however, are by no means connected, and are not enough to enable us to follow the story consecutively. It is interesting to observe that all these subsequent historic references are from the pens of these three men, John, Peter and Paul.

Paul, before his first imprisonment, had written of his desire to visit Spain. Writing from prison, he declared his expectation that he would be set at liberty, and would see Philippi again. In his latest letters, he spoke of visits made to Crete, to Macedonia, to Miletus, to Troas, and described himself in the very last letter as a prisoner, evidently again in Rome. Peter makes one historic allusion. He writes his first letter as from Babylon. John tells us the fact that he was a prisoner in Patmos.

The last historic glimpses of these men which the New Testament affords then are these: Paul was a prisoner in Rome; Peter was at Babylon, perhaps the new Babylon built on the Euphrates, perhaps Rome itself. John was exiled in

FINAL WORDS   271

Patmos. Here, then, we have the historic background for their last written words. Paul, from his Roman dungeon, wrote: "The Lord be with thy spirit. Grace be with you." Peter, from Babylon, wrote: "Grow in the grace and knowledge of our Lord and Saviour Jesus Christ. To Him be the Glory both now and forever. Amen." John, possibly from Ephesus, but with Patmos as his supreme consciousness, wrote: "The grace of the Lord Jesus be with the saints."

Let us think about all this. As I do so, I am impressed with three things. First, with the circumstances in which we last see these men; second, with the one thought that was evidently uppermost in the mind of each of them, that of grace; and finally, with the effect which grace had upon them, as it is revealed by these final words.

We begin with the circumstances. The discussion of differences of opinion as to dates here is unnecessary. I shall proceed upon the assumption of the accuracy of Sir William Ramsay's view as to Paul and Peter; that Paul died in 65, and Peter in 80. I am among the number of those who resolutely put the death of John latest of all, somewhere about the year 96.

Paul was in Rome, expecting his death shortly and violently. Said he in this letter: "I am already being offered." He was tragically alone. "Demas hath forsaken me, having loved this present age." "Crescens is gone to Galatia, Titus to Dalmatia. Only Luke is with me." He was conscious of the grave perils that were threatening the infant Church, as witness the whole of that second letter to Timothy.

Peter was in Babylon. There are those that believe his reference was actually to Babylon on the Euphrates, the new Babylon that had been built upon the site of the old. There are those who believe that when he used the word Babylon he used it mystically and was referring to Rome. I have no care to discuss the question. Either in Babylon upon the Euphrates or in Babylon upon the Tiber, Peter was expecting a violent death, for in his letter he said, "The putting off of my tabernacle cometh swiftly, even as our Lord Jesus Christ signified unto me." He was far removed from his own land, and from his own people. He also was keenly conscious of the perils that were threatening the Church, for his last letter is full of warnings concerning them.

John, as I have said, when he wrote the Revelation was probably in Ephesus, but the whole temper and tone of it was created by Patmos, the island in the Mediterranean, where he was a prisoner, and severed by the surrounding waters from his own land and all his own people. He also saw the failure of the Churches, as witness the seven letters in the Apocalypse.

From such somber surroundings these men wrote their last words, and each wrote about grace.

Peter was the elemental man; always stumbling; always climbing a little higher as the result of his failure; coming out at last to strong rock character and confirming the faith of his brethren. The last thing he wrote was this: "Grow in grace."

John was the mystic, seeing the unseen, hearing the inarticulate, sensing the infinite. He ended everything by saying: "The grace of the Lord Jesus be with all the saints."

Paul was the theologian, the philosopher, the mystic, the statesman. He concluded his message almost abruptly, in one blunt, brief sentence: "Grace be with you."

In each case the pen was laid down, for the last thing was said. All these men, the great human Peter; the mystic dreamer, John; the profound thinker, Paul; when they came to the end had one supreme consciousness. It was the consciousness of grace.

It is first interesting to notice how these men employed the term. It is pre-eminently Paul's word. Does that surprise you? Shall I confess that it surprised me? If I had been asked which of these men was the most likely to talk most about grace, I should have said John. It is not so. He mentioned it least. It was the great word of Paul. It abounds in every letter. We cannot read many sentences without coming across it. Peter, when he wrote his first letter, wrote it under the mastery of grace. In every section of the letter the word occurs. In his second letter, he opened with it, and he closed with it. John's use of the word is very rare. He was very reticent in his use of it. He seems to have reserved it for special use, for special occasions; and then to have left it to shed its own radiance over reaches in which he was always thinking in its atmosphere. We find it at the beginning of his Gospel:

> We beheld His glory, glory as of the only begotten from the Father, full of grace and truth. . . . And of His fulness we all received, and grace for grace. For the law was given by Moses; grace and truth came by Jesus Christ.

He never used it again in that writing, but the whole of it shines and shimmers in the light of it. In his first letter, grace is not mentioned. In his second letter, he employed it in greeting the elect lady. In the Apocalypse, the word is at the portal. He greeted those to whom he writes by using it. It is never mentioned again through all the mystic movements of the visions, until he has done, and then he wrote: "The grace of the Lord Jesus be with all the saints."

Paul, thinker, dialectician, theologian, statesman, must use the word perpetually to keep his spirit right, to reveal to those who should read his writings how he reveled in the glory of the infinite grace. Peter used it as the average man will use it. He is the typical human. John, who, I think, knew more about it than any of them, reserved it, was reticent about it, put it in here and there, so that the light of it flashes everywhere.

In order to gain an impression of what they meant by grace, we will take three passages, one from each of their writings, passages which I think are supreme in the revelation of what each understood by grace.

Let us begin with Paul.

"The grace of God has had its epiphany, bringing salvation to all men, instructing us to the end that, denying ungodliness and worldly lusts, we should live soberly and righteously and godly . . . looking for the blessed hope and appearing of the glory of our great God and Saviour Jesus Christ."

That is Paul's central word about grace. He first declared that grace hath appeared, has had its epiphany. Then he declared three things about the activity of grace, and they are all indicated by participles. The grace of God hath appeared; bringing, instructing, looking! Bringing salvation to men; instructing those who receive salvation, to the intent that denying ungodliness and worldly lusts they should live soberly, righteously, godly; looking for the appearing of the glory of our great God and Saviour Jesus Christ. This is Paul's concept of the activities of Grace. It brings salvation to men; it patiently instructs saved men through life; it looks for its issue to the second advent, the epiphany of the glory when God's victory shall be won.

Peter's central word is a phrase: "The manifold grace of God!" That may be literally translated, "The many-coloured grace of God." This fisherman, this practical soul, this man who stood in perpetual contrast to the dreamers, said one of the most poetic things about grace. The practical man became a poet. Grace made him a poet. When I read this, the word arrested me, and I thought that I remembered that Peter had used it before. At the beginning of the letter I found it. Many-coloured temptations. Over against that, at the close of the letter, he put many-coloured grace. Now where are my artist friends? I want them to think that out, and tell us all it means. I have seen some wonderful colours shining in and through it. Many-coloured temptations. The yellow temptation of jealousy. The red temptation of passion. Many-coloured grace. Heavenly blue shining down upon the yellow. Now, let the artists tell us what happens. When the blue falls upon the yellow we have the green of perfect earthly peace. When the heavenly blue shines on the red of earthly passion, what happens? Then appears the purple of priesthood and of royalty. Many-coloured grace falling upon many-coloured temptations; transmuting the yellow and the red into the green and the purple by the infinite mystic witchery of heaven's transfiguring love. Grace is the eternal rainbow of hope across all the arching blackness of the darkest day.

John, being a poet and a true mystic, wrote so simply, that it is difficult at first to grasp the infinitude that lies within the compass of his simple language. John's great passage about grace is found in the prologue to his Gospel:

"The Word became flesh, and pitched His tent among us (and we beheld His glory, glory as of the only begotten of the Father), full of grace and truth."

That is so simple that if we are not careful, we read it hurriedly and miss its sublimity. It is the simplicity of perfect poetry and the uttermost mysticism. John says in effect: Do you want to know what grace means? Look at Jesus! Behold Him, handle Him, listen to Him; and whether it be in the tears and tenderness of His eyes, or in the tones of His voice, or the vibrant holy anger of His accent, you are seeing grace! The grace of God was manifested in the Son of God.

Tell me, Paul, what is grace? Grace is the activity that saves, and instructs, and lights the dark horizon with the victory of the ultimate glory. Tell me, Peter, what is grace? The manifold colours of God, by which in mystic alchemy He transmutes the manifold colours of passion, and makes them contribute to the making of a man. Tell me, John, what is grace? Jesus! There is nothing more to be said.

From all these statements let us attempt to understand what grace really is. Grace is the activity of God. First, it is the activity which is of His very nature, which He cannot help or prevent because of what He is. Grace is love desiring to realize in every life the beauty of holiness, because in the realization of the beauty of holiness life finds its ultimate beauty and joy. Grace is not a quality in God which makes Him want to excuse sin. Grace is that love of His heart that intensely desires the highest, the best, the most glorious for men. Grace, therefore, is that which inspires and dominates His will. His will is inspired by His nature, and, therefore, "He willeth not the death of a sinner but rather that all should turn to Him and live." Therefore, grace proceeds to the accomplishment of its high purpose at all costs, and that means the cross. Oh simple words, so often said; yet what they mean no tongue can tell: "God so loved the world that He gave His only begotten Son." "He," the Son of God, "loved me and gave Himself for me." That is grace bringing salvation to men; instructing them patiently through the days in which they blunder, fall and fail; all the while lighting the distant sky with the promise of the advent, and the victory of glory.

That is grace, and it is manifold grace. There are colours breaking out from it perpetually. Grace is the rainbow, singing in tones of silent beauty its eternal anthem of final restoration.

Let us conclude by thinking of the effect that grace had upon these three men, as this is revealed in the fact that they wrote these words under such circumstances. Observe first their perfect personal satisfaction. Paul was in prison. Death was coming, and he wrote about it. "I am already being offered." But that is not all he wrote. He added, "The time of my departure is at hand." Departure is a nautical word. The time of my putting out to sea is at hand! But surely that was a mistake! He surely meant that he was approaching the harbour! He meant nothing of the kind. The Christian view of death is not that of reaching port. It is that of putting out to sea. Do you know Kipling's "Ship That Found Itself"? When did the ship find itself? In harbour? No, but upon the mighty deep. Departure is not running into harbour away from storms. It is going out into all the splendour of life. Is not there a hymn that opens something like this?

> Safe home, safe home in port!

and continues about:

> Rent cordage, tattered sails,
> And only not a wreck.

Miserable hymn! Terrible idea of dying! That is not the way. Paul thought of the end. Said he: "I am already being offered. The time of my putting out to the deep is at hand."

Paul, how are you going to finish this letter? I shall finish on the note of grace! Nothing else matters. But you are in prison? Grace is painting pictures upon the walls of the prison that make it more beautiful than the palace of a king. I am departing and the crown awaits me. I am perfectly content with grace! "Grace be with you!"

Peter also was going. He knew that he was about to

die a violent death. Tradition has it that he requested that he might be crucified head downward because he did not feel himself worthy to be crucified as his Lord was crucified. That may be true or not, I do not know. But this I know. Looking on, he said that he was going, and then he added this significant word: "As the Lord signified unto me." When he wrote that, in memory he was back by the sea of Galilee. He was remembering the early morning after the bad night of fishing; and he was listening to his Master saying to him: "Peter, when you were young you girded yourself, and you chose the way which pleased you; but when you are old someone else will gird you, and lead you where you do not desire to go!" John tells us He spoke signifying what death he should die. But the last thing Jesus had said was, "Follow Me!" Therefore, when Peter looked to the end, and saw it coming, he knew he would be crucified, but he knew that his Master had said it, that grace had arranged it! The colours playing out of the rainbow of grace made all the dark and the drab, purple with the promise of the day. He was perfectly content.

John wrote about tribulation. He said: "I am your brother; I am your companion in tribulation." But in that word there was not one note of complaint. To tribulation he added another word—And kingdom! And then another—And endurance in Jesus Christ.

These men had no personal anxieties! They knew the future: a dungeon, and loneliness, and death. But these things did not matter. The dungeon was made beautiful with the light of everlasting grace. Loneliness was canceled by the comradeship of the Lord of Grace. Death was transfigured with the glory of the manifold grace of God.

But again. I see the abounding confidence of all these men in the sufficiency of grace for the people of God.

Paul was writing to one man, a man who was in a place of peril, taking oversight of the church in Ephesus. He was giving him very careful instructions as to how he was to behave; and concerning his work, his church, and his responsibility as pastor. Now he knew that he must leave him in Ephesus, but there was no need to be anxious. "The grace of God be with you." Paul knew that grace was all that Timothy needed in Ephesus.

Peter was thinking in his writing, of the people of God in the time of their trial and difficulty, and his last word to them was this: "Grow in the grace and knowledge of our Lord and Saviour Jesus Christ." There was nothing else that mattered. He knew that nothing could harm them if they grew in that grace. Peter did not mean that they were to grow more gracious, though that would certainly result. He meant that, being in the grace, they were to grow. They were in grace; now, being in it, they were to grow in answer to it, they were to develop in response to its suggestiveness; they were to walk in its many-coloured light, and they were to do all that, by getting to know more and yet more perfectly Christ Jesus. Peter was perfectly content to leave them there.

John was thinking of all the saints. Grace is at the portal of the Apocalypse, and grace is its closing word. I go through that strange and wonderful book, and I think of the saints, waiting, watching, working, amid the terrific and bestial forces of evil in their dire and devilish conflicts. "John, tell me, how can they endure?" "The grace of the Lord Jesus be with the saints." John is perfectly at rest about the saints if that be so.

If these men had personal satisfaction, and abounding confidence in the sufficiency of grace for the people of God, they were all intensely desirous for the people of God, that grace might be with them, and that being therein, they might respond to its influence, and grow in its power.

And so, the historic references of the New Testament end in prevailing clouds and darkness, but all of them are illuminated by the light of grace. Thus it will ever be, until this period, ushered in by the epiphany of grace, shall triumphantly merge into that new period which will be inaugurated by the epiphany of glory. Therefore, we conclude once more with the wonderful words: "The grace of the Lord Jesus Christ and the love of God and the communion of the Spirit, be with us now, and forevermore. Amen."

CHAPTER XXII

THE STRENGTH OF THE NAME

The name of Jehovah is a strong tower: The righteous runneth into it, and is safe.
                                              PROVERBS 18:10.

LIFE IS FULL OF STRAIN AND STRESS. SOONER OR LATER WE ALL come to the consciousness of this fact. The illustrative figures of the inspired Scriptures all remind us of this fact.

Life is described as a race, for the running of which it is necessary that we should lay aside all weights, and forgetting the things we pass, as soon as they are passed, with eyes earnestly fixed upon the goal, so run that we may obtain.

Or life is described as a voyage, and the suggestion is that of the need the mariner has for skill and constant watchfulness, that he may escape the perils of rocks and sand-banks and shoals.

Or life is described as a battle in which the warrior must be fully panoplied and prepared to stand, and to withstand, in order that, having done all, he may stand.

Or life is considered as a great problem, full of perplexity, in which every day brings its new amazement, and all the way is a way in which the pilgrim passes through mystery and into mystery.

All these figures suggest the strain and stress of life.

There come to every one of us, sooner or later, days

when strength is weakened. These are the days of disaster or victory in human life, the days in which we find that of ourselves and in ourselves we are unequal to navigating the vessel, to prosecuting the battle to finality, to discovering the way along which we should walk, and to continuing therein in spite of difficulty. The day when we have to say *we cannot* is a day of disaster or a day of victory, and whether it be disaster or victory depends entirely upon whether or not we believe our text of the morning, and have entered into the full meaning of its profound and comforting suggestiveness. "The name of Jehovah is a strong tower: The righteous runneth into it, and is set on high."

Shall we first remind ourselves of the forces that are against us, in order that we may then consider what this text suggests as to the place of safety, in order that we may finally consider the proofs of safety.

Of the forces that have been and still are against us, the first are mystic and strange, and not perfectly understood; they are spiritual antagonisms. We have been conscious in the midst of life of the sudden assaults of evil. We deny absolutely that they came from within. They were not part of ourselves. We do not believe that they came from God, but we are quite sure of the assaults. Over and over again we are made conscious, whatever our philosophy may be, that there are spiritual forces, insidious and subtle, which suggest evil; and we are appalled by the overwhelming strength of these spiritual antagonisms.

Or, to speak of these things as they are personified according to Scripture, we have to take our way through life perpetually antagonized by one who has been described as "seeking whom he may devour," one who finds his way, if Scripture be true, into the immediate presence of God, there to slander and to ask permission to test us that he may sift us as wheat. The revelation of the antagonism of this evil spirit flames into supreme revelation in the Book of Job, and especially in one very remarkable sentence in that Book, where it is said that God inquires of him, "Hast thou *considered* My servant Job?" "Hast thou *considered?*" The question reveals an enemy who is patiently watching—watching for the weakest place in the chain, that there he may attempt to break it; watching for the least guarded door in the citadel of man-soul, that there he may force an entrance.

But there are other forces against us. The age in which we live is full of things that hinder us in our attempt to live the godly life. Let me name one or two of them. First, there is the fact that men are so eminently successful without God. That may sound a strange thing to say. The preacher is always denying it, and there is a sense in which we shall still continue to deny it. But it is impossible for the man of business, who is attempting to be a godly man, to look out upon his age without seeing how marvelously well men seem to get on without God.

Or, there is the problem of the long continued victory of evil in the world, the fact that time after time, when it seems as though morning were breaking, it suddenly darkens into midnight.

Then there is the problem of universal pain, the problem that floods me with letters, which I am always in amazed difficulty as to how to answer.

These are among the things that make life strenuous, and create the sense of strain, and demand some place of quietness and some place of peace.

Or, again, we have to do with the persistence of the self-life. I often feel that the enemy I dread most is not the devil, not the problems by which I am surrounded, but myself. The reappearance of the self-life is perpetual. Immediately a man thinks he has gained a victory over it, mastered it, it garbs itself in other vestments, and appears anew.

And then, there are the sorrows of life, the bereavements that come to us, the empty places in the home, the hope deferred that makes the heart sick, the disappointments that crush the spirit in personal friendships, the hour in which a man has to say:

> Yea, mine own familiar friend, in whom I trusted, which did eat my bread,
> Hath lifted up his heel against me.

These are some of the forces against us. Individually they defeat us; united they destroy us.

Now what are we to do? It is in the midst of a Book that is full of the revelation of these contrary forces, a Book that recognizes the spiritual antagonisms, that this wonderful verse flames out. It seems to be very much alone in this chapter of Proverbs. Yet, there is a wonderful fitness that this verse is put down into the midst of words that seem to have no connection with it. Into the chaos it comes with its suggestion of cosmos, into the darkness with its flaming light, into a sob and a sigh with its song. "The name of Jehovah is a strong tower: The righteous runneth into it, and is safe."

Let us attempt to interpret the meaning of this text by the Book, because the name of Jehovah is related to the whole of the old economy. I pray you remember the use these Hebrew people made of that name, the fact that they never pronounced it as we pronounce it, the fact that they never wrote it in fulness, so that they have created for us unto this hour a difficulty as to what the full name really was. On all the pages of their ancient Scriptures this particular name, to which the preacher now refers, stands revealed by four consonants, with no vowels, indicating a reverent reticence

THE STRENGTH OF THE NAME

in the pronunciation of a name so full of rich suggestiveness. And remember, moreover, that as you study these Old Testament Scriptures, you never find this name linked with any qualifying or distinguishing adjective. You never read, *the* Jehovah, or *my* Jehovah, or *the living* Jehovah. The Adonahy, the Lord; my Elohim, my God; the living Elohim, the living God; but never the, my, or the living Jehovah. It always stands alone as the tetragrammaton, four consonants from which the light seems to break. There was a singular reverence and reticence in the use of the name, and yet, it was the very center of the Hebrew religion, and the measure in which these people rose to any height of religious life was the measure in which they saw the light of that name, and took their refuge in its signification, and were made strong by all it said to them.

I know the difficulty of interpretation, but I do not hesitate to adopt the interpretation that it means the Becoming One—that is, the One Who becomes to His people all they need. It suggests the adaptation of Infinite Being to finite being, in order to bring about the strengthening of finite being with all the strength of Infinite Being. If it is difficult to follow that line, and to discover the mystery of the tetragrammaton, then let us turn to the name as it is illustrated for us in the Old Testament, in five pictures.

The first is that of Abraham on a mountain with Isaac. The second is of Moses on a mountain. In the valley are the hosts that he has led from Egypt's slavery engaged in deadly conflict with Amalek. Moses' hands are lifted in prayer, and while they are so lifted Israel prevails, and when they faint and droop Amalek prevails. The third is the picture of Gideon, the peaceful farmer, suddenly called to national service, commanded to gather an army and to strike a blow that shall break the power of Midian. The fourth is a picture of a prophet in prison—Jeremiah, exercising a ministry in which there is no gleam of hope as to immediate result; knowing this from the commencement, and becoming more profoundly conscious of it as he continues, until at last he is in prison, and in the prison house he is singing a song of hope. And the last is the picture of yet another prophet, an exile from his own land, by the River Chebar—Ezekiel, looking through all the clouds and the darkness by which he is surrounded, ever through and through until there breaks upon his astonished vision the ultimate realization of all for which he has long hoped.

We know the pictures: Abraham on Moriah; Moses on the mountain, with hands uplifted while Amalek fights Israel; Gideon acting to set his people free from Midianitish oppression; Jeremiah in the midst of utter failure, the prophet of failure; and Ezekiel in exile by the river banks.

Now all these men knew the meaning of my text, and knew it in one particular way in each case. In connection with these five pictures I find the name illustrated. Abraham on Moriah said, "Jehovah-Jireh." Moses on the mountain said, "Jehovah-Nissi." Gideon facing the conflict said, "Jehovah-Shalom." Jeremiah in the dungeon heard the word, "Jehovah-Tsidkenu." And Ezekiel by the river said as the last thing in his prophecy, "Jehovah-Shammah."

Jehovah-Jireh, the Lord will see and provide. Jehovah-Nissi, the Lord our banner. Jehovah-Shalom, the Lord our peace. Jehovah-Tsidkenu, the Lord our righteousness. Jehovah-Shammah, the Lord is there.

In these pictures, I find an interpretation of the meaning of my text which is full of value. "The name of the Lord is a strong tower: the righteous runneth into it, and is safe."

In the case of Abraham, we have an illustration of the obedience of faith in extremity. And by extremity I mean that he had come to the last test of his faith. Faith had been tried and tested and proved through all the years, but this was the final test. "Take now thy son, thine only son, whom thou lovest, even Isaac." All the promises of God were to be fulfilled in and through Isaac, and there was no other way in sight. Nevertheless, this man, in the hour of faith's stern and awful and overwhelming extremity, found the tower of refuge a place of strength, a high rock pinnacle where he was set above the stress and strain. "Jehovah-Jireh" means, quite literally, the Lord will see; but inferentially, and by intention, the Lord will provide. There is not a great distance between seeing and providing, vision and provision. Provision is the outcome of vision; and this man, when the command was given, and the altar was prepared, and he was at the end of everything upon which he had been learning, did not say, "I cannot see"; but he said, "God can see"; and thus he ran into the tower of refuge. The Divine vision and provision was the place of strength to a man when his faith was obedient to the very last extremity of its testing.

Again, the picture of Moses upon the mountain is that of the conflict of faith. The hour had come when the men of faith, who had been redeemed because of their belief in him who had endured having seen Him Who is invisible, were gathered in conflict; and in the conflict Moses knew that everything depended not upon the strength of their fighting, but upon the presence and the power of God. In that hour he uttered these great words, "Jehovah-Nissi," the Lord our banner. I like to imagine the picture from Moses' standpoint. There in the valley are the hosts of Amalek—cruel, overwhelming hosts. And there also is this little company of fighting Israelites. But what did Moses say that day when, conscious of the stress of the conflict, he ran into the name of the Lord? Like a banner floating and fluttering in the breeze he saw that name, and knew that victory depended upon God's presence with them. The name of the Lord to him was a strong tower, to which he ran and was set on high.

Or Gideon yonder is seen shrinking from service; and I have no criticism for him. I have already said that he was a farmer, a man of simple tastes, unused to the things of war. This man was apprehended, and appointed in the midst of his toil to be the deliverer of the people from long and brutal and cruel oppression. Oh, how he shrank, afraid even of the vision of the angel that had come to him for his commissioning. He said, I have seen the angel of the Lord, and I shall die. It was then that the great word came, "Jehovah-Shalom," the Lord send peace. And he went into the name of God, and was set on high above his own fears, above his own anxieties; and in that moment he became the intrepid leader who presently was content to fight with three hundred rather than thirty-two thousand, because such was the revealed will and method and purpose of God.

Or, I go once more to that dungeon, and see Jeremiah therein—a man who is the witness of faith in the midst of the most hopeless circumstances, and what is his hope? He says, "Jehovah-Tsidkenu," the Lord our righteousness. He knows perfectly well that there can be no civic strength that is not based on righteousness, no national restoration and uplifting that is not founded upon righteousness. And where is righteousness? Absent from the counsels of kings, absent from the policies of the men who were ruling, absent from the national leaders at that moment. Then he entered into the name of the Lord, "Jehovah-Tsidkenu," and was certain that because He was righteous the victory must be won; and he sang the song of the certainty thereof.

And, finally, Ezekiel by the Chebar, seeing his visions of

God, was a man of faith in the hour of exile, when all upon which human hope had been set was broken to a thousand pieces; and he saw through the mists and through the clouds, and as he looked to the ultimate, that on which he finally dwelt was not the glory of a temple or the prosperity of a people, but the presence of God. Ezekiel saw Jehovah present in the process, and consequently, present finally in the fulfilment of purpose. "The name of Jehovah is a strong tower."

I leave those illustrations, and I ask you for a moment to think with me of the proofs of safety. My brethren, all these I have referred to are in themselves proofs of how safe men are when they enter into this name. Abraham, Moses, Gideon, Jeremiah and Ezekiel; you notice that the illustrations coincide with the history of the nation. The whole history of Israel is in these illustrations. Abraham, the father and founder; Moses, the law-giver and leader; Gideon, the leader at a particular time of peril; Jeremiah, the prophet of failure; Ezekiel amid the failure. All these men were able to sing the song of victory, and to achieve a present victory, and pass its power on to coming days because they knew the strength of this great name. In every case these men were set on high above the tumult and the stress, entering into the place of peace even in the midst of conflict.

The Bible abounds with illustrations. Daniel knew conflict; he was persecuted, and they took him and put him in the den of lions. But if you tell me that Daniel was in the den of lions you have discovered only the most superficial truth. Where then was Daniel? In the name of Jehovah, in the den of lions; and when the king in the morning said, "O, Daniel, servant of the living God, is thy God, Whom thou servest continually, able to deliver thee from the lions?" Daniel answered, "O, king, live forever. My God hath sent His angel, and hath shut the lions' mouths." He went into the tower, and was set on high.

Or Job, who came to the fulfilment of his own life when he found his way through the flaming glory of the Theophany into the secret place of the name, and rested therein.

Or David, if indeed the psalm we read this morning was David's psalm. Did you notice the growth of experience and the growth of the sense of safety? At the beginning of the psalm he said, "I shall not be greatly moved," but before the song was done he said, "I shall not be moved." And how did he climb from trembling confidence to matchless assurance? Read the psalm again, and it will be seen that it is the psalm of God and the song of the name of the Lord—the song of a soul gathering courage and heroism in the secret place.

We need not confine ourselves to Biblical illustration. "Saints, apostles, prophets, martyrs," who passed through conflicts as severe, if not severer, than we can ever know, put their trust in this name, and found it safe. Or may I not appeal to some of you who are in the midst of conflict to prove the assertion of the text by the memory of things you have known in the lives of your loved ones? Will you let me help you by an illustration? I remember, seven and thirty years ago, when God took from my side—the side of an only boy—his one playmate, his sister. Do not ever indulge in the heresy that a child is incapable of sorrow. I remember coming back one morning—only a lad as I then was—from the grave where I had sat in loneliness, and I found in the house my father and mother. And, boy as I was, I crept up to where they were sitting together, and, if you like the heathenism of the word, it happened—there is a better word than that—my father's hand was resting on his Bible, and I looked at where his finger rested, and I saw these words: "The Lord gave, and the Lord hath taken away: blessed be the name of the Lord." And, boy as I was, I knew there was a connection between that verse and the light I saw on the faces of father and mother; and I never lost the impression of it. And, twenty-four years after, when my own first girlie was taken out of my own home, I got the Bible and turned up the same verse, and laid my hand where my father had laid his hand. "The name of the Lord is a strong tower: The righteous runneth into it, and is set on high."

The proof is scattered through the experience of the saints in all the ages, and is as near to you as father and mother's trust in God. Nay, verily, brethren, have you not yourselves proved it?

Of the supreme onslaught and victory, we have the story in the New Testament. Jesus knew the conflict of life as none other has ever known it. He knew the forces of spiritual antagonism. He lived in the midst of the problems that vex us. And the subtle forms of temptation with which we are familiar, He knew them and entered deeply and profoundly into them. He knew the sorrows of bereavement and difficulty; He was a man of sorrows and acquainted with grief. And how did He overcome them? To Him the name of the Lord was a strong tower into which He passed and was set on high. The supreme secret of all His victory over sin and sorrow is contained in His own confession, "I and My Father are one." In fellowship with Him He overcame. But there is a deeper signification in that story of Jesus. The name Jesus in itself is composed of the ancient name Jehovah, and yet another word that speaks of salvation. The name Jesus essentially means Jehovah is salvation. The name Jesus is Joshua. Now let my young friends take their Bibles and find out when the name was made. The Son of Nun did not bear it first. It was given to him. The significance is that of Jehovah and salvation interwoven, making the name Joshua, which is our name Jesus; and into that name finally we may run and be set on high.

> Jesus, name of sweetness,
> Jesus, sound of love,
> Cheering exiles onward
> To their rest above.

My brethren, what is the conflict to you this morning? Are you at the extremity of faith? Are you asked to walk a pathway that seems as though it must end in disaster? Are you sure it is God's will? Then, in comradeship with this Christ, Who walked the *via dolorosa*, and walked the way to victory, take your way along that pathway. Are you in conflict with foes in the valley that are against faith and against God? Let your hands be uplifted, and in that name Jesus there is a banner of Jehovah, and victory must come as you follow Him. Are you commissioned to some work from which you shrink, as did Gideon of old? In Jesus is the fulfilment of the great word "Jehovah-Shalom," for He is our peace; and we may enter into all service in perfect peace in Him. Are you feeling, rightly or wrongly, that you are strangely in company with Jeremiah, that all the foundations are breaking down around you, and that the national outlook is of the darkest? I pray you, in your dungeon, look higher and see "Jehovah-Tsidkenu." Or, if you would translate it into modern language, sing this: "Jesus shall reign where'er the sun doth his successive journeys run." And if today the thickening battle and the darkening gloom overwhelm you, stay a little by the river, and look far enough and earnestly enough, and beyond all the mystery of the hour you will see the glory of God's victory; and its chief word is this, "Jehovah-Shammah," the Lord is there. The crowned Christ, having won the kingdoms of the world, will make them His own to the glory of God.

CHAPTER XXIII

THE OPTIMISM OF FAITH

Faith is the assurance of things hoped for, the proving of things not seen.

HEBREWS 11:1.

THE HISTORY OF THE WORLD'S PROGRESS IS THE HISTORY OF the triumphs of faith. Faith, to all human seeming, does the most unwarranted things. It sings in prison. It fights while still in chains. It works without tools. You may put the men of faith into prison, but at midnight you will hear Paul and Silas singing. Sight sings in the morning when it has escaped from prison. Faith sings at night while it is in prison. You may put the man of faith into the dungeon and bind him with chains; but there, without a sword, with no carnal weapon, he will still fight a fight, and win a victory the issue of which will be seen in the days to come. Put the man of faith into circumstances devoid of all the forces upon which the man of sight depends, and he will begin to work, and in the long issues you will discover that his work is that which lasts, that which abides.

The literature of the prison is a wonderful literature. We confine ourselves to Biblical illustrations, and to one that is almost Biblical, Biblical in spirit. The great prophecy of failure and tears breaks out into its sweetest music when Jeremiah sings in prison. Find the central messages of hope, and they are messages which were written while he was in the dungeon. The clearest and most startling visions of God ever granted to the ancient people came to Ezekiel when he was an exile by the banks of the river Chebar. The great epistles of the New Testament were written in prison. Though you take the fisher of the Galilean Sea and banish him to the Isle of Patmos, there he sees through the mists and mysteries to the light and glory of the infinite consummation, and the Apocalypse is part of the literature of the prison. If you take the Bedford Tinker and shut him away in the prison house, there Bunyan dreams his celestial dreams and lays the world under a perpetual debt of gratitude to him. Why? Because these men were men of faith. If the test of a word is a work, if the test of a creed is a creation, if the test of a root dry and withered, is fruit luscious and beautiful, then faith is vindicated in the passing of the centuries. The men of faith have found:

> Glory begun below
> Celestial fruit on earthly ground
> From faith and love will grow.
>
> Lo to faith's enlightened sight,
>   All the mountain flames with light,
> Hell is nigh, but God is nigher,
>   Circling us with hosts of fire.

We may not be able to account for it, but I think no one here will be prepared to contradict the statement, that it is the men of faith who have made the great contributions to the world's progress; always the men of faith. I am not proposing to argue that tonight. My business is of a profounder nature.

I want to ask this simple question. Why is it that faith always triumphs? Why is it that the word of faith materializes into the work that lasts? Why is it that the creed of the man of faith vindicates itself in a creation? Why is it that this root—may I very reverently borrow a word that does not belong here—this "root out of a dry ground," this root which at the present moment is considered by the philosophies of men to be so entirely out of date, why is it that this russet, drab bulb, that seems to have no color and no glory and no light, why is it that it is forevermore breaking through and blossoming into beauty and triumph? Why is faith victorious? The answer is in my text. "Faith is the assurance of things hoped for, the proving of things not seen."

Let us first take two phrases from the text in order that in the briefest way possible we may remind ourselves of what they mean; "things hoped for"; "things not seen."

These are the unreal things, the intangible things, the imponderable and unlikely matters; the uncertain things of the future "things hoped for"; the uncertain things of the present, "things not seen." Mark, I pray you, that difference in suggestion. "Things hoped for" are always future. "Things not seen" according to the interpretation of this writer and this letter, are not future but present.

The "things not seen" are in existence now. How are you going to demonstrate them, be sure of them? By faith. The "things hoped for" are future. How are we to be sure of them? By faith. This is the statement not only of the two sides of the great fact, but of a sequence. "Faith is the assurance of things hoped for." Why? Because it is the "proving of things not seen." "Assurance of things hoped for" grows out of faith, because faith demonstrates, proves to certainty the "things not seen." "Faith is the assurance of things hoped for," therefore it sings in the midst of the process and in the prison house. Why does it sing? Why is it sure? Because it demonstrates, it proves the unseen things.

"Things hoped for"; these are things that lie ahead of us, things that we have not yet come into possession of, things that according to the philosophy of men and the appearances of the hour, it is improbable we ever shall come into possession of. "Things hoped for," the realization of our own ideals; the ultimate victory of good in the world; compensation for all the travail, the sorrow, and the loss of today; the striking of an even balance in the affairs of men, when justice shall reign supreme. We all sigh for these things; they pass, ever and anon, like a vision before our eyes, and we speak of it as a mirage, a disappointment, and ask, "Can our ideal ever be realized? Will there ever be the ultimate victory of good? Is there to be compensation for the stress and strain and sighing and sorrow of humanity? Will there be a victory of justice?" "Things hoped for" are the things we fain would see if we could.

"Things not seen." Is there anything unseen? Have we not done with reality when we have looked the last upon the things material? We are gathered together in this building; there are real, seen things in this building, light and life; men and women. Is that all? The man of the world says, "That is all you can prove." Faith, according to this writer, proves the unseen thing, not the unseen things that are distant, but that are near. What are the things that faith claims to prove? For the moment, I will not say faith has proved them. What are the things faith claims to prove? God, the spirit world, the hidden forces; angels sweeping up the mountain side that the prophet saw and his servant did not see, the angel ministers watching in Gethsemane, which Jesus saw and the disciples did not see. You say these are the uncertain things which the present age doubts, the unseen things. So much for our phrases. "Things hoped for"; the realization of ideals, the ultimate victory of good, compensation, the even balance and justice; the building of the city of God and the triumph of righteousness. "Things not seen." Oh, if there only were a

God, if only there were spiritual forces as well as material forces, if only the dreams of these men of old were true and the mountain flamed with light and angelic hosts; if only these things were real, then we should be quite sure that our dreams would be realized. Fail to believe in things unseen and hope dies, the song is silent, the fight ends, and the work is abandoned. Let the dust of the highway be everything, and the troops will weary upon the march and the territory will never be possessed. Let humanity come to the conclusion that the life of bread and raiment and dust is everything, and thereby is signed the death warrant of all high ideals and aspirations, and of everything noble. There is no assurance of things hoped for unless there be the proving of things unseen.

The writer of this letter declares that "*Faith* is the assurance of things hoped for, the proving of things not seen."

It is necessary that we take time to understand what this man meant when he wrote that word "faith." This letter to the Hebrews is peculiarly the letter of faith. It is a letter which supremely warns men lest they apostasize from faith in the unseen. From beginning to end, without waiting to turn to actual passages, sin is synonymous with unbelief; the sin that is in good standing around, that is, the sin that is popular, the sin that men never count vulgar, but which is so insidious that it weakens the nerve and dims the vision, and ends the possibility of strife, is unbelief. The master principle of victory is that of faith, the opposite of unbelief. This eleventh chapter, of which my text is but an introductory, explanatory word, deals with that whole subject. In this chapter, the writer makes pass before us the men of the ancient economy who wrought wonders, won victories, and made contributions toward the final consummation, and it was always by faith that they did these things. It is the story of faith.

What is faith? Faith is not merely intellectual conviction of a truth. Faith is more than intellectual conviction of a truth. Let me turn to one or two words here. In the third chapter of this letter, verses twelve to fourteen—

> Take heed, brethren, lest haply there shall be in any one of you an evil heart of unbelief, in falling away from the living God; but exhort one another day by day, so long as it is called Today; lest any one of you be hardened by the deceitfulness of sin; for we are become partakers of Christ, if we hold fast the beginning of our confidence firm unto the end.

Confidence is the word that I want you to remember there. Store that word in your mind.

Pass on to the nineteenth verse, and in close association with it read the eleventh verse of chapter four. "We see that they were not able to enter in because of unbelief." "Let us therefore give diligence to enter into that rest, that no man fall after the same example of disobedience."

Store in your mind the word *disobedience.* Turn on to chapter six and the twelfth verse—"Be not sluggish, but imitators of them who through faith and patience inherit the promises."

From this passage we will store in our memory the thought, *not sluggish but patient.*

In chapter ten, verse twenty-two—"Let us draw near with a true heart in fulness of faith, having our hearts sprinkled from an evil conscience, and our body washed with pure water."

The phrase I ask you to store in your memory hence is, "*with a true heart.*"

That is a somewhat wearisome business; but very important, for I hold that it is far more important for us to catch the real significance of the word, according to the mind of the man who wrote it, than that we should speculate about it.

In the reading of those verses, my hope is that some of you, my young friends particularly, will go back to read this letter through again and find what faith is. For the purpose of our present study let us observe that faith is not only intellectual conviction; it is that confidence reposed in a statement which produces obedience. I am not sure that faith is always perfect certainty. I am not sure that there may not be living faith which is not intellectual certainty. Faith is that which in the presence of a great statement, puts confidence in it, obeys its suggestiveness, risks something, ventures something upon the declaration in order to discover whether the declaration be true or not. I am growingly convinced that there may be living faith which is not based upon absolute intellectual certainty. I am inclined increasingly to say to men, "You will come to intellectual certainty by the exercise of faith." That is one of the values of my text. Faith is the proving of unseen things. That is the way whereby men find out whether there be a God, whether there be a spiritual world, whether there are forces other than the material. The declaration is made of the existence of God. The declaration is made as to the reality of the spiritual. The declaration is made that there are forces other than those of dust. You say, "I am not sure, my intellect is not entirely convinced; yet I will exercise faith, I will put confidence in the declaration, obey its suggestion; and I will do it with patience and diligence and a true heart. If I do that, and there is no answer, I shall have the right to deny the existence of the unseen and banish the hope of ultimate realization." I have no right to begin by denying the existence of the unseen and turning from the hope of the future, on the supposition that they are not. Faith is a risk, a venture, an adventure. That is the word, adventure. Abraham left Ur of the Chaldees. What was he doing? Making the great adventure. If there had been newspapers in Ur of the Chaldees, I can imagine the leading article on the morning after he had left—"We regret that our respected fellow-citizen has imagined!" It was a great adventure of faith, and faith was vindicated. What this letter calls men to is the proving of the great declarations of the unseen by stepping out in obedience to what these declarations demand, in order to discover. "If any man willeth to do His will, he shall know of the teaching, whether it be of God." Whereas that great word may have many applications—and I have heard many applications made of it, more or less correct—take its first significance. Christ was being criticized, men were denying the authority of His teaching and asking Him whence came His authority and His learning. Did He tell these men, "You must be intellectually convinced before you can be My disciple?" By no means. He said, "Do the thing I tell you, and in the doing of it find out whether it is true or not." This is the perpetual challenge that faces man, and faith is the great adventure. Might I not illustrate it on lower levels? Has anything ever been done in this world save upon the principle of adventure? Would the New World ever have been discovered if there had not been one man fanatical enough to sail and sail until he found it? "Oh," but you say, "it was there." If it had not been there, he could only prove it was not there by the same action. "Unseen things? Oh, they are not there." How do you know? You cannot deny until you have made the great adventure to discover. The testimony of the centuries is that the man who does make the adventure always discovers the unseen things.

When the writer of this letter here says that faith is the proving of things not seen, I want you to notice that he is not saying what I have been saying. He does not say that faith is the adventure. He says that faith is the victorious adventure. He declares that the man of faith demonstrates, proves the things that otherwise are absolutely uncertain. When a man will hear the declaration of the unseen and will square his life to the doctrine of the unseen, refusing to put upon his own personality the measurement of dust; when he will behave as though there were a God and eternity, and a spiritual world; that man shall come at last to certainty of God and certainty of the spiritual world. Faith is the proving of unseen things. One would like to go through this eleventh chapter not so much to tell again the ancient story, as to mark the working of the principle in the case of individual men.

"Faith is the assurance of things hoped for"—the realiztion of ideals. Faith is perfectly certain they will be realized. Faith says, "He will perfect that which concerneth me." Faith says, He shall present us faultless before the throne of God. Faith says these things. That is assurance, that is certainty. What is it based upon? He will "perfect that which concerneth me." That is an uncertain quantity. That is taking God for granted. That is the venture of faith. Faith is sure. Why? Because faith has proven the unseen. Faith has discovered God, is sure of God, and when faith is sure of God, faith is sure of the throne, and sure of the spiritual world, and sure of the reality of the things that lie beyond the material.

How am I to prove this to you? I cannot prove it to you. You must prove it for yourselves. While you challenge me to prove to you the reality of the unseen, let me give you a challenge in all earnestness and sincerity. You try to prove to that old woman that there is no God and see how you get on! She has never had more than the bread necessary for the day; her heart has been crushed with bereavement after bereavement; she has laid the sacred dust of loved ones in the grave until she is quite alone. Go to see her one day. Do you not know her? I will introduce you. She is in London. You will find her in every village. Go into her cottage. She will soon talk to you about the loved ones gone, and then suddenly with a light in her eyes that never was on land or sea, she will say, "I shall soon be with them. They will not return to me, but I shall go to them." "The Lord gave, the Lord hath taken away; blessed be the name of the Lord." Prove to her that she is wrong! You will not attempt it. You think she is wrong. You have no right to think so, until you have made her adventure, until you also have acted along the same line and have found out by that action of faith whether these things are so or not.

Mark the inter-action between these two statements. The proving of things not seen "is the assurance of things hoped for." Look at verse ten, "He looked for the city which hath the foundations, whose Builder and Maker is God." The assurance of the city resulted from the proving of things not seen. You say, This man was very foolish to leave a certain city for an uncertain city, to leave Ur of the Chaldees for some city never seen. Oh, but he was sure of the city. What made him sure? God. Let faith find God and faith sings the song of the city, and comes into fellowship with the future. That figure of the city runs all through the Bible until you get the figure of John in Patmos. He saw a city. Why was he sure of the city? Because he knew God. Why was his vision more detailed and more beautiful and wonderful than that of any other man? Because he had leaned his head upon the bosom of the Son of God incarnate, and had had fellowship with the Father through the Son. His song of the city was a song of the assurance of faith resulting from the proving of the things unseen. The proving of the unseen realities is the assurance of realized ideals. The proving of the unseen God is the assurance of the triumphing God. The proving of the unseen order is the assurance of ultimate compensation for all the strain and stress and sorrow. The proving of the unseen measures and weights is the assurance of the final victory of justice. Take away from me my certainty of God and of the unseen order and of the underlying justice, then I have no hope for the world. My hopes are not in parliaments, or in policies—and how much there is to shake a man if he put his hope there! London, Babylon, center of the world, celebrates the induction of its chief officer with military display and an animal feast that ought to shock civilization. When in the midst of London's poor, we can spend thousands of pounds on a feast such as that, I have no hope when I look at man. Underneath are the forces of eternity. The atmosphere of London is the fire of the ever-present God. The unseen things, men blunder through and never know them. God is not dethroned. He will build His city and bring in His triumph. Faith adventuring in obedience to the conception of the spiritual becomes certain of the spiritual and sings a song of hope on the darkest day that ever dawns.

Mark briefly in a closing word the effects of faith. Here again the chapter is better than anything I can imagine. The effect of faith is obedience. "By faith Noah, being warned of God concerning things not seen as yet, moved with godly fear, prepared an ark to the saving of his house; through which he became heir of the righteousness which is according to faith. By faith Abraham, when he was called, obeyed to go out unto a place which he was to receive for an inheritance; and he went out, not knowing whither he went."

Let there be in the soul certainty of God, and faith will be obedient in circumstances of contradiction and difficulty.

Not only obedience, but endurance; "By faith he," Moses, "forsook Egypt, not fearing the wrath of the king: for he endured, as seeing Him Who is invisible."

Endured, is the word. You say, That is an ancient story and perhaps it is not true. It is true in this house. There are men and women in this house who have done the same thing;

they have forsaken Egypt, they are enduring misunderstanding, persecution. How are they doing it? "As seeing Him Who is invisible." Beyond that, the writer goes on with illustrations every one of which one would like to dwell upon. From verse thirty on, he mentions names and then deeds. We will not stay with the names, but listen to the deeds, "Subdued kingdoms, wrought righteousness, obtained promises, stopped the mouths of lions, quenched the power of fire, escaped the edge of the sword, from weakness were made strong, waxed mighty in war, turned to flight armies of aliens."

Then from the major music of that melody, the writer drops suddenly to the minor melody which has in it more of victory than all the rest.

"By faith . . . women received their dead by a resurrection." You say, That is not so now. I know it is so now. By faith women, the most seriously smitten in the hour of bereavement, wrap their loved ones to their hearts and sing in triumph o'er the tomb. Faith is the victory. It is the inspiration of obedience and strength and might and endurance.

It is the spring of perpetual hope. Through rivers and seas of blood, men make their way onward toward the goal, lay down their life for lives in perpetual darkness of sin, lift their eyes ever toward the eastern sky though no streak of dawn be visible, and are full of exultation and expectation on the darkest day.

There is one other thing to say. Faith proves the unseen things not for itself only but for other men. By your faith you demonstrate the reality of the unseen to the world at large. You bring the unseen things into sight by your faith. By the victory your faith wins, you prove faith and prove the unseen things to the man of the world. By your strength in the hour of your agony, I come to believe in God more perfectly. By the magnificence of your overcoming, by the result of your faith, you demonstrate to me the reality of the things which you profess to believe. You say, God. I am not sure. But when you have ended your saying, I watch your doing; and I see that on the dark day there is light in your eye and a song on your lips, and I say, "You must be right; there is no secret for that triumph other than God." You demonstrate the unseen things by your faith. Faith brings out of your word a work, out of your creed a creation, out of your root, fruit full of beauty and sustenance; and men look on the work and believe the word, observe the creation and accept the creed, gather the fruit and are compelled to believe in the root. By your triumphs in the hour of pain and sorrow and agony, by your strength, by the victory with which you overcome in the pressing battle of life, you make men believe in the God you affirm to be the strength and sustenance of your life. By realization in personal life and conduct of victory, you prove to others the unseen things. Can I not put that in the simplest way possible? I put it so because it may help others. No man can ever persuade me not to believe in God, for this among other reasons. Had I no other reason, this for me would be sufficient to the end of my days. My father and my mother believed in God. Not because they said so did I believe in God, but because of what I saw their belief did for them. You cannot persuade me that they were mistaken. Their faith fastened upon facts, unseen, but facts, and I am trying to live as they lived, and I am demonstrating for myself the reality of the unseen.

So whether it be in the individual life, or in the life of the Church of God, or in the life of the world, faith is the victory. I am inclined to end tonight perhaps on your behalf, but certainly on my own, by saying to the Presence, the unseen Presence, in view of all the battle and all the sorrow and all the difficulties, "Lord, I believe, help Thou mine unbelief."

CHAPTER XXIV

THE VERDICT

What then shall I do unto Jesus which is called Christ?
MATTHEW 27:22.

THIS QUESTION OCCURS IN THE STORY OF THE APPEARANCE of Jesus before the Roman Governor Pilate. If we read the story superficially, we shall declare that Jesus was arraigned before Pilate. If we read the story carefully, determining to see its true inwardness, to discover its profoundest meanings, we shall say that Pilate was arraigned before Jesus. In the facts which were merely local and incidental and historical, Jesus was a prisoner at the bar of Pilate, waiting for verdict and sentence. In all the values which were essential and spiritual and age-abiding, Pilate the Roman Governor stood at the bar of Jesus waiting for verdict and sentence.

The Governor asked, "What then shall I do with Jesus which is called Christ?" as though the disposal of Jesus were in his hands. By the answering of that question, Pilate was deciding what it would be necessary, in the fulness of time and in the perfecting of the Divine economy, for Jesus to do with him. I do not mean by that to affirm that Pilate was lost because of his action upon that occasion. It is perfectly certain, that if Pilate never repented of his vacillation, never repented of that moment in which he seared his conscience to save his position, then his destiny was sealed. But who shall dare to affirm that this was so? It may be that in after years, when he had lost the position he had purchased at the price of disloyalty to conscience, the haunting memory of the face and regal mien of the Man Who troubled him that day, may have followed him until in penitence he turned to Him in submission; and if he did, then he found His grace sufficient to meet his need.

From this moment, I have nothing more to do with that old scene or with the local setting of my text, save for purpose of illustration. I am interested in the abiding principles, in the spiritual values, in the immediate and persistent application of this old-time story.

This is the final question of the Gospel according to Matthew, which is the Gospel of Jesus as King. He is presented to us here in the purple robes of His sovereign royalty. He is presented to us in the early chapters, first, in His relation to our own world; while Jesus was of our human nature He did not enter upon our human life by the will or act of humanity, but by the mysterious and direct intervention of God: second, in relation to the world above; after the Kingliness of work well done the wreath of Divine attestation was set upon His brow, "This is My beloved Son in Whom I am well pleased"; and the holy chrism, the anointing of the Spirit fell upon Him, fitting Him for specific Kingly work; finally, in relation to the under-world of evil; passing into the wilderness as King He met the enemy of the race and mastered him at every onslaught.

There follows the story of the Kingly Propaganda. First, the great Manifesto which we speak of as the Sermon on the Mount. Then the toil amid all the limitation of human life; the King is supreme in all spheres; master of material things; victorious in the presence of mental disorder as He flung the devils out and restored men to their right mind; triumphant in the moral realm, as He forgave sins and gave men power to sin no more. The King is next seen in conflict with the false rulers of the people, the shepherds who fed themselves instead of the people, the shepherds who sought their own safety instead of that of the people; defeating them, and rising superior to them on every occasion. At Cæsarea Philippi He challenged His disciples, and Peter made his confession "Thou art the Christ, the Son of the living God." From that moment He began to talk about His cross, and with calm and Kingly dignity He trod the Via Dolorosa that culminated in the tragedy of Calvary. The dead body of the King was laid by tender and loving hands in the grave.

On the first day of a new week the message came, the King is alive, and finally His authoritative voice is heard saying, "All authority hath been given unto Me in heaven and on earth. Go ye therefore, and disciple the nations, baptizing them into the name of the Father and of the Son and of the Holy Ghost; teaching them to observe all things whatsoever I commanded you; and lo, I am with you all the days, even unto the consummation of the age."

In that rapid survey of the gospel, the King is again presented. In the midst of the tragedy at the end, just before the flaming glory of the ultimate victory of resurrection, this question was asked, "What then shall I do with Jesus which is called Christ?" To answer that question I call you in the name of God, in the name of the King, in the name of your humanity. In the presence of the far-flung splendours of the unseen world, and the vast spaciousness of human life in the economy of God, I bring you this question and I ask you to make it your own and to answer it ere the day have passed, "What then shall I do unto Jesus which is called Christ?"

My business at this hour is to appeal for a verdict. I would fain bring you, my comrades in this human life, my fellow travelers to all the mystery and wonder of the life that lies beyond, face to face with the King and I would ask your verdict, "What then shall I do unto Jesus which is called Christ?"

In order that we may be helped, in order that we may be aided in our hour of decision, I propose to ask a series of questions, all of them leading up to, and culminating in the question of Pilate.

The first question I would suggest is this. What can I do with Jesus? I reply to that immediately. I can crown Him or crucify Him, and I can do none other than one of these two. Every one of us must give a vote for His crowning or for His crucifixion. There is no middle course because His claims are supreme, and His claims are superlative. He is either all He claims to be and all His followers have claimed for Him, or He is the most stupendous fraud that has ever been foisted upon human credulity. Have you ever really considered the words Jesus uttered as He stood in the midst of the promiscuous multitudes of men and women of all sorts and conditions; as He stood in the midst of men and women, with hearts wrung with sorrow, with spirits dejected by hope deferred; in the midst of men and women in the grip of sin and vice; in the midst of the physical pain and weariness and the dread tiredness of the multitudes? He said "Come unto Me, all ye that labour and are heavy laden, and I will give you rest." If that were a lie, it were the most cruel of lies. If it were the truth, it is the truth that we ought to live and die for, and proclaim to men, for this is what the world supremely needs. The Man Who can stand in the midst of human pain and agony and turmoil and temptation and say, "If you will come to Me I will give you rest," ought to be crucified if His claim is untrue or He ought to be crowned if it be true! What will you do with Him? What can you do with Him? Do not take the distant look alone, think of the claim He is making in London today. It is that He is able to take hold of the worst man and the worst woman, and so to touch them with forgiveness and with healing and with life that He will give them rest and make them the best man and the best woman. He is claiming today that He can lay His hand upon the flotsam and jetsam of humanity, upon men and women flung out upon the scrap-heap by the cruel grind of human laws, and that He can make of them such men and women that presently He will present them faultless before God, so that God shall not be ashamed of them, so that they shall not fail to command the respect of God. This is a superlative claim, and the Man Who makes a claim like this is a fraud, or so help me God He is my King. I want to be rid of the voice that makes claim like that if it is mockery; or I want that it shall be multiplied until every weary and broken-hearted man and woman has heard it, if it be true. I must crown Him or crucify Him. One of the most consistent and beautiful figures upon the page of the New Testament is that of Paul. Oh yes, he wrote one day that he was the chief of sinners, but he wrote that when he was standing in the presence of Christ. When a man stands in the presence of Christ he always feels he is the greatest sinner in the world. If you will compare Paul with other men you cannot but admire him. Before he knew Jesus, he was splendidly true, magnificently consistent, tremendously earnest. Mark the difference. Before he knew Jesus, he made havoc of the Church of God. Why? Because he believed that Jesus was an impostor, that He never rose from the dead, that all that His disciples were claiming for Him was untrue; and out of the pure honesty of his heart he was determined to stamp out His name. But there came a moment of illumination, a moment when a new light broke upon him, a moment when the conviction came that the Jesus Whom he thought dead was alive. What then? With an honesty that I would God other men shared, with a splendid intensity that was wholly admirable, he began to labour and suffer toward the hour when that Jesus should be the crowned Lord of all. What can I do with Him? I must crown Him or crucify Him.

Let me ask a second question. What does it matter what I do with Him? What difference does it make whether I crown Him or crucify Him? I will answer the question in the sense in which it is asked. There are a great many men; men I know in my business house, men I meet on the market, on the street, who have not crowned Him, but they seem to be doing very well. There are a great many people, thousands of people who are rejecting Him, but they seem to be doing very well. I put it so because that thing is said to me scores of times in one year in dealing with men about spiritual things. So I ask the question, "What does it matter?"

It makes all the difference first of all, to your character. It makes all the difference in the second place, to your influence. It makes all the difference finally, to your destiny. Character, influence, destiny.

These are the things men will not think of, but they are the supreme things. A man will think of his bank book, of his house, of his diet, of his education, of his amusement. None of these things are wrong, but they are secondary, by comparison they are unimportant. They are not the final things. I do not mean to say that Christ is not interested in these things, for I know He is interested in what a man eats, what he wears, where he lives; only His way of dealing with what a man eats, what he wears, and where he lives, is that of dealing with the man himself, and when He begins to deal with a man, He deals first with character.

Understand this, your character will depend, and does depend upon your attitude toward Christ. You cannot reject the Christ of this Gospel of Matthew without suffering deterioration of character. You cannot honestly crown Him without entering upon an ennobled life. Here is a thing I need not labour. There are men and women scattered throughout this house tonight, who if this were the time and place, would rise to testify to the fact that crowning Jesus changed their outlook and conceptions and therefore reacted upon them, so that they are not what they were. Crown Jesus and character becomes characterized by purity and love, and when you have uttered those two words you have said everything. When John looked at Jesus he said he saw Grace and Truth, love and life, compassion and holiness. That is the character that is produced. Not in a moment does it come to fulness of fruitage; oh no, some of us know how long the struggle is, how much He has to bear with, how patiently He has to wait when we turn from the pure to the impure, when we turn from love to the things that contradict it; but that is the pattern of character when Jesus is King, a stern endeavour after rightness and a strong moving toward compassion and tenderness toward other men. Reject this Christ of God, and gradually the standard of your morality is lowered; gradually you depart from the high ideals and accept the lower estimates of things; gradually you descend even from the respectable which you now worship to the vulgarity you now hate. Do you think any man lying drunk in the gutter tonight ever meant to lie there? Of course he did not. He has descended. Do you suppose any man in the grip of some hellish, devilish, dirty habit meant so to be gripped? He at first felt the shame of it, but gradually the shame passed, until today there are men who can sin without a blush. Character deteriorated, ruined, is always the outcome of refusing Christ.

Not character alone, but that which is the outcome of character, influence, is determined by relationship to Christ.

Crown Him, obey Him and—I quote from His Manifesto so that there shall be no speculation on my part—then what? "Ye are the salt of the earth;" the influence you exert is an influence that prevents the spread of corruption, and gives the man struggling in weakness his chance. "Ye are the light of the world," you shall live in the office, in the business house, in professional life, wherever you are, and your life shall be a life that helps men toward God and truth. Refuse to crown Him and your influence is the opposite. Instead of salt which prevents corruption, you will corrupt society. God help me, I am always afraid of generalities when I am after a verdict. Let me take one man, a young man in this house tonight. What will you do with Jesus? Crown Him and your character is ennobled, and I care not where you work or where you live, you will help men to noble things. Refuse to crown Him and your character will degenerate and the very stories you tell will help to damn men. Your influence depends upon what you do with Jesus.

Your destiny depends upon what you do with Jesus, for this life is not all. This life is but the place of probation. Life lies beyond, higher, deeper, profounder; and when presently, I shall cross the border-line, that crossing of the border-line will not change my character, will not change the essential facts of my personality. There is destiny. What lies beyond? Who dare say. Who dare invade the stillness and silence of the secrets of eternity? Not I. But I dare affirm that as a man shall choose in these days of opportunity so shall he abide in the days that lie beyond. I am not preaching to men who have never had an opportunity, or I might have another emphasis upon that message. If I were preaching to people who had never been brought face to face with Jesus Christ, and had never heard this evangel, I might have something else to say. I am preaching to men and women who know the name, and know the story, have seen the uplifted Christ, have witnessed the transformation of other lives. What you do with Christ settles not character and influence only, but destiny. It does matter.

Let us ask another question. Who can decide for me? The answer is swift and immediate. No one can decide for you. You must decide. The friends of Jesus cannot decide that you shall crown Him. Blessed be God, the foes of Jesus cannot compel you to crucify Him. Pilate washed his hands in water, and said, I am innocent. Pilate, it will never do! It is a base and hideous mockery. Listen, Pilate, you cannot wash blood out in water! Pilate, you stand at the bar of your own conscience. You are arguing between expediency and obedience, whether you shall do the straight thing though the heavens fall, or by some trick save your own position as Roman Procurator. You are trying to shift the blame upon those priests. God knows they are to blame, those evil inspirers of an evil deed. You are trying to put the blame upon the mob, crying for His crucifixion. You cannot do it, Pilate! You have asked a question more profound than you know, "What then shall I do?" When presently thou hast handed Him over to His cross, and thou hast written the superscription to mock the priests, and dost say "What I have written I have written," then thou sayest more than thou knowest. Thou hast chosen, thou hast written, and the clamour of His foes will not excuse thine action. The persuasion of His friends cannot finally decide thy choice. So it is in this hour. I have sometimes said, If I could, I would come and compel a man to Christ. Thank God I cannot. Every man stands in the awful awe-inspiring, tremendous dignity of his own power to choose, and no man can invade it. The friends of Christ tonight would fain persuade you, we are prepared to go so far as Paul when he said, "We are ambassadors therefore on behalf of Christ, as though God were intreating by us: we beseech you on behalf of Christ, be ye reconciled to God." But, you must decide. Every man chooses for himself. Do not forget that fact when the foes of Christ are trying to prevent you by their laughter and persecution, by their suggestion that you take the glamour and glitter of the things that perish. You must decide. This is a great congregation, but it is composed of lonely men and lonely women who within the next fifteen minutes will have decided each for himself, for herself, to crucify or crown Christ.

There is another question. When must I answer this? The answer to this is as quick and immediate as to the last. Now. Yesterday, I need not argue. Yesterday does not matter. Yesterday by your life, by your thinking, by your speaking, by your doing, you drove the nails and crucified Christ —for oh, men and women, remember that not the Jewish priests and Roman soldiers crucified Christ, but my sin and your sin. That is the deep mystery of the cross. By the sin of yesterday you crucified Him, so that there can be no further decision about yesterday. Tomorrow—you remember the saying of your childhood, more philosophic than you have thought recently—tomorrow never comes. There is no tomorrow for the activity of the soul. No man decides tomorrow. The soul is so close to God that its one hour of the clock is His now. You decide now and cannot escape it. When presently, the service over, you leave this building and walk through the streets amid the city's babel and noise, you go having given your vote for the crucifixion or the crowning of Christ. It is an immediate transaction.

One other question. What will be the result in the long issues? I have spoken of the near things of character and influence, and of destiny which may be a far thing but which begins here and now. In the long issues, what will be the result? Let me try to answer that question. There is a day coming when this same King shall appear again. He is coming into His Kingdom, blessed be God. That is the comfort of all such as work. That is the battle song that nerves us in the hour of turmoil and strife. He is coming into His Kingdom. It is not an idle song we sing, it is the profoundest thing in our souls: "Jesus shall reign where'er the sun doth his successive journeys run."

If the New Testament be true, He is to appear again. He has appeared, He has had His first advent, epiphany, appearing, which was an Advent of infinite grace. It was an Advent of awful loneliness, and pain and buffering, of prison and death; but He is coming again. There will be a second Advent as surely as there was the first Advent. There will be another epiphany, another manifestation, but how changed. The Son of man shall come in His own glory and the glory of His Father, and all the holy angels with Him. There is an hour coming when the world shall see again the King. Then this question will be reversed. The question is that awful, yet glad hour—and whether awful or glad depends entirely upon our present relationship to Him—will not be What shall I do with Jesus? but What will Jesus do with me?

He came, and they crowned Him with thorns; but He is coming with the diadems of the universe upon His brow. He came, and they put in His hand a reed, in mockery; but He is coming with the sceptre of the universe in His strong right hand; He came, and they lifted Him to die on the cross; but He is coming seated upon the throne of empire and dominion. When He comes again, He will do with men what men have done with Him when they had their opportunity to choose. If I have rejected Him, He will reject me, and that not capriciously, but by reason of the very necessity of the case. He will be compelled, in the day of the final establishment of

His government in the world and through the universe, to reject those who have rejected Him, for to retain them would be to ruin the new creation and blight and blast the established Kingdom.

Now finally, back again to Pilate's question. We have only attempted to emphasize it and insist upon its importance, and persuade you to personal decision by all the questions we have suggested. This is the last. What shall I do?

Would to God that the preacher could be entirely silent, or would to God that his voice might be heard simply as the voice of heaven. Each one is quite alone with God. I cannot see, neither can I know what takes place at this moment between your soul and God, and your neighbour cannot see or know. Thank God for the sacredness of our loneliness with God. I pray you be conscious of that. In that place of loneliness with God, ask Pilate's question, and answer it. "What then shall I do unto Jesus which is called Christ?"

What shall I do? Oh soul of mine, as though thou hadst never faced Christ before, as though thou hadst never come to this bar of judgment, now soul of mine, What wilt thou do with Christ? Everything depends upon the will. There is intellectual persuasion toward His crowning. He has made the emotional appeal to my heart. The call of my conscience bids me crown Him at all costs. Shall I do it? That is the question.

Courage my soul, dare to do it. And as though never before, in the presence of heaven and eternity, I lay down all the arms of my rebellion and crown Him Lord; He shall be King of my life.

It is hardly worth Thy taking oh King! It is bruised, battered; but oh, take it, and if Thou canst make a garden out of this desert, then do so; if Thou canst make any use of what there is of me, take me oh Christ, and make me in order to use me.

Is that what you say? God help you to make this real. Do not be deceived. In two or three minutes the service will be over, and going out of the building and along the streets you will go having voted for His death and crucifixion, or will have found the verdict that compels you to crown Him. Which?

God grant there may be hundreds of us who tonight shall crown Him to the glory of His name, for the saving of our own lives, in order that we may be soldiers of the King, servants of the King, workers together with God, for His name's sake.

CHAPTER XXV

SALVATION IN ZION

I will place salvation in Zion.
ISAIAH 46:13.

The forty-sixth and forty-seventh chapters of the prophecy of Isaiah constitute a complete message in themselves. The forty-sixth has to do with God's determination to destroy Babylon; the forty-seventh describes that destruction.

The reading of the forty-sixth chapter brings before the mind a condition of affairs that might almost be described as chaotic.

The city of God was in ruins; the people of God were scattered; the nation, peculiar to God for the fulfilment of His purpose in the world, was represented by the feeblest remnant. The chosen people of God are seen by the prophet, under the dominion of Babylon. Then the mind of Isaiah, illumined by the Spirit, sees a Deliverer—how far or how near perhaps he himself could not have told—and in the wake of that Deliverer Babylon destroyed, and the people of God restored to the fulfilment of the Divine purpose. In delivering this message, the prophet instituted a contrast between Babylon and Zion; between the city of God and the city of men; between all that man is able to do without God, and all that God is able to do in spite of man. It is a contrast between idols and God; a contrast between the gods of Babylon, "Bel boweth down, Nebo stoopeth," and the God of the chosen people, Jehovah. The contrast may be crystallized in two very brief declarations; idols are created and carried; Jehovah creates and carries. That is forevermore the difference between false and true religion, the difference between all idolatry and the worship of God, the difference between Babylon and Zion, between good and evil, between right and wrong. So that the contrast in this chapter, being peculiarly a contrast between religions, the conception of the prophet most evidently is, that what a nation is, depends upon the religion of the nation. Babylon has worshipped idols. Zion is the center of the worship of Jehovah. Idol worship means that men make idols and then have to carry them. They make them, carry them, and put them down; and they stay where they are placed, they cannot move. Their makers cry to them, but they cannot answer. When they move, it is because they are carried. In contrast, God creates, and whatever He creates He carries. Babylon makes an idol, and puts it down. It never moves. Jehovah makes a man, and carries the man; and if the man have vision and wisdom he worships Jehovah.

Of idolatrous Babylon, Isaiah saw the destruction. It was the vision of faith. Had we been there, with any other than the prophetic outlook, listening to any other voice than the voice of faith perpetually singing its song in the heart, we should have said that idolatry was strong and true religion weak. Behold Babylon, mighty Babylon; wealthy, equal to the conquest of the world; Babylon with its splendour and its pride! Behold Zion in ruins; her sons languishing, all her wealth gone, her power departed! But faith sees neither Babylon nor Zion pre-eminently; but the idols and Jehovah. Faith knows that the conflict is not between Babylon and Zion, but between idols and Jehovah. Faith foretells the downfall of

Babylon, and does so in an age when no one will believe the message save those who live by faith, and by faith see Him Who is invisible, and so are able to sing the song of ultimate triumph long ere the crash of battle commence.

The last word in the great movement which declares that Jehovah is determined upon the destruction of Babylon is the word of my text, "I will place salvation in Zion."

There are three lines of thought suggested for our consideration in this text. The great ideal is first suggested; salvation in Zion. Then the fact of failure is recognized; Zion without salvation. Finally, the prophetic word of promise declares that Zion shall be restored to the fulfilment of ideal, "I will place salvation in Zion."

The great ideal; "Salvation in Zion." For the interpretation of this phrase, the fulness and finality of the whole Bible is needed. Two antagonistic principles are discovered in the history of humanity as revealed in the Scriptures of truth. Whereas in our study of the Bible, we discover remarkable differences as between the old economy and the new, there are great underlying, unifying principles running from Genesis to Revelation. I am not going to deal at length with that principle of antagonism to faith which is represented by Babylon, but will state it in a few brief sentences. Babylon is first manifest as a confederacy without God in the history of Babel. From that moment throughout the whole of the Scriptures, whether Babylon be an actual city with an actual king, or whether the actual has passed and the principle of Babylon which is human confederacy without God alone remains, Babylon is against Zion. In the final book of the Bible, among the visions of the Seer of Patmos, we see at last the Lamb enthroned on Zion's hill, and immediately there follows the song of the multitudes "Fallen, fallen is Babylon the great."

Let us now restrict our examination to the other principle, and taking out of our text the two words "Zion" and "Salvation" attempt to see what they suggest.

When we read the Old Testament, the word Zion seems to thrill to the tireless music of a psalm. Zion is the synonym for everything of which the Hebrew thought with pride, with satisfaction, with gladness, and with rejoicing. What does Zion mean? That is a question that has not often been asked. We are so familiar with all that Zion stands for symbolically that we have been slow to inquire into the real meaning of the word. It means desert. That in itself is a suggestive fact. We find the first historic reference to Zion in the Book of Samuel, when after all Israel had made David king at Hebron, he captured Zion from the Jebusites. This Zion was a rocky fastness, devoid of verdure, in the center of verdant and glorious hills, so that presently men will say "As the mountains are round about Jerusalem, so is the Lord round about them that fear Him;" but itself was desert. A city had been built upon it long ere David captured it, and being a rocky fastness it was considered impregnable. When the Hebrews sang of Zion they never thought of the desert. The Hebrews associated with the name great essential values, and principles, and aspirations.

With the degeneration of the instrument through which God intended testimony concerning Himself to be borne to the world, the conception of Zion itself degenerated also, and men thought of it only from the civic standpoint, the national standpoint, the patriotic standpoint. These are all secondary things. A devout Hebrew who knew the secret mystery of his own life, and who lived in true consciousness of his relationship to Jehovah, sang of Zion and thought of Zion, as the place of Divine founding; the place of Divine dwelling; the place of Divine revealing. Zion for the Hebrew was the synonym of the Divine presence, the Divine government, the Divine unveiling; and the thought that came to the heart of the Hebrew when turning from those central verities to consider his own relationship to Zion was always the thought of the other word in my text, salvation.

Let us then inquire the meaning of this great word. The particular word, here translated "salvation," is somewhat rare in the Old Testament. The root significance is that of freedom. The idea here is that of safety based upon freedom. Zion was the home of the free; because it was the dwelling place of God, it was the place where bondage could not continue. Zion, the place of Divine dwelling and Divine revealing and Divine government, was the place of human security, and human realization, and human happiness. The captive exiles sang of Zion, and sighed for Zion, because Zion was the dwelling place of the great King, and consequently the place of the perfect Kingdom. Zion and salvation to the thinking of the Hebrew were always closely associated.

I turn from these Old Testament Scriptures to those of the New. Zion is first mentioned in Matthew, and finally in Revelation. In Matthew, it is mentioned by the citation of Hebrew prophecy, "Tell ye the daughter of Zion, Behold thy King cometh unto thee, Meek, and riding upon an ass, And upon a colt the foal of an ass."

The word occurs again in John's record of the same event; so that in the gospel stories, the thought of Zion is maintained in relation to the King Who came to establish the Divine order and bring in the Kingdom of God. When Paul was writing his great letter to the Romans he also quoted from the ancient prophecy and showed that the spiritual ideal was to be fulfilled in the Christian Church. The writer of the letter to the Hebrews, writing to the Hebrew Christians, tells them "Ye are come unto mount Zion, and unto the city of the living God, the heavenly Jerusalem." When Peter was writing to those of the dispersion in Bithynia and elsewhere, he told them that God had already laid in Zion a chief cornerstone, elect, precious, and that the preciousness of the cornerstone is made over to all such as believe in Him; and so the spiritual house is being built, the spiritual city is being constructed; the principles of the Divine government are being established in the world. We come at last to the Book of Revelation, and in chapter fourteen, we read these words, "I saw, and behold, the Lamb standing on Mount Zion, and with Him a hundred and forty and four thousand, having His name, and the name of His Father, written on their foreheads." That is the ultimate fulfilment of the Hebrew purpose and ideal; and closely associated with it is the declaration "Fallen, fallen is Babylon the great, which hath made all the nations to drink of the wine of the wrath of her fornication."

What then is the ideal suggested by this text? Let the local colouring fade. Let the immediate application of the ancient prophecy be forgotten, and the economy of God concerning Israel be out of sight. The principle revealed as a great ideal is that of the establishment of the Divine order in the world; Zion instead of Babylon. Babylon, the city and the life of godlessness. Zion the city and the life of godliness. All the prophetic writers and all the prophetic singers in the Old and New saw the ultimate victory, the victory of Zion over Babylon, of Jehovah over idols, of that religion which consists in worship of the One Who creates and carries, over that religion which consists in the creating of idols which men have to carry, and carry until overburdened by their weight they stoop to dust and destruction.

The startling recognition of the text is that it infers disassociation between Zion and salvation. It reveals the fact that there may be Zion without salvation. It suggests that the city may remain ostensibly the city of God, and yet not be a city of salvation. Is not that the story of all the trouble with which the prophets had to deal? Was not that the actual, local condition of affairs in the midst of which Isaiah and all those great Hebrew prophets exercised their ministry? Zion without salvation; the city of God, without God; the place of the Divine revelation, but no revelation; the center from which the law is to proceed for the benefit of the world, but no law proceeding from the center, the temple of worship with all its rites and ceremonies, but no worship; or in the words of the New Testament, form without power. That is the tragic side of the picture presented; the purpose of God, thwarted, prevented, hindered, unrealized. Zion, beautiful for situation, the joy of the whole earth, the city of the great King, the place to which captive eyes look with longing, the place to which the remnant of captives did return; but Zion without salvation, Zion, mark it well, under the yoke of Babylon, Zion mastered by forces which were antagonistic to Zion. That is the appalling picture. That is the condition of affairs in the midst of which the prophet exercised his ministry.

That is the perpetual peril of Zion, of the people of God, of those who name His name, bear His sign, profess His doctrines, claim to be His peculiar people; Zion without salvation, Zion under the yoke of Babylon; Zion, that ought to be against Babylon, preventing its victory, breaking its power; under Babylon's yoke, mastered by Babylon. That is the tragedy of the text. How comes it that Zion is mastered by Babylon? By the introduction of idols! How came the introduction of idols to Zion? By forgetfulness of God. Zion has made for herself idols, and Zion has had to carry the idols she has made, and Zion has been bent and bowed beneath the weight of her own idols. That was a subtle form of idolatry when Israel made the golden calf. What was the golden calf?

Read the story carefully and you will find it was a representation of God, for when they made the golden calf they did not ostensibly turn away from the worship of Jehovah. They worshipped God as they sang and danced around the calf. They made the calf to represent God. The golden calf was one of the ancient symbols of religion; the cherubim, the ox for service! Had you talked to the leaders who in the absence of Moses made the golden calf, they would have said, We are not turning from God, we are making something that will help us to worship God. That is idolatry on the part of the people of God. So surely as they make a likeness of God, presently they will worship the likeness and forget God. That is why God forbade the making of any likeness of Himself in order that men should worship. We are far away from the wilderness today, far away from the golden calf, far away in this assembly from image worship in any form, and yet idolatry abides in the Church of God today. The idolatry of the Church of God is seen in her mastery by Babylon, and in her weakness in every hour of stress and strain and strife. Her inability to interpret the will of God, the law of God, and to insist upon it in the world, is born of her complicity with Babylon, and that in turn results from the fact that she has put between herself and God rites, or ceremonies, or priests, or preachers. By such creation of false intermediation as between the soul and God, Zion bends to idolatry; and when Zion bends to idolatry, Babylon with her wealth and her pollution and her godless strength places upon the neck of Zion a yoke, and Zion has lost her power and lost her testimony.

There can be nothing more tragic than Zion without salvation, than the Church of God without the dynamic that makes men free, without the authority that interprets morality in the terms of the eternal, without the voice to which the world is compelled to listen. Zion captured by Babylon is the tragedy of all tragedies. That is the picture of the conditions to which this man delivered his message.

Now finally, hear the word of Jehovah, "I will place salvation in Zion." The ultimate victory of Zion will not be Zion's victory, but Jehovah's victory. Zion will come again to the place of power and testimony and witness through restoration, but the restoration will be wrought by God, "I will bring my righteousness near." Zion had her responsibility and it is clearly indicated. It consists first in a recognition of the difference between the idols and God. Remember that when you make your idol, you must carry your idol, and it becomes your burden. Remember, God made you and still carries you. Break down your idol and cease its worship, and worship the God Who makes and the God Who carries. Refuse to bend the knee to any other than God. Bend the knee to God, make His will supreme, His government the one and only law. Let the Church of God have done with the worship of the golden calf. Let the Church of God have done with her worship of her own rites and ceremonies. Let the Church of God have done admiring her own magnificent organizations. Let the Church embody the principles of Zion, and faith, and return to Jehovah, make His will supreme in all the affairs of her own service, and in all the affairs of the lives of her own people; let her remember and let her return, and then "I will place salvation in Zion." He will make the Church a city of free men, for bondage to God is freedom from all other bondage. The neck bent to His yoke is the most erect in the presence of every other form of tyranny. The man wholly submitted to Jehovah is the man who is master of lust and passion and the alluring forces of the world which only win a man, for his destruc-

SALVATION IN ZION

tion. It is the bondslave of God who is the free man in the world. That is the whole principle of Zion in a sentence.

From this consideration, we gather this application and these lessons. Anything in place of God, or anything that puts God at a distance, is idolatry. When we put something between the soul and God we at once become burden bearers. If our religion is something as between ourselves and God, though our creed be perfectly orthodox as to God, then are we idolaters.

How shall we know? We shall know by our relation to our religion. Let me put a question with all practical force. Are you carrying your religion, or does your religion carry you? That is the test question. There are men and women in this house tonight who are carried by God. They read the great word I read in your hearing, and they understand it, they know it. It is not poetry to them. It is poetry, but it is infinitely more, "I will bear; yea; I will carry." There are men here who, presently, will pass away from the sanctuary, the day's worship done they will take a night's rest, and tomorrow morning will settle back again into the work of the shop, the office, the hospital, and all the way will feel the lift and lilt of their religion. Those are the men who belong to Zion.

There are other men who lay their religion aside when the service is over, they have carried it, it is an observance. They come to the sanctuary because they ought to come once a week at least. It may be that in the morning hour, they will bend the knee in prayer, and also at night; but they are carrying their religion. It is something added on to their life, a department of their life which they lock safe up when they get to business and pleasure. It is a weariness to them, a burden. If they dared they would be rid of it. Then, even though they sing the song in this house, and attend reverently to the preaching, and never take the name of God in vain, they are idolaters, they belong to Babylon and not to Zion. The test of religion is whether you carry it or it carries you; whether it is a weariness and a burden, something that after all if you only dared you would fling overboard; or whether it is the inspiration, the joy, the strength of life. Idolatry is the making of an idol which you can put down in any given place—and you will find it there when you come back. It will not move. There is a good deal of that in the Christian Church. You go away today, you will find your religion here next Sunday; it will not move, but you will be away from it for a week. That is idolatry. True religion is the worship of God, which means that in the busy street, in the midst of perplexing questions in the office and the profession, and amid the thousand and one duties of the home, it carries you, and the song of His praise escapes your lips, and the gladness of His presence is in your heart. That is true religion.

There is Zion. There is Babylon. Oh soul of mine, art thou an idolater, or art thou godly? Dost thou belong to Zion, or dost thou belong to Babylon?

Leaving the thought of the individual, or multiplying it into the corporate whole, is this church Zion without salvation; or is salvation here? Are we a company of God's free men and free women and therefore able to pass the word of freedom to the slave, and able to help to snap his chains; or are we enswathed and hindered by the very chains of our religious observances?

How fine are the distinctions of God, and how searching the figures of Holy Scripture. Just where we thought we were safe from observation, He flashes upon us the light that shows that all the things in which we put our trust are false.

Zion; the house is there, the name is there, the songs are there, the sacrifices are there, the priests are there! But is salvation there? A man crosses the threshold, is he likely to be helped? Is he likely to touch the unseen, the eternal? If not —listen to me, my brethren—if not, Zion is a more terrible menace than Babylon. Babylon stands aloof and we know where we are. But if Zion is under the influence of Babylon then what can the world do? Let us see to it, I repeat, that Zion is the hill of God, that her citizens are men and women of faith, and then from her goes forth His law which is life and liberty.

My last word ought to be, and shall be a personal one. Go back to the vision of the Lamb upon Mount Zion with Babylon tottering to decay. That day has not yet come, but it is good to look at it. Thank God that the victory must be won. Yet go back over it, and shutting thyself up alone with God, brother mine, sister mine, in an act of lonely dealing with God say, art thou an idolater, or art thou worshipping Jehovah? If some man shall say tonight—God grant he may—I am an idolater, I have carried my religion—then fling it overboard now, and trust in Jehovah. He will carry you, and all your life shall flame with light and thrill with power, May He so bring us to Himself.

CHAPTER XXVI

THE RIGHTS OF GOD

He spake this parable; A certain man had a fig tree planted in his vineyard; and he came seeking fruit thereon, and found none. And he said unto the vinedresser, Behold, these three years I come seeking fruit on this tree, and find none: cut it down; why doth it also cumber the ground? And he answering saith unto him, Lord, let it alone this year also, till I shall dig about it, and dung it: and if it bear fruit thenceforth, well; but if not, thou shalt cut it down.

LUKE 13:6-9.

THE SIMILARITY BETWEEN THE SONG OF ISAIAH AND THE parable of Jesus is self-evident. In the song of Isaiah concerning the vineyard, the outstanding values may thus be stated; the Lord's vineyard, the Lord's plant, the Lord's expectation of fruit, the Lord's disappointment, and the Lord's judgment upon the vineyard. In the parable of Jesus the outstanding values may be stated in almost identical words; the Lord's vineyard, the Lord's fig-tree, the Lord's expectation, the Lord's disappointment. But there is a value in the parable which is absent from Isaiah's song, that of the intercession of the vinedresser. Judgment in the case of Isaiah was immediate because of failure. Judgment in the parable of Jesus is postponed because of the intercession of the vinedresser. It is, however, as certain in the one case as the other, if there yet be fruitlessness.

It is perfectly patent that the first application both of the parable of Jesus and the song of Isaiah was to the Hebrew nation. The principles have, however, a wider application.

The parable of Jesus was spoken in order to correct a false sense of safety. The earlier paragraph of this thirteenth chapter records that "there were some present at the very season which told Him of the Galilæans whose blood Pilate had mingled with their sacrifices." He reminded them also of others upon whom the tower of Siloam had fallen. The people to whom He spoke imagined that the judgment on the Galilæans, and that on the men of Siloam were evidences of exceeding sinfulness. Jesus said, "I tell you, Nay: but except ye repent ye shall all likewise perish." He then uttered the words of this parable.

The peculiar value of the parable, therefore, is that in it we find the true standards for the measurement of human lives. Men are still imagining that there are degrees of sin, that the Galilæans are sinners above all, that men overtaken by some catastrophe must therefore have been the most guilty. Christ declares that we cannot so measure sin. "Except ye"—the men whom Pilate has not arrested, the men upon whom no tower has fallen—"except ye repent, ye shall all in like manner perish."

Life ended by the brutality of Pilate may not have perished. Perishing is not the ending of material life by the accident of a falling tower. Perishing is something profounder, more terrible. You may live out all your days, according to human thinking, and die in quietness and peace, and yet perish, "Except ye repent, ye shall all likewise perish."

In face of so startling a statement, Jesus uttered the parable, and we will consider it carefully because it is one in which Jesus gives us the true standards for the measurement of human lives. Is not this what we supremely need? Is not this what we are supremely afraid of? Is there anything that we shrink more from than being measured by Divine standards? Are we not all in the habit of measuring ourselves by comparing ourselves as among ourselves? And when we do so we usually compare ourselves with those whom we know to be inferior to ourselves, and so we are uplifted in pride of heart, in satisfaction, in contentment.

The matter of supreme moment is not what neighbour or friend, or foe may think of us, but what God thinks of us. How can we find out? In the simplicity of this parable, Jesus has given us the standard of measurement, and the balances for weighing. Let us remit ourselves to Him for measurement and for weighing.

In order to do this, we must begin where we always must begin if we would understand or enter into the things of the Kingdom of heaven. We must listen to this parable as though we were children. This parable is indeed a picture of ordinary, everyday life; a picture of things with which we are all familiar. It is Eastern in colouring. The vineyard and the fig tree are peculiarly of the East; but you do no violence to the intention if you change the word vineyard to garden, and if you change the word fig tree to apple tree.

Three simple matters are suggested by the parable—

> The rights of the proprietor.
> The interference of the intercessor.
> The position of the property.

The first right of the proprietor is the absolute right of possession. The plant was in his vineyard. It was his plant. He had the absolute right of ownership.

The second right grows out of the first. It was the

moral right of expectation. He came seeking for fruit, and he had a perfect right to seek for fruit. What is a fig tree for? Ask a little child, and with magnificent abruptness, and with no waste of words the child will tell you, figs.

As I read on, I discover another right. He found no fruit; and he came years one, two, and three, and still found none. Then he said, "Cut it down; why doth it also cumber the ground?" He had a right so to say. His right to destroy was based first upon the failure of the tree to produce fruit; it was enhanced by his patience; but it was supreme because it cumbered the ground, that is, it took up space, soil, and strength which at the disposal of another tree would have produced fruit. That is the first phase of the picture.

Before proceeding to the others, let us inquire into the spiritual suggestions of this. They bring us face to face with the rights of God. This is a phrase which I sometimes think we are a little in danger of forgetting today, especially when we are dealing with human life. I hear a great deal about the rights of man. I do not hear very much in the common speech of today about the rights of God. I am not speaking about man's right in regard to his fellow man, but about man's rights in regard to God; what a man has a right to expect from God. Some men have even been daring enough to write what they would do if they were God. The impertinent suggestion smacks of blasphemy; as though it were possible for a finite mind to come to final understanding of what the infinite Mind ought to do; as though it were possible for a being bounded by horizons that are not many miles away, or at most bounded by one small planet which is but as dust in the balances to the immensity of the universe, as though it were possible for such a being to imagine the things that he would do if he were God. Yet, that attitude of mind is being admired and worshipped today.

Let us attend to this teaching of our Lord in which in the simplest parable possible He has reminded humanity of the rights of God in regard to human life. To my own heart it is full of comfort, whilst full of fire.

The first truth is that of God's absolute right in all human lives. The sovereignty of God is based upon the fact that every man is the creation of God, and so the offspring of God. I am a thought of God. I am God-created; physically, mentally, spiritually, intellectually, emotionally, volitionally; analyze as you will, but over all your analysis write the inclusive declaration, man in the image and likeness of God, made by God. I am the property of God. I like to begin there when I am preaching to men about eternal things. I like to look into the face of every man and say, "Thou art not the property of the devil; thou art not the result of the forces of dust. Thou art the property of God." There are senses in which man is the bond-slave of the devil; the bond-slave of sin; the servant of lust, passion; but in the deepest fact, the essential fact of his being, every man belongs to God. The absolute right of proprietorship is enhanced by the fact that all our lives are lived in God's world. It is said that this is a sad and wicked world. That is not true. It is a glad and beautiful world. When Bishop Heber sang his missionary hymn he sang a great truth,

> Though every prospect pleases,
> And only man is vile.

If there be a touch of evil upon the world, it is the touch of the human hand that has lost its cunning, because it has sold itself to the forces and resources of evil. This is God's world; His sunshine, His rain. Evil has never made a blade of grass; it has destroyed many. The devil never made anything; he has destroyed much. Evil is destructive, not constructive.

It makes nothing, it only breaks. I am in God's world, a world that He has encompassed with a sky of blue, over which He scatters the clouds in a profusion of glory, gladdened by the setting or the rising sun, until I am appalled by the magnificence around me. It is God's world. All the forces of my life are forces which He has given me. I am in this world, of the world in measure, but not wholly and finally. God owns me in His world. His is the right of absolute proprietorship; a more wonderful right than any figure of speech can show forth. The man who owned the vineyard and planted the fig tree therein, did not make the fig tree; but God Who owns the world made it, and every man in it. His right of proprietorship is based upon His creation. What a revolution there will be when we can bring men back to this first, fundamental truth about human life; the right of God as proprietor.

The rights of God are also those of moral expectation. Have you ever noticed how constantly Jesus made the men to whom He spoke juries to decide upon their own actions and activities, and pass verdict upon themselves. I think He meant to do that when He uttered this parable. Do you differ from any of the things He said when He spoke these words? Have you not a right to expect apples from an apple tree in your garden? No one will quarrel with that. Then apply the truth you admit in the higher realm. If man is God's creation; if all the forces of his being have come to him from God; if man is living his life in God's world in the midst of resources which God has provided; God has a right to expect fruit.

What fruit? What has God a right to expect from a man? Here again, be true to the simplicities of the parable and you will touch the sublimities. Ask a boy what a man has a right to expect from a fig tree, and he will say, figs. What have you a right to expect from an apple tree? Apples. Do not be afraid of the simplicity of our illustrations. What does God expect from a man? Manhood. That is all. What does God expect from a boy? Boyhood. From a girl? Girlhood. What does God expect from a woman? Womanhood. I shall thank God if the statement startles you into the frame of mind for consideration. God does not expect that you will ever be an angel; but he does expect that you should be a man. "Oh," but you say, "surely if you preach the gospel you will tell us that God expects us to worship, to pray, to give, to be religious." I decline to make use of those minor and partial terms of description. I will make use of that which includes them all. God requires from a man manhood. God is not seeking angels in London; and that not merely because He is not likely to find them there, but because to the heart of God, men and women are more than angels. When Father Taylor, the sailor preacher, lay dying, his daughter said, "You will soon see the angels." He replied, "Folks are better than angels." He spoke out of a great comradeship with God.

As God comes into His garden seeking for fruit, and examines the plant of my life, can He find the fruit He wants? That is the question. Can He find manhood? We can only answer that question by asking another, "What is manhood?" There is only one answer to that inquiry. The meaning of humanity has once been perfectly revealed in the Man of Nazareth. That is Manhood. We test our lives, as I have already said, by comparison with others; we stand in the public place of assembly still and say: "I thank Thee that I am not as other men, or even as this poor publican." We sing our way through life upon the basis of a satisfaction in the fact that there are many worse than ourselves. The measurements are false. What is a man? Behold the Man. I am to find out what I am by comparison with the life of Jesus; and when I use the word Jesus in this respect I am speaking of His humanity for the moment, the actual, positive, warm humanity with which we are familiar in the gospel stories. Behold the Man, and measure thy life by His. He was the revelation of God; and of man also. Has it ever occurred to you that we do not know the real meaning of our own lives until we have looked at Jesus? We are conscious of the contradictions of our own personality. We state the fact in differing ways. We say there is in us the angel and the beast, forever fighting. We speak of strange aspirations after high and noble things, and of grovelings amid low things. Oh yes, express it how you will, in the language of the new formula or philosophy the old truth abides, we were born in sin and shapen in iniquity. We are engaged in a battle as between the forces of good and of evil. We are broken human beings from the start. I look at the Man of Nazareth and see man after God's own heart, the archetypal Man, a perfect revelation to me of the true meaning of my own nature. I cannot find the key to my own life in any other man. I have lost it entirely as within my own personality. Song and sigh, aspiration and groveling! What is man? I am unable to answer until I have looked at the Man of Nazareth. How can I tell the story of His Manhood? We are familiar with Him. I will only do it in briefest words. He was a Man homed in the will of God, absolutely at the service of His brother men. That is the Man of Nazareth. Hear the law from His own lips: "Thou shalt love the Lord thy God with all thy heart, and with all thy soul, and with all thy mind . . . Thou shalt love thy neighbour as thyself." These things He did; but have I done them? As the measurement of that life is placed upon my life; as my life is put into the balances and weighed in the balances of the sanctuary against that life, the life that answered the impulse of the love to God and love to men, that in singing and by suffering served to help others; oh God, how I have failed!

Profane swearer! No, thou hast never been that, neither have I. Brought up in Christian homes you and I were graciously, tenderly sheltered from blatant, vulgar sins; pre-eminently satisfied with ourselves may we be, if we measure ourselves as among ourselves; but if Jesus is the standard then the Proprietor comes into the vineyard expecting fruit, and finds nothing but leaves. My life is a failure when measured by that standard.

Therefore, let it be stated carefully—not with anything of the tone of triumph in the fact, but with solemn consideration of it—because man has failed, God's right is established to destroy him; and not merely because man has failed, but also because God has had long patience with man.

> Nothing but leaves! The Spirit grieves,
> O'er years of wasted life.

No drunkenness, adultery, profanity; but no fruit that gladdens and satisfies the heart of God. No worship in the way of love to Him. No service in the way of helpfulness to my fellow men. And all this in spite of long patience. Every man who so lives cumbers the ground in that economy of God. It may be that you are not a cumberer of the ground in the economy of the British nation; but in the economy of God the man who is bearing no fruit cumbers the ground. Has it ever occurred to you that another man occupying your place in the office might exert an influence for the healing of humanity's wounds, and the bringing in of the Kingdom of God, which you are not exerting? I remember in earlier years walking through the streets of New York with my friend Albert Swift. He pointed out a great orphan institution in which hundreds of bairns were being cared for. I said, "What a sad thing it is to think of all those children without father or mother." I was startled by his reply; he said, "I don't know; I am not sure it is as sad as you think." I asked his meaning, and this was his answer; "In scores of instances those children only had their chance of life when father and mother were dead." It is appallingly true, and it is more true than we think. It is not merely true of the slum children in the gutter. It is true of the children in the suburbs. You feed your children, clothe them, educate them; but what chance have they of spiritual manhood with your example? Has it occurred to you, young man, that if another man sat at your desk in the office, the next man would have a better chance of purity than while you sit there? In the sanctuary, we see things from the standpoint of the sanctuary. We hear that searching word of Jesus, "He that is not with Me is against Me, and He that gathereth not with Me scattereth." There are only two moral, spiritual forces at work in the world, gathering and scattering; centripetal, and centrifugal forces. That is equally true in the spiritual world. The force of your life is gathering or scattering, hastening the Kingdom of God, or hindering it. The man who fails to be a man after the pattern of God's economy is cumbering the ground, wasting God's earth and sunshine, and all of God's resources. That is the solemnity of the parable. I am not standing in judgment upon this congregation. God knows I am before the judgment bar with you. It is by the words of Christ that we are to be judged, and we stand together before those words tonight. He comes to us with the revelation of the rights of God, the absolute right of proprietorship, the moral right of expectation; and after He has measured us, and found us receiving God's resources, dwelling in His world, planted in His vineyard, but bringing Him no fruit, He has a right to cut down because of failure, because of His patience, because we cumber the ground.

Thank God there is yet another thing in this parable. It is the story of the intercessor. We will go back for two or three moments to the picture itself. What is this picture of the intercessor? Mark this simplest of things about it. What is the purpose in the heart of the vinedresser? If you say that his purpose is that of mercy upon the fig tree, it is not so! There is no word that speaks of mercy upon the fig tree. Is that astonishing? Look at it carefully. What is the underlying purpose of the vinedresser? Exactly the same as that of the proprietor, *fruit*. "Lord, let it alone this year also." What for? "Till I shall dig about it, and dung it: and if it bear *fruit* thenceforth, well; but if not thou shalt cut it down." There is no quarrel between the vinedresser and the proprietor. Let it reverently be affirmed, there is no quarrel between God and Christ about man. Jesus Christ did not come into the world to persuade God to have mercy upon the man who is going to be failure through eternity. Christ came into the world to produce in man the fruit for which God is seeking. There is no difference in the ultimate intention of God and Christ. I am constrained to say, out of profound and ever-growing conviction, that the evangelism which suggests to man that Christ has done something which is merely to provide a way of escape from penalty, is false evangelism. He does that, but how? By freeing men from the disastrous failure, by remaking them that they may be what God wants them to be. Jesus Christ the Lord is not leading into the dwellings of light and glory a vast multitude of failures, of incompetent men and women. If you want to know the kind of people He will introduce to His heaven at last, hear it in the words of inspiration, He will "set you before the presence of His glory without blemish in exceeding joy." If there is any man who names the name of Christ, sings the songs of the sanctuary, professes to be a member of the Church of Christ, and his life is still barren, he is not a Christian. Unless the love of God is shed abroad in the heart, unless that love is expressed in service to our fellow men we are not Christians. We may be Christianized pagans, with a creed upon our lips, wearing the livery of the sanctuary, but we are not Christians. Jesus Christ did not come to ask God to let off the man who refuses to bear fruit. He came, to use the figure of the garden, to dig about the tree, and dung it. He came to provoke it to fruit-bearing by introducing to it new life, and fruitful resources. He came to touch the tree with a new life which shall make it respond with fruit.

And if not, if after all His digging, and all His introduction of new forces, the tree is still barren, then He says, "Thou shalt cut it down." He is one with God in purpose. He is one with God in ultimate verdict and sentence. He is one with God in the desire for fruit, and in that operation whereby He seeks to perfect men to fruit-bearing.

The spiritual values are perfectly patent. What is it that Christ offers to do for me? Why is the judgment postponed upon my guilty soul? In order that he may bring new forces to me; a barren, fruitless, failing man! That I may become fruitful, abounding in fruit to the glory of God. That is the basis of appeal. He does not ask God to be pitiful, to excuse the fruitless tree. He asks God to let Him deal with the tree, to make it fruitful. No man is ever going to be admitted into the high and holy presence of the dwellings of the saints in the light of God, on the basis of pity but upon the basis of perfection. Let us make no mistake about the purpose of Christ.

The last matter may be dismissed in two or three sentences. What is the position of the tree in the vineyard? One word covers the whole story. Fruit! If at last there shall be fruit, then the tree will abide, it has fulfilled the purpose of its being. If at last there be fruit, then the demand of the proprietor has been met, and he will be satisfied. If at last there shall be fruit, the vinedresser will be repaid for all his patience and toil.

What is the first and final matter about my life, and thy life, my brother man? Fruitfulness according to pattern. That I become what God would have me be. That I become a man God-centered, God-governed; a man expressing my love for God in my love for my fellow-men, and my service to them. If that be produced, then my safety, my salvation is assured. If that shall be produced, God's requirement will be met, and He will be satisfied.

If that result be produced in me, then the Christ of the cross will see in me of the travail of His soul and be satisfied.

In a very few moments the Sabbath evening service will be over. We shall be taking our way back to our homes, and if these transitory lives of ours be spared and tomorrow's sun dawn, we shall be away to the city, following our profession, in the midst of the daily avocation; but now we pause as in the very garden of God, and He is seeking fruit. What does He find? That is a question not to be answered by one man to another. I am asking no confession. It is a question to be answered by the preacher in the pulpit as in the presence of his God; by every man in the house as in that same great presence.

May all others be reverently patient while I say this final word. There are those who are saying, "If these be the standards, then we come short of the glory of God; if these be the balances, then weighed in the balances we are found wanting. Then what shall we do?" This is the hour of the

Vinedresser, and He seeks at this moment to communicate to all who know their failure, the values of His own death and life; whereby failing men and women can be made fruitful; whereby those who fail because they are in the grip of the destructive forces of habit and of passion and of sin, can be made masters over all of them in the power of His indwelling life.

The most appalling and overwhelming thought of the hour is this, that in the magnificence of the dignity of human will you can, I can, refuse the ministry of the Christ, and choose the barrenness and the failure until the hour of doom and the day of judgment. But in that same magnificent dignity of human will, I can yield my life to Him, all bruised and battered, fruitless; and He will place at my disposal forces whereby it shall be remade, so that not only shall the fig tree in the vineyard flourish and blossom and bear fruit; but the very desert shall blossom as the rose.

In the presence of that Christ, and in the power of that Spirit, by those standards and measurements, found wanting; shall we not begin again by handing our lives over to Christ that He may produce in us the fruit that will glorify God?